THE ORIGINS OF RIGHT
TO WORK

THE ORIGINS OF RIGHT TO WORK

Antilabor Democracy in
Nineteenth-Century Chicago

Cedric de Leon

ILR PRESS

AN IMPRINT OF

CORNELL UNIVERSITY PRESS   ITHACA AND LONDON

First published 2015 by Cornell University Press
First printing, Cornell Paperbacks, 2015

Printed in the United States of America

Library of Congress Cataloging-in-Publication Data

Leon, Cedric de, author.
    The origins of right to work : antilabor democracy in nineteenth-century Chicago / Cedric de Leon.
        pages cm
    Includes bibliographical references and index.
    ISBN 978-0-8014-5308-3 (cloth : alk. paper)
    ISBN 978-0-8014-7958-8 (pbk. : alk. paper)
    1. Open and closed shop—Illinois—Chicago—History—19th century.
2. Labor—Illinois—Chicago—History—19th century.   3. Labor movement—
Illinois—Chicago—History—19th century.   4. Working class—Political
activity—Illinois—Chicago—History—19th century.   5. Political parties—
Illinois—Chicago—History—19th century.   6. Chicago (Ill.)—Politics and
government—19th century.   I. Title.
    HD6488.2.U6L46 2015
    331.88'92097731109034—dc23   2014043953

Cornell University Press strives to use environmentally responsible suppliers and materials to the fullest extent possible in the publishing of its books. Such materials include vegetable-based, low-VOC inks and acid-free papers that are recycled, totally chlorine-free, or partly composed of nonwood fibers. For further information, visit our website at www.cornellpress.cornell.edu.

Cloth printing   10 9 8 7 6 5 4 3 2 1
Paperback printing   10 9 8 7 6 5 4 3 2 1

Printed with Union Labor

For my sisters and brothers in GEO and LEO,
Locals 3550 and 6244, American Federation of Teachers Michigan

Contents

Preface

As a graduate student of sociology at the University of Michigan, I spent as much time organizing on behalf of my union as I did writing my dissertation. In 1998, when I arrived in Ann Arbor, I immediately joined the graduate assistants' steering committee, and by 2001, I had become local union president. Instead of taking a tenure-track job in San Diego when I graduated in 2004, I took a lecturer position in my department and became lead organizer of the lecturers' union. Throughout my time in Ann Arbor, Michigan, teachers went on strike and either fought their employer to a draw or won resounding victories. Of course, I knew that globalization had badly weakened Michigan workers, especially in the auto industry, but my own experience had been that the labor movement remained defiant and strong.

I should have known better. By 2011, conservatives were blaming my fellow teachers for a financial crisis which, as far as I knew, had begun with the predatory lending practices and credit default swaps of Wall Street. Then the unthinkable happened: Michigan, the cradle of the modern U.S. labor movement, joined the ranks of mainly southern "right to work" states, where workers receive the benefits of union contracts without having to pay the dues or fees that support the daily operation of unions. By the winter of 2012, workers in other union strongholds like Ohio, Indiana, and Wisconsin had come under similar attack.

This might not have been so surprising to me had I been on the ground, but in 2007 I left Michigan for my first tenure-track job at Providence College, where I focused on getting sociologists to take the study of political parties seriously. The shock of this monumental setback, however, stirred in me the impulse to return to my labor roots and the central claim of my dissertation, which was that the United States emerged from the crucible of the Civil War as an antilabor democracy, one that undermined the right of workers to bargain collectively with their employers.

The parallels between that time and ours were inescapable. My sense of security in leaving behind a strong labor movement reminded me of the promise of the northern victory in the Civil War which, for nineteenth-century American workers, was the prospect of land out West and an escape from wage dependency in the nation's cities. The splash of cold water to my face recalled the rude awakening that these same workers must have felt as they realized that they would not become independent farmers and instead remain in industrial servitude. Finally, the fact that the current raft of right to work legislation was passed in states where the Republican Party controlled all branches of government was a stark reminder that the postbellum political establishment was responsible for one of the most brutally repressive moments in American labor history.

This book argues that the current generation of workers and trade unionists, like other generations before it, has come face-to-face with a long-standing inheritance: a democracy—born in the epic fire of civil war—that safeguards the individual worker's right to access the American Dream while simultaneously denying a collective route to its fulfillment. In this, the present work makes two major contributions. First, while other scholars emphasize the role of social classes, unions, and the law in shaping this critical moment in American history, I emphasize the changing relationship between political parties and workers. Second, if observers of neoliberalism often trace the contemporary attack on organized labor to the Thatcher and Reagan era, I contend that its modern ancestry goes back to the postbellum order, when the political establishment revised the English common law doctrine of conspiracy to equate collective bargaining with the enslavement of free white men. Consequently, my claims are also at variance with accounts which hold that America's well-deserved reputation for antilabor politics originated at the turn of the twentieth century or shortly thereafter.

However much I am reminded of Civil War–era politicians and workers, the process of writing this book has been much more about the generosity of the living. Julia Adams and Nitsan Chorev helped me establish contact with Cornell University Press. Indeed, I might not have written this book had it not been for a compliment that Nitsan paid me during a visit to Brown back in April 2011. The support of my editor, Fran Benson, at Cornell ILR Press has been overwhelming from the start. I never thought that pitching a book could be so fun. Behind the scenes, my developmental editor, Cecelia Cancellaro, helped me from first contact to book contract and on to the submission of the draft manuscript. My friend and colleague, Melissa Wooten, a font of professional wisdom, introduced me to Cecelia.

I want to thank the many fine scholars who have been supportive of my research from the beginning, especially Julia Adams, Lis Clemens, Diane Davis, Julian Go, Jeff Haydu, my adviser Howard Kimeldorf, Richard Lachmann, Isaac Martin, Mark Mizruchi, Jeff Paige, Kent Redding, Lynette Spillman, Mills Thornton, and the late Mayer Zald. For collaborating with me on our own distinctive approach to political parties, I owe a great intellectual debt to Manali Desai and Cihan Tuğal.

My arguments are anchored in a case study of Chicago, which was home to the nineteenth century's leading politicians and labor leaders, not least Stephen A.

Douglas and Albert Parsons. For bringing Chicago to life, I must thank the staff of the University of Michigan Graduate Library, including the Joseph A. Labadie Collection, the Newberry Library, the University of Illinois Library, and the Chicago History Museum. I am especially indebted to John Hoffman, curator of the Illinois History and Lincoln Collections at the University of Illinois Library, and Lesley Martin, Debbie Vaughan, and Anne Marie Chase at the Chicago History Museum Research Center.

Libraries were important at home, too. The Rochambeau Library, which is my local library, was an important source of friendship and political engagement. The Providence Atheneum furnished an inspiring alternative workspace. And Phillips Memorial Library at Providence College never once failed to supply me with the secondary materials I needed; Beatrice Pulliam was especially helpful.

I finished this book while on post-tenure sabbatical. By supporting me through the years, my colleagues at Providence College made this burst of productivity possible in the first place. My wife, Emily Heaphy, generously endured a year of financial strain in the hope that I might eventually take a break (I did). The sociology department at Brown University provided me with the resources and time to complete the project. I am particularly grateful to Michael Kennedy for securing the visiting scholar position and to José Itzigsohn and Josh Pacewicz for making me feel so welcome. While at Brown I had the pleasure of working with several talented graduate students—Aisalkyn Botoeva, Diana Graizbord, Johnnie Lotesta, Michael Rodriguez-Muñiz, Yibing Shen, and Trina Vithayathil.

Finally, the beating heart of this book is the fond memory of my sisters and brothers in GEO and LEO, Locals 3550 and 6244 of the American Federation of Teachers Michigan. Their steadfast loyalty to their students and each other is an inspiration to all of us who struggle for justice and democracy. This book is dedicated to them.

TRACING THE ORIGINS OF RIGHT TO WORK

On December 6, 2012, a Republican-controlled Michigan legislature passed "right to work" legislation, allowing workers in this longtime labor stronghold to receive the benefits of union contracts without having to pay the dues or comparable service fees that support the daily operation of unions. Amid mounting protests from thousands of union members outside the state capitol in Lansing, Republican governor Rick Snyder said that the law was "about being pro-worker, about giving the freedom to choose who they associate with." Though "right to work" laws make it extremely difficult for unions to represent their members and secure strong contracts, Governor Snyder added, "I support the unions in many regards; I support their right to organize. This has nothing to do with collective bargaining. I continue to be an advocate of collective bargaining in Michigan." State Senate majority leader Randy Richardville echoed Mr. Snyder's sentiments. He said, "I have long been a supporter of collective bargaining, but whether you support collective bargaining or not, it should be the worker's freedom to choose whether or not he or she belongs to a union . . . what this ultimately comes down to is the individual worker" (Skubick 2012).

A century and a half earlier, in another midwestern town just three hours west of Lansing, Republican mayor and *Chicago Tribune* editor, Joseph Medill, spoke before throngs of Chicago workers striking for the eight-hour day. In a move of either astonishing faith in his fellow man or outright effrontery, Medill declared, "Journeymen have the lawful right to combine by trades or unions and determine the conditions on which they will exchange their labor for wages, but they have no legal right to compel any outside worker to accept their conditions or to sell his labor only at their price, for that would be to destroy his personal freedom and liberty of action" (*Chicago Tribune*, May 16, 1872, 4).

Though separated by 140 years, the two sets of statements are based on the same premise. The spokesmen of the Republican Party, past and present, concede the right of workers to assemble and to set rules for their own organizations, but employ the rhetoric of liberty in ways that delegitimize the workers' most effective strategies for improving their wages and working conditions. In each case, the weakening of workers' collective power is justified as a safeguard to individual freedom. Governor Snyder speaks of the worker's right to associate with whomever he or she likes, while Medill cautions against infringing on the individual worker's "personal freedom and liberty of action." Although free riders are often reviled for reaping all the benefits of the team's efforts while doing none of the work, these appeals insist that the free rider is entitled to shirk his duty. They encourage workers to accept the higher wages and benefits that unions are able to negotiate relative to nonunion workplaces, while not contributing financially to house and staff the organization, advertise its objectives, and mobilize the rank-and-file behind a common list of demands. Beyond shrinking the operational budgets of labor organizations, the "right to work" dulls the urgency of collective action. If workers are unwilling to contribute dues, they are unlikely to put themselves out in other ways as well: they might choose not to sign a public petition, attend a rally, or walk a picket line. In sum, the "right to work" encourages wholesale divestment from the financial and organizational means through which unions can bring pressure to bear on recalcitrant employers and then frames the resulting power imbalance as the moral imperative of a free society.

This book is about the bait-and-switch that has historically constrained American workers' freedom under liberal capitalist democracy; enticed with the American Dream, they are simultaneously denied a collective route to fulfill its promise. I trace the present moment back to the time of Joseph Medill when employment relations were being rewritten in the context of slave emancipation. It was then that the United States became an antilabor democracy—one that, despite occasional assurances to the contrary, was hostile to the notion that workers possessed any rights beyond the ability to bargain one-on-one with their employers.

This is not to say that American workers are forever doomed by history or that a more progressive future was somehow foreclosed by the end of the nineteenth century.[1] It is to say, rather, that workers have had, and must therefore always be prepared, to defend their hard-won collective rights in the face of a political and economic system that was set up to preserve only the right of individuals to negotiate the terms and conditions of their employment.

That outcome was hardly preordained, for both antebellum politicians and workers were deeply critical of the individual wage contract, often calling it wage "dependency" or "slavery," because it rendered white men subservient to a master class. This arrangement was less troubling when it was still possible for most workers to start their own businesses and become master craftsmen themselves, but political discourse shifted as workers became permanently mired in wage labor. The cost of doing business increased even as workers earned and saved less, thus putting a life of economic independence out of reach to all but the wealthiest merchants, manufacturers, and commercial farmers. Accordingly, during the Jacksonian era (1828–1844), the Democratic and opposition Whig parties often framed their competing economic policies as ones that would enable white men to escape wage dependency and become self-sufficient farmers. Between 1846 and 1861, as Americans colonized the land that would become the continental United States, the major parties fractured over whether slavery should be permitted in the new western territories. All factions agreed, however, that the goal of land policy should be to preserve a path to self-sufficiency for less affluent white men. Indeed, it was only in the years immediately after the Civil War that the wage contract became understood in mainstream political discourse as a safeguard to personal liberty. Politicians, in what became known as the doctrine of "free contract," held that even the poorest white man was free, because no one could make him enter into a wage contract unless he agreed to the terms. Yet even then, it was the political establishment that espoused that view, while workers rejected it as a fancy reinterpretation of wage slavery.

If free wage labor is the central feature of capitalism—its sine qua non as Marx, Weber, and countless others have argued—then the emerging industrial order had something less than the full-throated political support of antebellum actors. Accordingly, any adequate examination of workers' place in the transition to liberal democracy must reconcile the persistent critique of wage dependency with the outpouring of support among Northern workers for the cause of "free labor" prior to and during the Civil War. The ensuing chapters address the following puzzle: Why did the critics of wage dependency reorganize in favor of liberal capitalist democracy only to reject it shortly thereafter? While other accounts (e.g., Hattam 1993; Stanley 1998) emphasize the importance of the law and social actors on the ground (e.g., classes, ethnic groups, voters), I argue that mass parties pressed formerly adversarial class and ethnic voting blocs into the service of liberal capitalist democracy and then incurred the wrath of immigrant workers when they abandoned the critique of wage dependency in favor the doctrine of free contract and its core implication, the right to work.

Specifically, my answer unfolds in a narrative of the changing relationship between political parties and workers, for the key is to understand that while the critique of wage dependency persisted, its target changed through three phases of partisan struggle. In the Jacksonian era, the close relationship between Democrats and workers was built on that party's populist critique of economic dependency, on the one hand, and the increasing inability of workers to escape such dependency, on the other. But in 1846 both the Democrats and the Whigs became internally divided over the question of slavery extension. The crisis shifted the terms of political debate away from the critique of wage dependency under capitalism toward a critique of dependency under slavery. Instead of arguing about the tyranny of banks and other economic institutions, parties and workers debated whether southern planters would monopolize western lands and thereby prevent workers from becoming independent farmers. In the North, the specter of a "slave power conspiracy" reshuffled the parties' electoral bases, uniting previously antagonistic class and ethnic voting blocs (i.e., elites and nonelites; native-born and foreign-born) into a grand free labor coalition under the leadership of the Republican Party.

This is only half the answer, however, for while the first two phases explain why the critics of wage dependency came to the defense of free labor, antebellum politics do not explain why workers later rebelled against the very social order they helped to establish. This is where the third phase in the relationship between parties and workers comes into play—a phase during which Joseph Medill loomed large. Northern workers bought, and Republicans sold, the claim that barring slavery from the western territories would allow them to escape wage dependency in the nation's cities. What workers did not—and could not—know is that the North's triumph in the Civil War would be used to delegitimize collective bargaining.

As labor unrest mounted during and immediately after the war, the major parties despaired of a strategy to settle the so-called labor question and return to issues like the tariff that once peaceably organized the terms of political debate. Eventually, both parties advanced a contractual vision of free society. In contrast to its previous incarnation as a slaveholding republic where some laborers were forced into the service of their masters, the republic—now formally without slavery—would protect the right of all workers to exchange their labor freely in a one-on-one negotiation with their employers. Workers, recognizing that the doctrine of free contract was merely a glorified version of wage dependency, were persuaded by trade unionists, socialists, and anarchists to reject the major parties' appeal in favor of strikes, boycotts, independent third parties, and revolution.

The political establishment responded by drawing a powerful implication from the doctrine of free contract, the right to work, and used it both as a rhetorical tool to mobilize those frightened by labor's uprising and as a rationale for antilabor state violence. A trade union, politicians argued, coerced individual employers and workers into a collective agreement that was tantamount to the enslavement of free white men. Collective agreements prevented the individual's "right to work" at whatever wage he wanted, while simultaneously prohibiting another individual, the employer, from paying that wage. Revising the English common law doctrine of labor conspiracy, postbellum political elites imposed a double standard on the modern employment relation. Though late nineteenth-century employers were incorporated increasingly as combinations like partnerships, corporations, and companies, the right to work framed the employer combination as a free rights-bearing individual, a "corporate person," and the labor combination as a conspiracy in restraint of trade. Having constructed both trade unionism and the slave power as plots subversive of individual liberty, northern party leaders ordered the police and military to break strikes and eradicate the labor movement just as they did the Southern rebellion. Thus, the Northern victory in the war was prolabor to the degree that it ended the institution of slavery, but antilabor in the sense that it enabled political elites to forcibly subdue workers' collective attempts to address economic inequality under capitalism.

To bring these complex dynamics to life, I use the case of Chicago, Illinois from the beginning of the Jacksonian era in 1828 through the Gilded Age, ending with the infamous Haymarket Affair of 1886–1887. I weave the national and local contexts together by showing that factionalism among state and local parties disrupted coalitions of voting blocs in the electorate. I track ward-level electoral returns over time as well as the shifting rhetoric of party leaders and workers on the issue of wage dependency. The data suggest three things. First, the base of the Jacksonian Democratic Party was a coalition of immigrant (primarily German and Irish) majority-worker wards. Second, the Republican base during the political crisis over slavery was a coalition of German majority-worker and native-born middle-class to affluent wards. Finally, the industrial strife of the postbellum period alienated Chicago workers from the major parties, leading the former to establish revolutionary organizations and a Workingman's Party. Throughout this period, the grist of Chicago politics was the discourse of dependency, but its character changed and its capacity to bind workers to the two-party system waned. When that happened, the political establishment used the right to work to justify and ultimately enact its repression of the labor movement.

I extend the long-standing scholarly conversation on democratic transitions, American exceptionalism, and related dynamics, through a focus on political parties. Parties politicize and depoliticize—in theoretical parlance "articulate"

and "disarticulate"—social divisions such as region, race, and class as they struggle for power and in the process occasionally remake the social order. In that
capacity, parties may mobilize coalitions for and against democratic reform and
incline or disincline communities toward certain types of social organization
such as capitalism or socialism. Parties, however, are not omnipotent. When they
fail to do the work of articulation or when their articulatory projects fall flat, the
governed may withdraw their support, and political elites, in turn, may resort to
violence to preserve the social order as they did in the postbellum era. Nor are
party politics by any means the whole story. The economic, legal, and ethnoracial
contexts of this period each played a role in inaugurating the right to work and
the antilabor democracy that it justified. Adding the context of partisan struggle,
however, enriches our knowledge of this critical moment in American history,
for politicians interpreted, altered, and even directed these other areas of social
life. What is missing from existing accounts, in short, is the rough-and-tumble
world of party politics.

Alternative Theories of Antilabor Democracy in the United States: First Order Implications

In my critical overview of the literature, I distinguish between the "first" and "second" order implications of my argument. Although the act of "bringing parties
back in" contributes to a wide range of research, not all of it bears directly on the
relationship between labor and American democracy. By first order implications,
then, I refer to those bodies of work that address this relationship head-on. These
are the literatures on American exceptionalism, which examines the antilabor
tendencies in U.S. political culture, and democratization, which theorizes the
conditions favorable to democratic transitions and expansions. By second order
implications, I have in mind scholars for whom the relationship between labor
and democracy is a tangential or non-issue, but who are nevertheless impacted
by the claim that political parties shape social life. These include analysts of class
and racial identity as well as electoral politics.

American Exceptionalism

American exceptionalism denotes the vast literature that arose in response to
Werner Sombart's ([1906] 1976) now century-old question, "Why is there no
socialism in the United States?" Those familiar with this research will know
that it supplies several alternative hypotheses to the one I propose here, ranging

from the complex to the monocausal and ahistorical. The latter include several accounts of the putative "conservatism" of the American worker. I do not refute these more problematic examples of the genre, because others have capably dispatched them elsewhere (see, for example, Katznelson 1981; Kimeldorf 1988; Voss 1993), but I discuss three highly sophisticated answers to Sombart's puzzle that are of a historically sensitive variety.

Kim Voss's foundational book, *The Making of American Exceptionalism* (1993), was a response to the ahistorical accounts alluded to above. Contrary to claims that American workers were intrinsically allergic to socialism, Voss insisted that the Knights of Labor, the hugely popular late-nineteenth-century labor federation, had cultivated a homegrown working class radicalism that was every bit as critical of capitalism as its European counterparts were, going as far as to call for the abolition of the wage system itself. However, the Haymarket Affair of 1886–1887, in which anarchists were accused of throwing a dynamite bomb at police in Chicago, led to the violent suppression of the Knights nationwide and forced the American labor movement in a more conservative direction.

Though Voss rightly emphasizes the centrality of antilabor state violence in the postbellum order, her periodization is somewhat at odds with the historical record in two respects. First, the Knights' critique of wage dependency had a long pedigree and was once pervasive among political elites—that stratum of actors that would later order the police and military to forcibly subdue the labor movement. Second, large-scale antilabor violence occurred well before Haymarket (for instance, in the nationwide railroad strike of 1877), yet those episodes of state coercion failed to put the labor movement in a defensive crouch. To bridge these gaps, we require an alternative account that can accommodate both the early critique of wage dependency and the growing divergence between workers and political elites on that question over time.

Another highly influential group of scholars in the American exceptionalist tradition consists of those who emphasize the enduring hold of the English common law doctrine of labor conspiracy as well as its institutionalization in the judicial system (see, for example, Hattam 1993; Steinfeld 1991; Tomlins 1992). Victoria Hattam's now canonical work in this area is a prime example. Her research was largely a response to other legal scholars, who held that an early Massachusetts Supreme Court case, *Commonwealth v. Hunt* (1842), essentially legalized labor unions in the United States (Hattam 1992, 47–48). In contrast to the *Hunt* thesis, Hattam argued that antilabor prosecution under the conspiracy doctrine continued well after 1842, picking up precipitously from the Civil War to the 1880s, when judges began to use the injunction as a new tool to thwart strikes. The implications of her research went beyond legal studies to explain

American exceptionalism, for, she argued, it was the judiciary that compelled the labor movement to advance a more conservative set of strategies in improving workers' lot under capitalism.

Legal scholars have contributed mightily to our understanding of the U.S. labor movement, but they have largely sidestepped or downplayed the importance of political parties in this process. In formulating her judiciary thesis, for instance, Hattam directly undercut the notion, first propounded by Sombart, that the American two-party system smothered progressive third party alternatives (1993, ix). Another example of this tendency is Amy Dru Stanley's (1998) *From Bondage to Contract*, according to which social scientists, abolitionists, labor reformers, and jurists—but not parties—placed freedom of contract at the center of the postbellum social order.

The deliberate exclusion of parties runs into several problems. To begin, in the American system of "party government," politicians controlled the very means of violence that the state used against labor and shaped jurisprudence on worker rights by becoming judges themselves, often running, and being elected, on a party slate. U.S. Supreme Court justice Melville W. Fuller, for instance, was a staunch Chicago Democrat and was instrumental in crafting that party's anti-labor position before he was elevated to the court. Indeed, free contract and the right to work together comprised a language of mass mobilization that the political establishment had hoped would galvanize a silent majority, who were terrified of labor's revolutionary fervor. This was so much the case that in Illinois, labor conspiracy was encoded not in a body of jurisprudence handed down by judges based on legal precedent, but in *statutory* laws authored by politicians in the state legislature in direct response to large-scale job actions. The role of political parties remains an untold part of the story that Hattam and others have capably begun to tell.

I end this commentary on the American exceptionalist tradition with a book that is peculiar for placing parties at its center: Ira Katznelson's (1981) *City Trenches*. On his account, political parties, beginning in the antebellum period, mobilized workers according to ethnic identity, while relatively tolerant labor laws (e.g., *Commonwealth v. Hunt*) allowed American workers to resolve their workplace grievances through trade unions. The historical split in American workers' consciousness—class identity at work, ethnic identity at home—has prevented a more progressive and structural challenge to capitalism, which would apply a militant class analysis not only to the workplace, but to society as a whole.

Katznelson did what few other analysts had done apart from Sombart himself, which was to argue for the role of parties in precluding socialism in the United States. Yet, putting aside the problematic characterization of the *Hunt* ruling, *City Trenches* is hindered by an overemphasis on the politics of ethnicity. Katznelson's claim regarding the nature of urban electoral coalitions was based on an influential school of historiography at the time of the book's publication that rewrote antebellum political history to reflect the dominance of ethnoreligious divisions (Benson 1961; Formisano 1971). But as more recent syntheses suggest, ethnicity was only one of several important modes of political identification in the American case. For example, I argue here and elsewhere that the mid-nineteenth-century Republican Party articulated workers as northern subjects. This unified formerly antagonistic foreign- and native-born ethnic groups in the free labor coalition and thereby undermined ethnic politics in their previous form. John B. Jentz and Richard Schneirov (2012) have likewise shown that Chicago workers embraced a multiethnic class-based political identity after the Civil War. I would add that workers did so, not in isolation from parties, but in direct interaction with them: the politics of community and work were intertwined in Chicago, and those politics were as motivated by class as they were by ethnicity. There is little room in Katznelson's otherwise useful account for the politicization of alternative or intersecting identities over time, due to a relatively inflexible view of urban parties as ossified ethnic machines. This, in turn, prevents an examination of the erratic trajectory of Chicago workers' support of free labor from the Jacksonian era, through the political crisis over slavery, and on to the Gilded Age.[2]

Democratization

In reviewing the democratization literature, we go from inquiring into the absence of a particular social order—socialism, to the presence of one—liberal capitalist democracy. The most prominent studies on that subject hold that democratization occurs because of the mobilization of competing class coalitions, though they differ on which social class is the most consistent vanguard of democratic change. For Barrington Moore (1966), it is the bourgeoisie. For Guillermo O'Donnell and Philippe Schmitter (1986), democratic coalitions result from bargaining among antagonistic factions of the elite. For Dietrich Rueschemeyer, Evelyne Huber Stephens, and John Stephens (1992), the working class is the most consistent advocate of democratic reform; whereas for Jeffrey Paige (1997), neoliberal democracy's prime movers in late twentieth-century Central America were the informal urban sector and rural workers.

The exclusive emphasis on class dynamics, however, leaves a number of questions unanswered about the case at hand. Take, for example, Moore's famous typology of the three routes to the modern world. That typology is essentially a story of winners and losers. The fascist or reactionary route is taken when a weak bourgeoisie joins with powerful landowners to repress peasants and work-ers. The communist route to modernity entails the opposite outcome: workers and peasants successfully mobilize to dispossess landed and urban elites. Finally, when a strong bourgeoisie unites with nonelites to defeat large landowners, the outcome is liberal democracy (Moore 1966, 413).

Thus, in the American case, a strong northeastern industrial class led mid-western farmers in a war that eventuated in the defeat of southern planters. The bourgeois-farmer alliance, Moore argued, was made possible by the North-east's increasing reliance on midwestern consumers and the simultaneous turn in southern trade toward Great Britain in the 1850s. Shifting markets allowed northeastern industrialists and southern planters to walk away from each other despite a long history of economic interdependence. In addition, the conver-gence of northeastern and midwestern class interests shattered a preexisting agri-cultural alliance between the Midwest and the South, which "helped to make unnecessary for a time the characteristic reactionary coalition between urban and landed elites" (Moore 1966, 140–141).

There are numerous empirical and analytical problems with this account. Though the North's victory in the Civil War served the interests of capital more than those of free white labor, and though a cross-class coalition was critical to the rise of liberal democracy, Moore was wrong about the class coalitions of the antebellum period, due largely to his inattention to political parties. Farmers and workers of all regions, even in the South, tended to vote for the Democratic Party, whereas industrialists and planters tended to vote for the Whigs. Antebel-lum class coalitions, according to Moore's typology, were thus predictive of the fascist and communist routes to modernity. Furthermore, the bourgeoisie was by no means in a strong position to rule, for the Whig Party was perpetually in opposition, while the Democrats dominated antebellum politics. If Moore was right about the Northeast-Midwest alliance that eventually prosecuted the war, then he left a crucial question unanswered: Why did rank-and-file Democrats leave their party to unite with their adversaries in the Whig Party, over whom they enjoyed at least political, if not economic, dominance?[3]

Looking ahead to the postbellum period, we might ask another question: If the Northeast-Midwest coalition made a reactionary alliance against farmers and workers "unnecessary," why did the end of the war witness the violent repression of precisely these sectors of society? As one anonymous reviewer of this book insightfully pointed out when comparing U.S. Reconstruction to the Arab Spring in Egypt, we must explain why bad things end up happening to good people. The problems with the democratization literature, then, are really not just about the focus on social class with its resulting inattention to party dynamics, but also about a focus on the moment of transition itself, with much less emphasis on its aftermath. Yiching Wu's (2014) work on the Chinese Cultural Revolution refers to this vexing moment as "demobilization," because Mao and his allies were confronted with the challenge of having to wind down the revolution after they themselves had incited it. Similarly, we might ask whether Reconstruction was a moment in which Northern political elites felt it necessary to confront the revolutionary fervor of the free labor coalition, as workers connected the dots from the emancipation of black slaves to their own unrequited emancipation from industrial servitude.

Alternative Theories of Class, Racial and Electoral Politics: Second Order Implications

Having thus pointed out the gaps in the literatures that bear directly on the relationship between labor and American democracy, we turn now to those scholars for whom that relationship is less central. This section explores the ways in which an inattention to parties leads to a number of open questions about the factors affecting voting behavior and the formation of class and racial identity.

Subjectivist Theories of Working Class Formation

A book about collective bargaining and the frustration thereof presupposes that workers at some point became conscious of the need for collective action. In the humanities and social sciences that process is often called "working class formation" or just "class formation." Though the details of this process have been debated since Marx's time, the debate reemerged with renewed vigor in the second half of the twentieth century. The two great camps in that debate correspond to what Pierre Bourdieu (1989) once called the "objectivist" and "subjectivist" moments of class.

For objectivists, workers are always and already a class by virtue of their structural location at the bottom of the capitalist system. The fact that workers do not own the means of production (e.g., factories, land) while their employers do, automatically places the two groups in different social classes, whose competing economic interests all but ensure that theirs will be a relationship of mutual hostility (see, for example, Anderson 1980, 40; Dahrendorf 1959, 148–149; Marx and Engels [1848] 1998; Wright 1990, 272).

Subjectivists countered that such arguments lead scholars to unfairly chastise workers for not behaving in appropriately revolutionary or "classlike" ways (Mann 1973, 32–33; Parkin 1979; Somers 1997, 77). Accordingly, subjectivists advanced a more forgiving framework. On their account, workers must first identify as a class before one can say definitively that such a class has come into existence. Moreover, workers arrive at that identity in their own way and time, often in the course of labor disputes with their employers. The myriad historical and cultural factors impinging on a specific case of class formation imply that the process may or may not culminate in the revolutionary endgame that objectivists hope for and expect given workers' exploitation under capitalism (see, for example, Katznelson and Zolberg 1985; Steinmetz 1992; E. P. Thompson 1963, 9, 11).

The subjectivists prevailed in that debate, owing largely to their openness to the plain fact that workers have not always, nor in the same fashion, embraced an insurrectionary class politics. Indeed, one might plausibly argue that subjectivist theories of working class formation are flexible enough to accommodate the erratic trajectory of workers' politics in the mid-nineteenth-century United States.

Subjectivists generally assume that when workers embrace class identity, they do so in the context of the workplace and in opposition to their employers. Yet the trajectory of class formation in mid-nineteenth-century Chicago does not fit neatly with that assumption. The anger of Chicago workers was directed not only at their employers, but also at southern planters and political parties. The first political organization of Chicago workers was a land reform league established in 1848 to protest the expansion of slavery into the western territories. Workers organized the city's first unions as the slavery issue subsided in the early 1850s, but organizing dropped off as the controversy over slavery extension reemerged. Unions surfaced again during the Civil War, and it was then that workers began increasingly to identify as a class unto themselves, instead of as northerners together with the farmers and employers of their section. Moreover, while workers' analyses of their deteriorating conditions in the postbellum period referenced unscrupulous employers, they reserved a distinct animosity for the major political parties, whom they accused of abandoning the critique of wage dependency in favor of free market liberalism. In short, the historical development of Chicago working class politics requires an alternative theory based on contexts outside the workplace.

New Immigrant Groups and White Racial Identity

The Republican Party mobilized northern workers of European descent by arguing that the westward migration of southern planters would render them industrial slaves, no better than their agricultural counterparts to the South. Organized worker opposition to slavery extension, which began in the 1840s as the parties took up the issue, was therefore partly an attempt to claim the privileges of whiteness, chief among these being access to cheap land.

This claim requires a serious engagement with "whiteness studies," a subfield in the scholarship on U.S. race relations. The latter proceeds from the assumption that racial identity is fundamentally a relational construct: the notion that some people are "black," for example, is meaningless outside a racial cosmology or hierarchy in which others are not. Students of whiteness seek to shift scholarly attention from people of color toward the dominant racial group, without whom the very notion of "color" would be impossible. From there, this perspective advances two key analytical claims. First, Anglo-Americans did not automatically view other immigrants of European descent (e.g., Irish, Jews) as white and therefore one of them. Accordingly, the research on whiteness has tended to focus on the ways in which new immigrant groups mobilized to claim the "privileges" or "wages" of whiteness. These include access to coveted jobs, low-interest home mortgages, college admissions, and political power. Second, the literature suggests that whites justify the imbalance in resources that such privileges engender by resorting to the rhetorical themes of abstract liberalism such as individual freedom and choice. For example, numerous studies point out that whites rationalized their opposition to residential desegregation during the Civil Rights era by insisting on their freedom to pick their friends and to send their children to neighborhood public schools (Bonilla-Silva 2003; Brodkin 1998; Citron 1969; Cohen 2003; de Leon 2011; de Leon et al 2009; DuBois [1935] 1998; Hirsch 1983; Ignatiev 1995; Jackson 1985; Katznelson 2005; Lassiter 2006; Lipsitz 1998; MacLean 2006; Mills [2002] 2004; Oliver and Shapiro 1995; Roediger 1991; Sugrue 1996, 2008). Thus, Mills writes that the "framing of the United States as . . . [a] liberal democracy . . . has facilitated and underwritten . . . massive evasions on the issue of racial injustice" ([2002] 2004, 239).

Though whiteness studies have greatly extended our understanding of U.S. race relations by focusing attention on the "unmarked" dominant group, the field is nevertheless somewhat ill-equipped to handle the case at hand in two respects. To begin, the aforementioned privileges are said to result largely from state transfer payments, laws, and regulations that favor whites and disadvantage nonwhites. But as Stephen Skowronek famously observed, the early to mid-nineteenth-century American state was fundamentally a weak state of "courts and parties" (1982, 24). That is, it did not possess the administrative capacities of the New Deal welfare state, for instance, which was responsible for institutionalizing many of the white privileges in question. Thus, a more precise account of nineteenth-century U.S. race relations must inquire into the ways in which political parties and the judiciary used their own authority to mobilize support for racial privileges. There is also the related problem of "periodization," the way in which scholars view the development of white racial identity over time. Mills and others rightly suggest that the rhetoric of liberal democracy has been used to justify a racialized distribution of power and resources, but liberalism, as I imply above, only began to eclipse competing ideologies like the critique of wage dependency after the Civil War. Indeed, the idea of a free society based on voluntary individual contracts was liberalism's way of justifying wage dependency in a political and economic order suddenly without slavery. Any research designed to explain the trajectory of European immigrant workers' racial identity from the early to the late nineteenth century must therefore necessarily begin with an examination of white racial formation *before* the advent of liberal democracy. Yet, with the notable exceptions of Theodore Allen (1994), Noel Ignatiev (1995), and David Roediger (1991), the literature on whiteness has tended to center on post–Civil Rights race relations. Furthermore, when antebellum race relations are taken seriously, it becomes clear that whites did more than just resort to the convenient rhetorical themes of abstract liberalism to preserve or gain access to resources: the partisan appeal to white racial identity was one of several factors that made liberalism possible in the first place.

Voter-Centered Approaches to Electoral Politics

Lastly, a book on the interaction of parties and workers pulls for an engagement with the scholarship on electoral politics. The dominant approaches in that field are voter-centered, meaning that the outcome of an election or series of elections is said to be due primarily to dynamics within the electorate itself (e.g., the entrance of women into the workplace or the growing number of immigrant voters). The goal of much of this literature is to identify the determinants of "vote choice," why a given voter casts her ballot for one party or candidate but not another. I have described the competing schools of thought elsewhere as the "social voter," "partisan voter," and "issue voter" perspectives (de Leon 2014). The social voter or "sociological" approach holds that individuals vote the way they do out of loyalty to a social group such as one's class or religion (e.g., she votes for the Labour Party, because she is a worker; he votes for the Islamist party, because he is Muslim) (Berelson et al. 1954; Knoke 1976; Lazarsfeld et al. [1944] 1948; Lipset and Rokkan 1967; Manza and Brooks 1999). The partisan voter or "social psychological" approach holds that the way one votes depends on her or his long-standing familial loyalty to a political party, otherwise known as "party ID" (e.g., she votes for that party, because her father and grandfather did) (Campbell et al. 1954, 1960; Converse 1964, 1966; Key and Munger 1959; Miller and Shanks 1996; Smith 1989; Stokes 1963). Finally, the issue voter perspective explains differences in vote choice based on one's rational policy preferences (e.g., I am voting for that candidate, because I agree with her on abortion) (Black [1958] 1963; Downs 1957; Enelow and Hinich 1984; Fiorina 1981; Hotelling 1929; Key 1966;

Kinder and Kiewiet 1981; Merrill and Grofman 1999; Nie et al. 1976; Pomper 1972; Smithies 1941).

The trouble with the social and partisan voter approaches is that individual demographic characteristics and familial loyalties are generally stable. If a voter is Protestant, for instance, she is unlikely to become Catholic in the next election cycle or even in her remaining lifetime. Likewise, if one's family has traditionally voted for a certain party, that pattern is not likely to be overturned in the short term. Yet in the decade and a half just prior to the Civil War, the allegiances of voters across the United States shifted erratically. Between 1846 and 1848, for example, the traditional voting blocs of the Whig and Democratic parties split and recombined in unprecedented coalitions. In the next six years, the status quo ante slipped back into place as the erstwhile strongholds of the major parties became strongholds once more. The mid-1850s, however, witnessed a mass exodus of voters from the major parties into the upstart political organizations that eventually prosecuted the war. Antebellum voting behavior begs the following question: Why did the old parties lose control of their coalitions in the mid-1840s and reestablish their hold between 1848 and 1854, only to squander it so completely by 1860? Any account of the mid-nineteenth-century American case must explain the volatility of electoral politics in that period, and stable loyalties, whether to social group or party, are unable to do so.

The social voter approach in particular is hard pressed to explain why some social cleavages or differences (e.g., class, race, religion) become politically salient at a given time, while others do not. To use another example, the distinction between free and slave states—the so-called sectional cleavage between North and South—had, by 1860, existed in the United States for almost a century without a civil war. Similar debates over slavery had occurred in 1789, 1819, and 1833, all of which eventually receded as economic issues quickly returned to the fore. We might therefore ask why the political crisis over slavery came to a head in 1860 and not before.

The theoretical traditions that comprise the issue voter approach are better able to account for short-term shifts. The realignment tradition, for example, holds that the advent of new issues (e.g., civil rights, the environment) in the electorate has the power to disrupt existing patterns of party dominance (see, for example, Abramson et al. 2010; Beck 1974; Brady 1988; Burnham 1970; Carmines and Stimson 1989; Key 1955, 1959; Sundquist 1983). One might argue that in each triumph and reversal above, voters' rational policy preferences simply changed.

There are at least three problems with this perspective. First, although scholars of realignment employ competing metaphors (e.g., "flash points," "evolution") to describe the rise and fall of political regimes, most theories assume that power shifts rhythmically from one party to another over time (de Leon 2014; Pierson 2004). This sense of time, or "temporality" as academics call it, has a mechanical feel in stark contrast to the turbulent temporality of partisan struggle in practice. Second, the role of parties is unclear: one gets the sense that political organizations are at the mercy of voters' preferences, as if those preferences are not themselves shaped by political campaigns. Finally, and perhaps most important, there is the problematic assumption of rationality. If we assume that the divergence in antebellum voter sentiment was due in part to the competing "interests" of Northerners and Southerners, then we come face to face with a vexing analytical conundrum, namely, that Northern and Southern interests predict precisely the wrong political outcome. The dispute between the North and South turned on whether slavery should be permitted where it had never before existed. If Northerners had let the South secede, they could have claimed title to the West and prohibited the extension of slavery unilaterally. One might very well argue that it was in the interest of Northern voters to let the South go without a fight. Conversely, in seceding, Southerners effectively forfeited their right to the western territories. One might suggest that it was in the interest of Southerners to remain in the Union, reach a compromise, and thereby ensure slavery's expansion into the West albeit on a limited basis. Of course, as we now know, the exact opposite occurred: Northerners moved to crush the Southern rebellion, Southerners seceded from the republic and suffered the end of slavery in defeat, while the total "cost" of that conflict (to put it in rational choice terms) climbed to upward of 750,000 lives, the largest death toll of any war in American history (Hacker 2011).

Political Articulation

I resolve the foregoing dilemmas by building on the theory of "political articulation," according to which, "*party practices naturalize class, ethnic, and racial formations as a basis of social division by integrating disparate interests and identities into coherent sociopolitical blocs*" (de Leon, Desai, and Tuğal 2009, 194–195).

The theory may be broken down into three parts. First, parties make divisions or cleavages such as class, race, and religion politically salient. This is not to say that demographic differences are fictional. Catholics, Protestants, Jews, and Muslims, for example, each have distinct (if related) traditions to be sure, but whether they matter for the purposes of political division depends on whether or not parties articulate them as a basis of contention. Next, parties go through the trouble of politicizing social differences, because victory depends on the parties' ability to mobilize an enduring majority coalition; that is, to frame their own supporters as the natural majority who should rule and their opponents' supporters as the illegitimate minority who should not. Third, political articulation is not just about the successful naturalization of cleavages, for the converse implication is that coalitions unravel when parties fail to do the work of articulation or else advance a vision of the social order that falls flat in the face of competing political projects. The reproduction of political power hinges on the ability of parties to not only achieve but also maintain what Antonio Gramsci (1971) called "hegemony," the acquisition of mass consent to govern. Consent is by definition impermanent and thus always at risk. When the governed withdraw their consent, power may then pass from hegemony to domination, such that political elites give up on cultivating support through persuasion and instead coerce the unruly masses into submission. It is this ongoing struggle between competing political projects and the tension between coercion and consent that accounts for both the short-term shifts leading up to the advent of antilabor democracy in Chicago and the ensuing repression of the labor movement.

By comparison, the American exceptionalist tradition is somewhat limited in its capacity to explain the historical emergence of the postbellum antilabor regime, because it either sidelines the role of parties in government (e.g., in writing labor conspiracy laws and commanding the police and military) or assumes an unchanging relationship between parties and workers (e.g., as primarily ethnic in character). The political articulation framework solves this analytical problem by pinpointing the rise of antilabor democracy at the end of three sequences of party-worker interaction, when political elites abandoned the critique of wage dependency in favor of the doctrine of free contract and the right to work.

The puzzle of U.S. democratization has two parts. The first is why midwestern nonelites realigned with their erstwhile political adversaries in favor of a liberal capitalist democracy. Here a focus on parties allows us to argue that Republicans used the specter of a slave power conspiracy to shift the terms of political debate away from a critique of wage dependency under capitalism to a critique of wage dependency under slavery, thus unifying formerly adversarial voting blocs into a northern free labor coalition. The second part of the democratization puzzle is the reactionary response of political elites to the labor question. This I interpret as an instance in which political parties, having attempted and failed to acquire the consent of the governed, then secure the latter's cooperation by force.

Moving on to second order implications, the seemingly paradoxical trajectory of working class identity in this period likewise rests on the rise and fall of party projects. Antebellum parties deployed the critique of wage dependency to articulate white workers first, as a class of "producers" together with white farmers, and then, as northern "free labor" together with the white elites and farmers of their section during the political crisis over slavery. The immediate postbellum period was an instance of failed articulation, for the parties' contractual vision of a free society offended workers who remained suspicious of wage dependency. Trade unionists, socialists, and anarchists were then able to articulate workers to their organizations as a class.

The scholarship on U.S. race relations must contend with (a) the fact that the antebellum state was insufficiently developed to distribute racial privileges in the way that the New Deal state later did; and (b) the fact that liberalism only began to eclipse other political ideologies after the Civil War and thus cannot account for why white racial identity had by that point already been so bound up with the expectation of economic independence. I address these problems by demonstrating that the concept of white privilege was advanced, not by the antebellum state, but by antebellum politicians, who promoted territorial expansion and land reform to workers of European descent as a solution to wage dependency.

Finally, the dominant voter-centered approaches to electoral politics are unable to account for the political volatility of this period, both because of their emphasis on long-term stable factors such as partisan and social group loyalties and because of a focus on rational interests, which in this case lead away from civil war. The trajectory of party development, by contrast, tracks much better with the political behavior of American workers than these dominant approaches to vote choice. The antebellum parties were once able to keep the focus of the polity squarely on economic issues and away from slavery. However, the unexpected defeat of Martin Van Buren for the Democratic presidential nomination in 1844 touched off a chain of partisan reactions and counter reactions, including a final backlash that badly undermined the American party system's ability to contain the politicization of slavery. Specifically, Van Buren's defeat fueled a pivot in public policy toward territorial expansion, which begged the question of the status of slavery in the new territories. The ensuing debate led to the exodus of Free Soil Democrats and their base among immigrant workers into the Republican Party, a brand new party that unified Democrats, Whigs, and all others who opposed the westward expansion of slavery. After the war, when politicians pivoted yet again and embraced the wage contract as a metaphor for freedom, immigrant workers defected from the mainstream party system to unions, labor parties, and revolutionary organizations.

By solving the above analytical problems in this way, this book aligns with a long-standing, but now resurgent, scholarly emphasis on the influential role of political parties in social life. Beyond Gramsci, scholars will no doubt recognize that my arguments bear a remarkable resemblance to Adam Przeworski's earlier work on the ways in which socialist parties cultivate working class identity (e.g., Przeworski 1977; Przeworski and Sprague 1986). In addition, this book shares much in common with classic historiographical accounts of the contentious relationship between nineteenth-century American workers and political parties (e.g., Hugins 1960; Montgomery 1967; Pessen 1967; Wilentz 1984). My claims also dovetail with recent arguments about the role of political parties in abortive democratic transitions (e.g., Redding 2003; Riley 2010), transitions to social democracy (e.g., Desai and Riley 2007; Heller 1999), and transitions to free market economies (e.g., Tuğal 2009).[4] Scholars of U.S. race relations tend to focus on the antagonism between social groups (e.g., whites vs. non-whites) and racial states (e.g., apartheid South Africa). Yet at least a few insist that political parties may either downplay or heighten supposed racial differences (e.g., Chen 2009; Frymer 2008; Gerteis 2007; Hiers 2013; Redding 2003; Roediger 1991). With respect to the research on electoral politics, an intrepid handful of sociologists have dared to say that parties help us understand the sometimes infuriating outcomes of democratic life. Apart from Manali Desai, Dylan Riley, Cihan Tuğal, and yours truly, the list includes Ron Aminzade's (1981, 1993) earlier work and the current work of Stephanie Mudge (Mudge and Chen 2013) and Adam Slez (Slez and Martin 2007).

I am not the first sociologist in recent years to argue that parties matter. What makes this book different from my colleagues' work, however, is that it makes political parties the focal point of synthesis, bringing together these otherwise isolated bodies of work to explain the dynamics of labor movements, class and racial formation, democratization, and electoral politics simultaneously. On this account, parties stand at the intersection between the state and civil society. That is, parties divide civil society into competing coalitions or blocs as they struggle for power; in that role, they often shape and reshape class and ethnoracial identity. At the same time, parties control the system of nominations, appointments, and elections to political office, which is to say that they hold the reins of state power. They are thus able to further politicize social differences by, for example, providing social services or tax breaks to some, while denying them to others. But perhaps more insidiously, when the people reject the parties' proffered vision of society (i.e., who is the majority and who is the minority; who is good and who is bad), from their perch atop the state, they are able to make laws, appoint loyalists to the judiciary, and unleash the police and armed forces—all to the disadvantage of their adversaries. As I demonstrate, the dual influence of political parties on both the state and civil society has had vast repercussions for the freedom of workers under liberal democracy.

Methods, Case Selection, and Data

Any case study of large-scale social transformations must confront three challenges. The first is the methodological legitimacy of single case analysis. In fact, comparative historical methodology has moved beyond the notion that a single case is merely a single observation or data point, and thus can only generate tentative theoretical claims. As Rueschemeyer has argued, case studies "can test theoretical propositions as well, and they can offer persuasive explanations," in part because they must go through "frequent iterations of confronting" alternative "explanatory propositions with many data points." This iterative process of fitting theoretical ideas to the complexities of a single case, "allows for a close matching of conceptual intent and empirical evidence" (Rueschemeyer 2003, 318).

But if a single case can do so much, one might still ask, "why Chicago"? As the queen city in the home state of both Abraham Lincoln and Stephen A. Douglas (the 1860 presidential nominees of the Republican and Democratic parties respectively), Chicago was a key theater in the political crisis over slavery. It is no coincidence, for example, that the Republicans chose Chicago to host the fateful Republican National Convention of 1860, which nominated Lincoln for the presidency. Douglas's primary residence was in Chicago, and it was there that he died two months after the South fired on Fort Sumter. Beyond housing the leadership of the nation's two great parties on the eve of battle, Chicago supplied the vanguard of labor unrest that swept across the North during Reconstruction and the Gilded Age. Not only the infamous Haymarket Affair of 1886–1887, but also the nation's first May Day strikes for an eight-hour day took place in Chicago. The city's English-language trade union paper, the *Workingman's Advocate*, was both the organ of the Chicago labor movement and one of the most influential labor journals in the country. With leadership comes grave responsibility, however, and Chicago workers bore the brunt of labor repression in this period. For example, in the Great Railroad Strike of 1877, police, military, and paramilitary groups killed approximately thirty men and boys, many of whom were buried anonymously in lime pits, while another 200 were wounded, the largest number of casualties of any city in the nationwide job action. This suggests that an important rupture occurred in the politics of American workers during the postbellum period and that Chicago was at the epicenter of that rupture.

Third, a case study of this importance must provide data that are sufficiently persuasive of its central claims at the local level but also "scale up" to the state, regional, and national levels of analysis. With respect to voting data, proponents of the dominant voter-centered approaches to electoral politics may insist that only individual-level survey data can provide evidence for the arguments advanced here. To this, I apply Adam Przeworski and John Sprague's famous line that "this study is a study of voting, but not of voters" (1986, 3–4, 10–11). That is, my focus is not on the individual-level determinants of vote choice, but rather the effect of party development and practices on large-scale social trans-formations. In any case, individual-level survey data are simply unavailable for the period in question: pollsters and social scientists only began administering surveys in the 1930s. Accordingly, I cross-check individual-level manuscript census data on ethnic and socioeconomic settlement patterns in Chicago from Einhorn (1991) and Hirsch (1990) against archival ward-level electoral returns to present the most accurate picture possible of changing voting patterns by ward. I also track the development of the critique of wage dependency through a content analysis of party and labor newspapers and the minutes of labor meetings and rallies. For insight into the importance of patronage, factionalism, and other "backstage" party dynamics, I look to the private papers of party leaders and operatives. Lastly, because Chicago and Illinois politics were so central to the political crisis over slavery and the titanic clashes between capital and labor after the war, I make a special effort to draw on archival data that put local players in direct conversation with statewide, regional, and national figures.

Chapter Organization

For those eager to plot the arc of the narrative, I provide a brief preview here. Chapters 2 through 5 are the key thematic chapters that drive the momentum of the narrative, from the Jacksonian era, through the political crisis over slavery and the Civil War, and ending with the doctrine of free contract, the right to work, and antilabor state violence after the war.

Chapter 2, the first thematic chapter, answers the question: What was the critique of wage dependency and just how mainstream was it? It examines the ways in which the Democrats and Whigs sought to articulate workers to their respective parties through economic policy. This political project was anchored in a framework of civic standing that celebrated self-sufficiency especially among farmers and artisans and stigmatized wage workers, slaves, and women for relying on others for their own survival. The leaders of each party accordingly worked to frame their policies as ones that would enable less affluent white men to become or remain economically independent.

In Chicago, the foregoing national narrative manifested itself in the dominance of the Democratic Party under the leadership of *Chicago Democrat* editor and U.S. congressman John Wentworth. The early Democratic organization was strongest in the north and west sides of Chicago, where German and Irish immigrant workers predominated, and weakest on the Lakeshore where the affluent native-born minority resided.

Chapter 3 addresses why the critics of wage dependency reorganized in favor of a liberal capitalist democracy. The answer lies in the back-and-forth political struggle to articulate workers and other constituents as northerners in the decade and a half before the Civil War. A battle for leadership succession in the Democratic Party in 1844 prefigures this monumental transformation, for the losing faction in that conflict would later oppose the expansion of slavery to the western territories as Free Soil Democrats and eventually as Republicans. Free Soil Democrats insisted that the westward migration of southern planters would prevent white workers from resettling as farmers in the West.

The split over territorial policy led to a rift between the Illinois Democratic organization led by Stephen A. Douglas and the Chicago Democratic machine led by John Wentworth, who took up the Free Soil banner as Congress debated the status of slavery in the newly conquered northern half of Mexico known as the Mexican cession. The emergence of the Free Soil cause, in turn, prompted Chicago workers to establish their first political organization, a chapter of the National Reform Association, which likewise sought to bar slavery from the western territories for fear that planters would monopolize the land and condemn workers to a life of industrial servitude. Eventually, the Democrats' once dominant coalition of Irish and German majority-worker wards fractured and gave way to a Republican free labor coalition of German majority-worker and native-born middle-class to affluent wards.

Chapter 4 answers the relatively straightforward question, "What was the relationship between Chicago parties and workers during the war?" Though workers responded enthusiastically when their political leaders called on them to fight at the start of the war and rallied behind their assassinated leader Abraham Lincoln at war's end, in between they had become observably alienated from the political establishment. By 1864, Chicago workers had organized a multiethnic citywide labor federation called the General Trades Assembly and published their own newspaper, the *Workingman's Advocate*, in a bid to establish a prolabor lobby. The political strategy of Chicago's incipient labor movement was to support only prolabor candidates, regardless of party affiliation. These developments comprised an intermediate stage on the way to organized labor's wholesale repudiation of the party system during Reconstruction.

The last narrative chapter answers the question, "What were the implications of the North's victory in the Civil War for the political relationship between parties and workers?" While Chicago workers continued to protest their deteriorating conditions, now in an emerging liberal democratic order formally without slavery, the major parties responded by equating collective bargaining with the slave power as related conspiracies against individual freedom. When liberalism's contractual vision of a free society failed to peaceably articulate Chicago workers into mainstream politics, party leaders used state violence to subdue labor's revolt and rationalized their military offensive as a safeguard to the right to work.

Workers meanwhile saw the parties' abandonment of the critique of wage dependency and the antilabor violence it permitted as a betrayal of their military service and the promise of the war, which they saw as nothing less than the emancipation of white men from permanent industrial servitude. Accordingly, Chicago workers took the cause of their economic independence into their own hands by striking for an eight-hour day, which they thought would provide some semblance of independence by allowing equal time for work, rest, and leisure. In addition, they organized a Workingman's Party and established revolutionary organizations. Throughout this period, white workers increasingly referred to themselves as a class at odds with the class of capitalists and their allies in the political establishment.

The concluding chapter circles back to the first and answers the question, "What can the origins of right to work teach us about the condition of American workers and the U.S. labor movement under neoliberalism?" It teaches us first that the antilabor ethos of nineteenth-century liberalism is alive and well. Contemporary right to work rhetoric derives from the original postbellum claim that workers must be free to bargain with their employers on an individual basis. Second, it tells us that workers are not likely to take the status quo lying down. As they did during Reconstruction and the Gilded Age, contemporary American workers have come out en masse to resist the widening economic inequality of the neoliberal order. Finally, the story of antilabor democracy in Chicago suggests that though workers are not doomed by liberalism, they nevertheless face their forebears' battle to preserve labor rights in a context that has been historically hostile to collective bargaining. The state is not their only obstacle, however, for the peculiar intersection of race and class in the founding of American liberal democracy framed economic independence (or in contemporary parlance, a middle-class lifestyle) as a distinctly white privilege. Rather than challenge the racialized basis of this fantasy, the Obama administration has revived its promise by closely courting the support of white middle-class suburban voters, secure in its prediction that racial minorities, including now Latinos, will flock to the president's standard for lack of any viable party alternative. The potential for rebirth in the U.S. labor movement will hinge on its ability to forge a path of political independence, rejecting both the hostility of the Republican Party and its status as a captured constituency in the Democratic Party.

THE CRITIQUE OF WAGE DEPENDENCY, 1828–1844

And where is that band who so vauntingly swore,
That the havoc of war and the battle's confusion
A home and a Country should leave us no more?
Their blood has wash'd out their foul footsteps' pollution.
No refuge could save the hireling and slave
From the terror of flight or the gloom of the grave,
And the star-spangled banner in triumph doth wave
O'er the land of the free and the home of the brave.

—Francis Scott Key (1814)

In this third verse of "The Star Spangled Banner," Francis Scott Key draws a distinction between the United States and Great Britain. Key, like many of his countrymen at the time, believed that Britain was ruled by an aristocracy, and that as in any such arrangement, those who fought in defense of the aristocracy did so only because they were fundamentally unfree; unfree, in that they were wholly dependent on their lords and masters either for wages, as in the case of "the hireling," or for their room and board, as in the case of "the slave." Thus, when Key writes that neither could be saved "from the terror of flight or the gloom of the grave," he is in fact boasting that even as the British shelled a Baltimore fort in 1814, the minions of the monarch could not be saved from the terrible onward march of American liberty.

"The Star Spangled Banner" evinces a central feature of early American political discourse, namely, a deep distrust for any form of government that would nurture dependency as the natural condition of men. It is anchored in what Nancy Fraser and Linda Gordon (1994) have referred to in another context as the "discourse of dependency." This discourse, which finds its ideological origins in the republicanism of the American Revolution, placed a premium on a man's capacity to live independently of naked economic interest (Banning 1978; McCoy 1980; Pocock 1975; Wood 1969, 1992). By this logic, those who were dependent on others for their own survival—wage workers, women, children, and slaves—could not be trusted with the welfare of the republic as a whole.

In their desperation, they might be persuaded to sell their political support in exchange for some monetary remuneration (Boydston 1990; Roediger 1991; Wood 1992). By contrast, white male artisans and family farmers were viewed as the icons of independence, for it was imagined that they lived comfortably enough off their own labor that they could steer the course of the republic without prejudice to their own enrichment. Dependency and citizenship were therefore not categories that applied evenly to everyone: they referred to specific racial, class, age and gender groupings. One of the central preoccupations of the Jacksonian two-party system, then, was enabling the economic and political independence of white men.

This chapter foregrounds what most other studies of large-scale social transformation have slighted—that 1) political parties used evocative discursive tropes to shape voters' identities and interests; and 2) voters must recognize themselves in the rhetorical appeals of politicians for social transformation to take hold. Although I take economic change as seriously as other scholars of this period do, I contend that such change does not lead inexorably to a certain kind of politics. In the last century, we have seen fascists, socialists, nationalists, and liberals press the theme of economic change into the service of radically different political agendas. Likewise in the Jacksonian era, Democrats argued that the emerging "market revolution" would result in the economic dependency of the common man, while the opposition Whig Party countered that the market revolution signaled a new age of shared prosperity and insisted that the Democrats' demagogical resistance to commercial measures would stall progress and deprive farmers and workers of a shot at economic independence in the new economy. In doing so, the Whigs argued, Democrats made the common man the party's political dependent. In sum, neither "the economy" nor "economic interest" has an objective face—they are continually interpreted and reinterpreted by parties in struggle.

The articulation of competing electoral coalitions and cleavages notwithstanding, politicians are not free to interpret these matters in any way they please. Rather they are constrained by a common set of inherited rhetorical devices that they deploy to frame and counterframe the fundamental divisions of American society in ways that authorize their own party as the "natural" governing party and disqualify the opposition as the embodiment, for instance, of all that is "un-American." To use a contemporary international example, post-Soviet Russian politicians use the specter of Stalinism to undermine the credibility of their political adversaries. Similarly, in the Jacksonian era, each party stigmatized the other as the agents of dependency, alike in every way to the British aristocracy, while drawing a direct line of succession between their own party and the patriot ranks of the American Revolution.

The Common Ground

Whig and Democratic rhetoric shared at least three themes in common: a critique of the wage system, a celebration of independent farmers and artisans (also known as "mechanics"), and a memorialization of independence from British colonial rule. These themes manifested themselves as much in silences and innuendo as they did in overt statements.

Take, for example, the Democratic Party's favorable review of a tract written by fellow partisan and labor advocate, Orestes Brownson, who denounced the wage system as being far worse than black bonded slavery itself: "We say frankly, that, if there must always be a laboring population, distinct from proprietors and employers, we regard the slave system as decidedly preferable to the system of wages." He adds, "Wages is a cunning device of the devil, for the benefit of tender consciences, who would retain all the advantages of the slave system, without the expense, trouble, and odium of being slave holders" (*Chicago American*, September 11, 1840, 2). Here Brownson claims that wage labor is no better than chattel slavery. If anything, it is worse, because it conceals "for the benefit of tender consciences" the effective enslavement of free white men. What is perhaps more interesting, however, is that the Democrats' hearty approval of the Brownson tract appears as a reprint in Chicago's Whig paper, the *Chicago American*. The Whigs use the statement as evidence of Brownson's hostility toward religion and private property, but are palpably silent on the claim that wage dependency is a form of slavery hidden in plain sight.

If there is any doubt that the Whigs were less critical of the wage system than Brownson and his fellow Democrats, we need look no further than their commentary on factory life. In 1841, for example, the *Chicago American* published a poem titled "The Little Factory Girl." Without even reading the poem, one expects a Dickensian piece about the evils of the factory system. To let the piece stand on its own without any editorial commentary, a convention in newspapers at the time, would have constituted a sufficient indictment of wage labor, but the Whig Party introduces the poem as a representation of British employment relations in particular, though significantly Britain is nowhere mentioned in the poem itself. The Whig editor then vouches, with solemn disapproval, that the "sufferings" detailed have an unfortunate basis in reality. If this insinuation proceeds from the same suppositions that were self-evident to Francis Scott Key, then the Whigs were up to more than offering context to the reader; they were evoking memories, real or imagined, of the American condition before Independence. The poem reads,

> 'Father, I'm up, but weary,
> I scarce can reach the door,
> And long the way and dreary—

Oh! Carry me once more.
To help us, we've no mother,
And you have no employ;
They killed my little brother—
Like him I'll work and die. . . .
The overlooker met her
As to her frame she crept,
And with his thong he bent her,
And cursed her as she wept. . . .
The sun had long descended,
But night brought no repose.
Her day begun and ended
As cruel tyrants chose. . . .
At last the engine ceasing,
The captive homeward rushed;
She thought her strength increasing,
'Twas hope her spirits flushed. . . .
Again the factory's ringing,
Her last perception tried,
When from her straw bed springing,
'Tis Time!' she said—and died.

(Chicago American, November 17, 1841, 4)

The author of this poem, like Brownson, equates wage dependency with slavery. The little factory girl is described here as being a "captive," subject to the whims of "overlookers" who whip her with a "thong." Further, her time is not her own, for her day began and ended "as cruel tyrants chose"; her last words came at "the factory's ringing," and those words were "'Tis Time!" The factory girl is bereft of any instinct or capacity for self-government, having scarcely a moment to sleep, let alone to contemplate the welfare of her country.

Contrast the depiction of the little factory girl to the celebration of the farmer. "There is no situation in the world," the *Democrat* opined, "in point of real comfort, and enjoyment, and independence, to be compared with that of an honest, temperate, and industrious farmer . . . These habits are indispensable, in fact, to men in all professions" (*Chicago Democrat*, April 20, 1836, 2). The image of Longfellow's "Village Blacksmith," which was eagerly republished in the *American*, has a similar ring:

His brow is wet with honest sweat;
He earns whate'er he can,

> And looks the whole world in the face,
> For he owes not any man.
>
> (*Chicago American*, October 12, 1842, 2)

The farmer and blacksmith evince a willingness to work hard of course, but what distinguishes these icons of independence from the factory girl is that the former are men who enjoy a modest degree of autonomy. The blacksmith sweats, but he does so honestly; he is free of debt and is therefore able to look upon the "whole world." Likewise, the farmer is "industrious," but he, too, is "honest" and experiences "real comfort . . . and independence." One gets the sense from these passages that economic independence cultivates, or is at least linked to, basic decency and civic virtue.

Antebellum party papers are filled with such examples, each contrasting the condition of hirelings with that of small independent producers and alluding to the haunting menace of British aristocracy, which would, given half the chance, transform producers into dependents. This is as much as the competing parties shared in their use of the discourse of dependency, for they differed markedly in their policy strategies for making economic independence attainable in a time when it seemed farther and farther out of reach. Indeed, the clash of these opposing uses of the discourse prompted one student of early Illinois politics to refer to it as "The Spoils Aristocracy and the Paper Aristocracy," in reference to those supposedly dependent on the spoils of political patronage (Democrats) and those allegedly dependent upon the Bank (Whigs) (Leonard 2002, 156). It is this difference that accounts for the fact that Chicago's majority-worker neighborhoods tended to support the Democratic Party more consistently than they did the Whig Party.

The Paper Aristocracy

Democratic Party rhetoric drew on the widely held notion that liberty emerged perfect and complete at the founding of the republic. Thus, the party's stated aim was to undo the corrupting influence of time by restoring the nation to "the pure and simple design" of early America (Wilson 1974, 7). That design was the utopian vision of a small holder republic, the enlargement of which would ensure that white men would at least have the opportunity to one day be masters of their own domain (Ashworth 1983; Blau 1954; de Leon 2008; Ford 1988; Huston 1998; Meyers 1957; Sellers 1991; Thornton 1978; Watson 1981, 1990; Wilentz 2005; Wilson 1974). Witness the following advice copied from a history of the American Revolution, the compliance with which "would have saved Illinois much trouble: . . .

'Honor the men who, with their own hands, maintain their families, and raise up children who are enured [*sic*] to toil . . . [and] a great majority of your country must and will be yeomanry, who have no other dependence than on Almighty God . . . From the great excess of the number of such independent farmers in these states, over and above all other classes of inhabitants, the long continuance of your liberties may be reasonably assumed'" (*Chicago Democrat*, February 9, 1842, 2). On this account, the country's political independence is anchored in the economic independence of individual men; that is, on their capacity for self-government, specifically to "maintain their families" "with their own hands." "The long continuance" of liberties, in turn, is contingent on the extent to which the government embraces policies that allow them to flourish. Note, too, that independent farmers were to be cherished in this way "over and above all other classes of inhabitants." Conspicuously absent from the homage were the industrial sectors of the republic.

Complementary to the notion of a timeless, perfect republic was the Democratic commitment to an "economy of nature," which was pervasive among party activists as well as farmer and labor advocates (Huston 1998, 24–26; Welter 1975). For if the republic emerged perfect from its inception, it was in part because it had been built upon an economy in which everyone knew physical labor, and survival was guaranteed only by sheer exertion and skill in the transformation of raw materials. This assumption would have resonated with the denizens of an underdeveloped country like the United States, since farmers and mechanics experienced the unforgiving character of a natural economy firsthand.

Accordingly, the Democrats visualized the rights of property, not in terms of ownership per se as it is largely conceived of in the present-day, but in terms of a just reward for physical labor. The party's war with the Second Bank of the United States rested on the belief that the banking system reversed the natural order of private credit between individuals, in which there was reciprocity of burdens and benefits. In the Jacksonian era banking system, the interest that should have gone (in the Democrats' estimation) to the honest producers who received bank notes in exchange for their labor or mortgages, went instead to the very banks that issued them. Moreover, for their trouble, the same producers who propped up the banks through their receipt and expenditure of bank notes were regularly imprisoned for unpaid debts (Holt 1999, 5; Welter 1975, 85–87).

In response the Democratic Party passed stay and exemption laws to protect debtors, and mechanics' lien laws to protect unpaid tradesmen. The Democrats thereby challenged the very concept of property in its contemporary form. Bankers and other speculators were believed to traffic in unreal property, for real property was understood as the fruit of physical labor. It could not accumulate on its own or "work for you"; it had to be reaped from the ground or forged through craftsmanship. Property was fundamentally intended for use, and Democrats were determined to obliterate the power of property to do anything else (Welter 1975, 97). Thus, when Democratic president Andrew Jackson vetoed the rechartering of the Second Bank of the United States, he wrote, "when the laws undertake to add . . . artificial distinctions, to grant titles, gratuities, and exclusive privileges, to make the rich richer and the potent more powerful, the humble members of society—the farmers, mechanics, and laborers—who have neither the time nor the means of securing like favors to themselves, have a right to complain of the injustice of their Government" (Howe 2007, 380).

The vision of an economy of nature, typified in Jackson's veto message, was refracted in Chicago Democratic politics through the critique of wage dependency. When the editor of the *American*, for example, supported the General Land Office's decision to sell land to a speculator named John Kinzie instead of a far less connected M. M. Connel, the *Democrat* insulted the editor declaring, "he is a mere menial of the aristocracy," and condemned the "would-be nobility of this city . . . who now think that with their money they can not only govern the affairs of Chicago, but the balance of Illinois" (October 12, 1836, 2). The idea that wealth could be employed for the purposes of influencing government policy, then, was anathema to the Democrats. The practice was a marker of nobility, and any supporter of the practice, in turn, was predictably referred to in the language of wage dependency as a "menial" of that nobility.

Because they called for both "a return to the beginning" and an economy of nature, the Democrats condemned any interference with small-scale agriculture or artisanry as a presumptuous attempt on the part of aristocrats to deprive freemen of their birthright (Wilson 1974, 8). This view of the republic achieved its fullest expression in matters of national policy. An article from the *Democrat*, titled "Impositions of the Day," brings together a critique of the high tariff (advocated by the Whigs for the protection of domestic manufacturing) with the theme of wage dependency: "We notice the whigs are getting possession of many of our literary, agricultural and mechanical papers and turning them into organs for the advocacy of a high tariff, that blight and mildew of agricultural progress . . . shifting the burthen of taxation from the rich upon the poor. All democrats should frown upon base impositions upon the laboring interest by the hired menials of the aristocracy of our country" (October 11, 1843, 2). A crucial feature of this passage is the distinction made between "the laboring interest" and "hired menials," which mirrors the existing social distinctions between farmers and mechanics, on the one hand, and wage workers, on the other. The implication is that if a tariff is passed, the laboring interest will become hired menials themselves, doomed to shoulder the burden of both indirect taxation through the tariff and thus the "impositions" of the aristocracy. Rather than risk this fate, farmers and mechanics—in a word, Democrats—must rally to defeat the measure.

Of all the debates of the Jacksonian era, however, no other issue in Chicago aroused more suspicion of the incipient market economy than the re-chartering of the Second Bank of the United States, which was then the largest corporation in the country. It handled all of the federal government's financial transactions, made loans to banks and individuals, sold U.S. Treasury securities to foreign buyers, and expanded or contracted the country's money supply in response to the business cycle. As we have seen, the Bank was attacked for having too much power, for trafficking in unnatural property, and for being aloof to the wants and needs of ordinary Americans (Howe 2007, 374, 376).

In this, the critique of wage dependency once again figured prominently, not only in reference to workers and farmers who were framed as the Bank's victims, but also in reference to Whig politicians, who were assailed as hirelings of the Bank. For example, the Democrats charged that the Whig editor of the *Chicago American* was "in the *pay* and *service* of the *United States Bank*," while Whigs in general were men who "sell themselves when they are not wanted"—a sharp contrast to Democrats who comprised "A class of men who cannot be bought nor sold, and who will not be transferred like cattle" (*Chicago Democrat*, July 15, 1835, 2; September 2, 1835, 2). Take as another example this extract from the *Chicago Democrat*: "Let us wage a war of extermination against Bank minions, Bank advocates and Bank owners! . . . The battle field is before us—the golden troops of Biddle [head of the Second Bank of the United States] are in martial array, and let us vanquish them or perish in the last ditch" (August 16, 1837, 2). As in the tariff question where the aristocracy and their hirelings were the enemies of the laboring interest, so, too, is there a distinction made here between "Bank owners" and their dependent "Bank minions," on the one side, and Democrats, on the other. Elsewhere in the same issue, U.S. congressman John Wentworth (see figure 2.1), who was editor of the *Democrat* and head of the Chicago Democratic Party, lampooned the Whigs for arguing that the remedy to the financial Panic of 1837 was government reform. He insisted instead that because banks encourage men to ruin themselves and the country by borrowing beyond their means, the remedy must be the wholesale destruction of the banking system itself. Wentworth began, "To prop up their vascillating [*sic*] credit, men will sell themselves to Banks." To "sell" one's self—as a wage worker would have done—was an odious matter, signifying as it did total desperation and servility to one's patron. For the Democrats, this was contrary to the principles of a natural economy in which sheer physical labor could produce all the necessaries of life. Wentworth continued, "Granting that any other remedy was necessary than the immediate return to the pursuits of honest industry—that a firm reliance upon the adequateness of the productions of our soil to the wants of the inhabitants, and an adaptation of our expenditures to our income, does that remedy belong exclusively to the Government?" Answering his own question, Wentworth concluded that "the proper cause" of the panic originated in the "foppery, extravagance, dissipation, and amusement" of Whig aristocrats (August 16, 1837, 2).

Democratic rhetoric was therefore based fundamentally on the claim that the preservation of national independence relied on the economic independence and self-government of mechanics and especially farmers. Conversely, the descent of farmers and mechanics into a condition of dependency, personified by the hirelings and paid soldiers of the aristocracy, would precipitate the decline of national independence. Because the Democrats relied so heavily on the image of the hireling to advance their party platform, our understanding of their policy solutions to the problem of dependency (e.g., the dismantling of the Second Bank of the United States) would be overly thin without also understanding that

FIGURE 2.1.   Cabinet photograph; ICHi-68764; Portrait of John Wentworth; Chicago, Ill. (n.d.). Photographer: Brisbois, Mosher Gallery. Courtesy of the Chicago History Museum.

wage labor was not free labor. The critique of wage dependency would also form the bedrock of the Whigs' rationale for state-led economic development.

The Spoils Aristocracy

If the Democratic Party claimed that a timeless liberty could be preserved only by a vigilant watch over first principles, then the Whigs' commitment to state-led economic development arose out of a belief that American liberty was a process that was "cumulative and ongoing" (Wilson 1974, 4–5). The Whig legislative program, called "the American System," advanced a vision of progress that "included high protective tariffs to nourish American manufacturing and create a home market for American agricultural products, a national bank to provide a sound and uniform currency, and federal subsidization of internal improvement projects [e.g., canals, roads] to ease the movement of goods" (Holt 1999, 2, 7).

Apart from the republican ideology of the revolution, Whig political culture drew heavily on evangelical Christianity. Evangelicals, who comprised an important constituency of the Whig base, insisted on the individual's freedom of conscience in communing with God; the Christian's conscience alone should guide human behavior, and any outside interference was accordingly viewed as a moral violation. This religious injunction fused with republicanism to frame party discipline—the organizational pressure to tow the party line—as a civic sacrilege. As the preeminent historian of the Whig Party, Michael F. Holt, writes, "because party discipline required men to sacrifice their own views for the good of the organization, because it encouraged blind obedience rather than independent action, party organization crushed freedom of conscience and made men moral slaves" (Holt 1999, 30–31; see also Howe 1979, 9, 14, 18).

Whig politics were not without secular influences. Faculty psychology, for example, which studied the ability of rationality and conscience to offset the influence of animal passions and mechanical needs, animated the Whig distrust of party spirit and the call to arms that so often characterized Democratic exhortations to the public. Faculty psychology, in turn, was complemented by other intellectual trends such as the renewed interest at the time in classical rhetoric, whose practice was also intended to tame the passions with cool-headed statesmanlike rationality (Howe 1979, 31). In addition, the utopian socialism of Robert Owen and Charles Fourier were then very much en vogue. Fourierism in particular was the most popular such movement, at one point boasting twenty-six "phalanxes" (experimental communities), two dozen clubs, and upward of 100,000 members nationally. Horace Greeley, one of the most important powerbrokers in the Whig Party, established his own phalanx in upstate New York, convinced as Fourier himself was, that small cooperative communities, operating on the scientific laws of unity, would spread across the country and necessarily contribute to social harmony and progress (Guarneri 1991, 2, 60). Together with evangelical Christianity, these secular influences animated a contemplative and orderly corporatist worldview within which the putative conflict between elites and nonelites was only a chimera created by Democratic demagogues. Economic independence could be sustained, and also enhanced, if only the people would grant a Whig mandate to transform the republic into a prosperous commonwealth in which all white men would cooperate to assure the well-being of each (Howe 1979; Quist 1998; Welter 1975).

Despite the distinctly solidaristic flavor of these influences, the Whigs nevertheless relied on the critique of wage dependency to advance their rationale for state-led economic development, though they preferred to fasten the stigma of dependency on partisanship rather than on economic institutions. That is, the Whig Party deployed the critique in their insults of Democratic Party leaders, who, they claimed, inculcated slavish loyalty among their constituents and were dependents themselves on the spoils of party patronage (Holt 1999, 29). The tone of contempt in these jabs was animated by a cherished belief that independent men could meditate on the welfare of the republic without being distracted by opportunities for private gain. Any other system, like the British, invited corruption. Free white men were therefore not to be bought or sold on the political market, and a popular way of attacking the opposition for transgressing this inviolable norm was to call them wage workers or hirelings, since the latter were supposedly among the only people desperate enough to take political bribes.

In 1836, for instance, the Whigs accused the Democrats of buying votes with patronage, and likened the practice to wage work, which they characterized as selling one's self to the highest bidder. In the following extract, the editor of the *Chicago American* begins sarcastically, giving the hired voter the benefit of the doubt, and then artfully questions his own judgment:

> Why they may even box in the same twenty four hours every point in the political compass, turn every imaginable somerset, and "play such fantastic tricks, as make the angels weep," and are they not independent? What better evidence want ye of the possession of independent spirit, than perfect freedom of action? And yet some unversed in the science of political action, would stigmatise such vacillation and *weathercockism* the most consummate and degraded dependence that can be imagined,—would brand such voters, such democrats, or what not, with the brutal appellation of "Cattle," and broadly insinuate that

such voters are bought and sold!—that they set themselves up in the political market to the highest bidder—that like the Swiss and Hessians they fight for pay, and are so fond of doing well by their trade, that they will turn around at a moment's warning for higher wages or, more "approved security." (August 6, 1836, 2)

Although their invective is clearly aimed at the Democratic Party, there is nevertheless another obvious target as evidenced by their use of "pay" and "higher wages"—that of the wage system itself. If there was any doubt that Francis Scott Key was alluding to wage dependency in his use of the word, "hireling," the editor—for emphasis it seems—makes reference to "the Swiss and Hessians" who were universally despised by Americans for fighting for pay on the side of the British during the Revolutionary War and the War of 1812. Then, in addition to comparing wage dependency to slavery as in the use of "Cattle"—a device used to invoke the specter of the white slave—the Whigs inform us that political dependency, like wage dependency, is "stigmatized" in their time.

Wentworth graciously republished an attack on himself in an 1835 issue of the *Chicago Democrat*, in which his relationship to the "Kinderhook Magician," Democratic leader Martin Van Buren, was at issue. Of Wentworth, a Whig editor wrote,

> This hireling was imported from New York by the Kinderhook Magician . . . and this menial and tool is to do the dirty work in which he is engaged . . . they appear determined to crush or drive him from the station to which the *unbought* freemen of Illinois had called him . . . and from thence he visited Kinderhook where he received his *orders*. (*Chicago Democrat*, Sept. 2, 1835, 2)

The author of the attack ends by referring to Wentworth as "the imported Swiss," again exploiting the memory of Britain's hired mercenaries to insinuate that Democratic operatives like Wentworth were political dependents. Note, too, the sharp distinction made between "the hireling" who does "the dirty work" on the one hand, and the "unbought freemen of Illinois" on the other. If freemen were not bought, then hirelings—alone in their likeness to slaves—were very much so, an implication which suggests that wage workers in the Jacksonian era were on a par in status with blacks in bonded servitude.

Not surprising, the Whigs portrayed Democratic administrations as hives of waged, and, therefore, political dependency:

> The General and State Governments together control 87,000 [public positions]. This is exclusive of army, navy, and the troop of persons employed by the executive officers of the national and State

governments. The dependents upon all these swell the number to half a million, and makes what may well be regarded as a frightful picture of power upon one hand and dependence upon the other. (*Chicago Daily Journal*, October 8, 1845, 2)

This passage is intended to expose the substance and scope of Democratic power. Substantively, the Whigs imply that the Democrats stand not on principles, but on the mechanism of patronage, which secures the cooperation of party workers by making them economically dependent on the party for their livelihoods. The scope of this influence is vast, for the sum total of federal and state patronage appointments including the armed forces consists of half a million well-placed functionaries, whose only job is to carry out the will of party leaders, irrespective of the future damage to the welfare of the republic. As one address to Illinois Whigs predicted, though "we may wear for a while longer the forms of freemen," under Democratic leadership, "our spirits will be effectually enslaved" (Holt 1999, 32).

If the ideological origins of Democratic opposition to commercial measures would be somewhat opaque without also understanding that wage workers were a dependent population, so, too, would the Whig rationale for state-led economic development. The lone obstacle to their plans of moving the republic up the scale of civilization was political patronage, which they attacked by likening it simultaneously to wage and bonded slavery.

Economic Change and Audience Reception

In 1989, the eminent sociologist Michael Burawoy published an important essay criticizing Adam Przeworski and John Sprague's (1986) attempt to offer a party-centered explanation of working class formation. The latter famously argued that class voting, and thus presumably class identity, were fundamentally "an effect of the activities of political parties," especially socialist and labor parties (1986, 3–4, 10–11). Burawoy countered that Przeworski and Sprague lacked an account of the "micro-foundations" of workers' lives under capitalism, which are "grounded in production and the lived experience it generates" in the workplace (Burawoy 1989, 82–85). This section seeks to halve the distance between Burawoy and Przeworski.

As I have argued already, economic change has no objective political face. Economics matter, but how they matter or are interpreted depends in part on the trajectory and content of institutional politics. This is not to suggest that workers have no interpretations of their own apart from those fed to them by parties in struggle. This would be misleading in general, but especially so with respect to the mid-nineteenth-century American case. The Democratic Party was able to articulate urban workers together with farmers as a class of producers, because antebellum workers had developed their own critique of wage dependency based on the micro-foundations of life under early American capitalism. Labor republicanism, in turn, allowed workers to "recognize" themselves in the Democrats' populist opposition to the Whigs' probusiness agenda.

The National Scene

If the Democratic Party was able to articulate workers and farmers as producers, then it was to some degree because the widening ambit of the market economy in this period led to the erosion of a way of life. Before the age of sweating and factory production, urban workers would have belonged to one of three groups, each corresponding to a stage of craft expertise. Masters, who were usually tradesmen themselves, owned the shop and typically attended to customers, ordered supplies, and kept the books. Apprentices were the lowest ranking workers in the shop, uninitiated in the mysteries of the craft and set to work on the most menial tasks. They were usually teenagers who were taken on as trainees and given board and lodging in return for their labor. Masters often promoted their apprentices to the position of journeymen between the ages of eighteen and twenty-one, marking their passage into manhood with a suit and a wage. A journeyman was a master-in-training, having already been authorized as a bona fide practitioner of his craft, and typically spent his energies saving enough to start a shop of his own. One distinguishing feature of the craft tradition, then, was the mobility between the various positions in the shop. Though the distinctions had real consequences for their work and livelihoods, and though journeymen worked for wages, the constituent groups of the workshop by and large saw themselves as part of a fluid hierarchy (Laurie 1989; Stanley 1998, 89).

Journeymen had nearly complete control over their own work, not only in terms of autonomy (they could do their job without much interference from the master of the shop), but also in terms of the labor process, since they alone did everything necessary from start to finish to turn out the product of their trade. Their work, in other words, was not split into countless infinitesimal movements along an assembly line; the tradesman was an entire assembly line unto himself. Because early nineteenth-century mechanics had a substantial degree of free time on the job, their days were a mixture of work, spirited conversation, fun, and drinking. In fact, it was the job of some apprentices, depending on the trade, to ensure that beer was in constant supply throughout the workday. Moreover, most urban dwellers would have been raised on farms before coming to the city, and were not used to the industrial discipline of even the smallest workshop. Such workers could be found fishing or hunting during the workday or going home to do farm chores. The masters for their part were largely uninterested in speculation or expansion, instead preferring gradual and modest gains, otherwise known as "competencies" (Laurie 1989, 32, 35–37, 44).

All this was changing during the Jacksonian era. As Stanley Lebergott's foundational analysis reports, if the self-employed (e.g., master craftsmen) outnumbered employees (e.g., journeymen) by a ratio of over 5-to-1 in 1800, then by 1860 employees had for the first time in U.S. history overtaken the self-employed (Jentz and Schneirov 2012, 2; Lebergott 1961, 292). This means that the Jacksonian era was the midpoint of America's transition to a primarily wage-based economy. Scholars have argued that this transformation resulted from at least two major changes.

First, the Jacksonian era witnessed the rise of the merchant capitalist, whose main goal was to sell unprecedented quantities of goods at cheap prices. Their proliferation across the market landscape increased competition dramatically, putting added pressure on masters to cut costs by speeding up production in their shops and cutting the wages of journeymen. As the merchant capitalists' hold on market access tightened, masters became their agents, resulting in colder, more impersonal labor relations in the shop. Where once masters were teachers and moral exemplars, they soon became entrepreneurs and employers. If master craftsmen were once members of the same craft societies as their journeymen, bent as they were upon fetching the highest price for their employees' work, they eventually deserted them. Further, in their quest to drive down the costs of production, merchant capitalists began investing less in commerce (their stock-in-trade), and more in manufacturing capital, thereby generating the conditions both for the rise of the factory and sweating systems and for the decline of the small artisan (Lambert 2005, 25; Pessen 1967, 4–5).

Second, revolutionary improvements in transportation entrenched the merchant capitalist still further in the new economy. Though railroads did not become pervasive until the 1850s, roads, harbors, and canals did. The most famous of these projects, the Erie Canal, completed in 1825, had lasting effects throughout the Jacksonian era especially for northeastern and midwestern merchants who gained access to each other's markets for the first time through its construction. Waterways and roads made it possible for large quantities of goods to move cheaply about the country, setting master mechanics in one regional market against those in another, and thereby increasing pressure to ratchet up production and reduce wages even further. Shipping costs by wagon were $0.30 to $0.70

per ton-mile in 1812, but by the 1830s, canal costs were down to as little as a penny per ton (Laurie 1989, 21–23; Pessen 1967, 4–5). Together, the advent of the merchant capitalist and infrastructural improvements led to what Charles Sellers (1991) has called the market revolution, and as a direct result, to the decline of small-scale production.

Though long-term aggregate statistics imply a steady increase in antebellum wage rates, they tend to conceal hidden dynamics that were deleterious to the condition of workers, including steep declines in wages during periodic depressions such as that which occurred in the aftermath of the Panic of 1837, when fully one third of the nation's workers were unemployed and wages decreased between 30 to 50 percent. Nor do aggregate statistics track other trends like deskilling and labor speedups. For example, as Robert Margo (2000) observes, the wage increases of skilled workers were markedly less than those of unskilled workers in this period. Further, just as real wages fluctuated with uncomfortable regularity, the price of consumer goods sometimes increased to almost unlivable levels, due in part to an erratic paper currency. The Federal Reserve's cost-of-living index for the Jacksonian period dropped 6.9 percent from 1829 to 1830, returned to its 1829 rate by 1833, plummeted again in 1834 by 12.1 percent, and then rose a full 41.2 percent to a period high in 1837. This resulted in an increase in the wholesale prices for all commodities across the board, while wages failed to keep step (Fogel 1989; Glickstein 2002; Margo 2000; Pessen 1967; U.S. Bureau of the Census 1961).

In urban centers, where the lie of antebellum material abundance was perhaps most in evidence, the depression of wages made it less possible for journeymen to save enough money to start shops that could compete with the new workplaces, which were greater in size and required more capitalization (Lambert 2005, 25; Laurie 1989, 36). In addition, because the capital requirements to do business were growing, banks flourished due to their lending power. The result was that even master mechanics began to acquire permanent debt, sometimes going to prison upon failing to repay their loans (Hugins 1960, 27; Pessen 1967, 5).

The modicum of control that journeymen did retain was over the labor process, and even this was starting to change. One path toward this development was the factory system, which accounted for a relatively small but growing percentage of manufacturing work, especially in textiles, heavy industry, small segments of the building trades, and the book and periodical branches of the printing trades (Wilentz 1984, 113–114). But as Bruce Laurie (1989, 41–42) points out, such establishments were ahead of their time. The more pervasive and no less unsettling path toward the transformation of the labor process was the "bastard artisan" or "sweating" system. Sweating was carried out in homes and shops where production relied principally on hand tools. In these smaller workplaces, the labor process was subdivided among increasing numbers of underpaid workers, including women, children, and convicts. There is evidence to suggest that such deskilling or "cheapening" had been happening since around 1825 in New York City, but it was occurring on a far grander scale in the 1830s and 1840s to the point that a new generation of journeymen could hardly be called skilled craftsmen at all, though many of them retained the title (Lambert 2005, 25; Laurie 1989, 28, 39–40; Wilentz 1984, 112–114).

The resistance of American workers to this transformation was typically Jacksonian in the sense that it reflected an "anxiety" about the precariousness of their economic independence and the promise of what we today call the American Dream (Glickstein 2002). As Sean Wilentz writes, artisans "elaborated their own variant of American republican ideology, bound to their expectations about workshop production" (1984, 15). Organizationally speaking, this reaction took the form of trade unions and "ten-hour" leagues, which pressed for a shorter workday.

Apart from protesting their low wages, workers called for an end to the newest incursions on labor autonomy and the labor process, which amounted to the progressive devaluation of skill within the trades. They opposed the unregulated hiring of cheap labor in the sweating system, which worked to depress wages and subdivide skilled labor into nothing more than a set of discrete, mindless tasks. Further, workers demanded time for leisure and mental improvement. The Boston Trades Union demanded an adult education system, in which workers could keep abreast of the latest improvements in the mechanical arts and sciences. Perhaps most famously, workers across the country struck for and won the ten-hour day, declaring that the "sunup to sundown" system, which was a carryover from agriculture, was against the laws of "justice and humanity." Indeed, in 1835, Theophilus Fisk was even urging workers to fight for the eight-hour day, firm in the belief that "eight hours for work, eight hours for sleep, [and] eight hours for amusement and instruction" was the "equitable allotment of the twenty-four" (Pessen 1967, 42).

Workers' view of the hours of work as a matter of citizenship and dependency turned on the aforementioned republican principal of civic virtue. Overwork and lack of education interfered with workers' capacity for self-government, and antebellum conceptions of citizenship were defined precisely in terms of this capacity. To repeat, the economically insecure were deemed too desperate to take an interest in the public welfare, and perhaps more ominously could be bought in exchange for their votes. The prospect of a degraded citizenry, on this account, boded ill for the republic as a whole. The labor reformer William Sylvis once said, "Remember, too, that all popular governments must depend for their stability and success upon the virtue and intelligence of the masses; that tyranny is founded upon ignorance; and that while long hours, low wages, and few privileges are the strength and support of the one, they are entirely incompatible with the other" (Lambert 2005, 30).

The platforms of early American labor organizations also included demands for union rights, so that workers might legally defend their independence against the onslaught of masters, factory owners, foremen, and merchant capitalists. They demonstrated against the use of strike breakers and insisted on the right to strike, the right to organize unions, and the closed shop, which required that all employees become union members. These demands emerged in part as a reaction to the phenomenon of conspiracy trials in which courts tried and convicted labor leaders for strike activity (Hattam 1993; Pessen 1967, 21–22 passim; Tomlins 1992).

Workplace issues, in turn, informed workers' opinions about the mainstream political issues of the day. Because the price of staples rose and fell erratically in response to a fluctuating paper currency, Jacksonian era workers opposed the use of paper money, referring to it routinely by the name fastened upon it by the Democratic Party: "rag money." Because more and more mechanics were being imprisoned for debt, workers also opposed the banking system in general, reserving special venom for the Second Bank of the United States, which they called the "Monster" as Andrew Jackson himself did, and against which they incited their members to engage in a "war of extermination." The invocation of "war" in this context does not refer to a class war as in revolutionary socialist discourse, which would appear somewhat later, but instead recalled the ethnic cleansing "Indian Removal" campaigns that made Andrew Jackson a war hero and, in turn, a presidential contender (de Leon 2010; Howe 2007, 376; Hugins 1960, 24, 28, 33–34).

What is interesting about workers' rhetoric in this period was its continuity with Democratic political discourse. It was precisely their activity on behalf of the Democrats that led governors like William L. Marcy of New York to restrict convict labor, the sweating system, and the state banking system. The New York labor leader George Henry Evans joined forces with the Democratic Party, becoming especially active between 1832 and 1834, at the height of President Jackson's war with the Second Bank of the United States (Hugins 1960, 22 passim; Wilentz 1984, 209–210). It was the Democratic opposition to the Bank in particular, that led the Workingmen's Political Association (Evans's radical coalition) to say of Jackson that "there are few who do not prefer him [over the Whig, Henry Clay] for his support of the most important measures which the workingmen advocate" (Hugins 1960, 27). Even when the New York Democratic Party had gradually grown-favorable to banks, effectively repudiating its pledges to the workingmen, the latter forged their own faction within the party and subsequently reunited with the elements of a "purer Tammany" during the Panic of 1837. This was "not . . . to institute a new party" (in the place of the old Tammany Hall organization, which comprised the leadership of the city's Democratic machine), but rather, "to form a union with those of their fellow-citizens whose political principles are truly Democratic" (Hugins 1960, 40). The New York Workingmen, along with similar organizations across the Northeast, therefore did not disavow the Democratic Party; quite the contrary, they insisted that they were the "original Democratic party" reincarnated (Hugins 1960, 41; Wilentz 2005, 420). Their place within that organization is perhaps best symbolized by the memorialization of the labor advocate and Democratic Party editor William Leggett, who, despite having once been labeled a "disorganizer" of the Democracy, was honored as a veritable saint of Tammany Hall upon his death in 1839 (Hugins 1960, 48).[1]

The key question for the purposes of this book is whether the Democratic Party's critique of dependency resonated sufficiently with workers' own anxieties about the market revolution to win their support. To return to the example of New York, it is clear that despite their differences with the Democrats in terms of policy, antebellum workers and Democrats deployed the discourse of dependency in very similar ways (Wilentz 1984, 213–214). Though some like Wilentz (1984) have argued that this consensus allowed the Democrats to co-opt and destroy antebellum labor organizations, an alternative Gramscian interpretation is that the Democrats *acquired the consent* of workers to rule, so that, for instance, their associations regularly endorsed Democratic candidates. My argument, then, is not that antebellum labor politics were somehow reducible to antebellum party politics, but that the social dislocations of early American capitalism and the inherited critique of wage dependency from revolutionary republicanism allowed the Democratic Party to articulate workers together with farmers into a dominant electoral coalition of producers.

Chicago

Within the national arc of the market revolution, Chicago's own economic transformation was spurred by the prospects of the Illinois and Michigan Canal, which promised to link the Great Lakes to the Mississippi River for the first time. Speculators from the East traveled West to transform Chicago from a former French-Indian fur trading post and military fort, into a midwestern boomtown. But even before the completion of the canal in 1848, Chicago's economy had grown exponentially. With the dredging of a town harbor in 1835 that opened up the Chicago River to large vessels traveling through Lake Michigan, the city became a premier link between the growing outposts of the West and New York and Europe by way of the Erie Canal in the East (Cronon 1991, 55–60; Einhorn 1991, 29–31). The pace of population growth resulting from the Northeast-Midwest connection was staggering. After Chicago's own program of "Indian Removal" (called the Black Hawk War), the city's white population grew from 350 at its incorporation in 1833 to 20,023 in 1848, an increase of fifty-seven times its original size in just fifteen years. The largest immigrant communities were Irish-born (20 percent) and German-born (17 percent) and were initially drawn to Chicago in 1836, when construction on the canal began (Einhorn 1991, 31; Levine 1992, 182–183; Pierce 1937, 43, 44n4; Skogan 1984). The growth of trade was just as astonishing. In 1838, Chicago's first shipment of wheat was 78 bushels; by 1848, that number had increased to 2.5 million bushels (Andreas 1886; Fehrenbacher 1957). And in ten short years, from 1840 to 1850, manufacturing increased from $62,000 in capital investment and 414 total "persons" employed, to $1,068,025 in capital investment and a total of 2,081 total "hands" or wage workers employed. Other estimates report a manufacturing work force of 5,000, annually producing goods worth $8,000,000 to $10,000,000 million (Levine 1992, 182; U.S. Census Office 1840 (3), 87, 302–309; U.S. Census Office 1850 (4), 223).

The data on workers' political allegiances during Chicago's "speculative era" are not as robust as those for the period immediately following or as the data for the same period among workers in New York and Philadelphia, but they are strongly suggestive nonetheless. First, if small-scale farmers and workers comprised the base of the local Democratic Party, then we must of necessity inquire into the reasons for this electoral alliance. One important reason is that workers aspired to become farmers in order to escape wage dependency in the nation's cities. As Reeve Huston writes, an exclusive focus on workers as propertyless wage earners "offers a narrow definition of 'labor' that would have seemed alien to most antebellum workers." Workers and farmers had a "shared sense of identity," because both groups thought of themselves "as members of the 'producing classes'" (Huston 1998, 21).[2] In this, Chicago workers were no different, for while many of the aforementioned immigrants were tradesmen, the latter were drawn to Chicago as much by the prospect of land, as they were by the prospect of jobs. "Preemption" laws gave immigrant workers two advantages in the great land grab of this period. First, before federal lands were sold at auction, where the wealthy invariably had a leg up on ordinary working people, preemption laws gave male heads of household already resident in a given state or territory the right of first refusal. This meant that nonresident speculators and developers could only purchase land that residents decided to forego. Second, preemption laws allowed residents to buy land at the federal minimum price instead of having to outbid more affluent players at auction. According to the distinguished historian Bessie Louise Pierce, "In Chicago, as elsewhere, the ease with which land was obtained through pre-emption rights and settlers' agreements, by which immigrants could set up for themselves at small expense, 'encouraged mechanics and labourers, on arriving, or soon after, to abandon their appropriate trades and occupations for a bright hope of soon making their fortunes under the pre-emption laws.'" Accordingly, despite the notable flood of immigrants to the city, the local economy experienced chronic labor shortages (Pierce 1937, 193). Pierce's observation is telling. Had wage labor not been stigmatized, one might logically have expected immigrant tradesmen to stay in the employ of master mechanics or even to start their own shops, but what we see instead is that Chicago's first wave of immigrant workers sought to bypass the worsening condition of both the journeyman and master and become farmers instead. Workers were thus also and at the same time aspiring small-scale agriculturalists, constituents who tended in this period to vote Democratic.

As we saw in the case of New York, unions and other Jacksonian era labor organizations comprised the radical left-wing faction of urban Democratic parties. Chicago workers were clearly familiar with, and supportive of, the movement for a ten-hour day. Josiah Lambert (2005, 36) notes that workers across the country first struck to shorten the workday in the mid-1830s. The city's own ten-hour struggle started at the same time but concluded slightly later. Local workmen began agitating for an end to the agrarian sunup-to-sundown rule in 1836. At a meeting of the "Mechanics of Chicago" on May 14, 1836, the workers, led by H. Volk and J.R. Gavin, voted unanimously in favor of the resolution "That ten hours be considered sufficient for a day's work." The minutes of the meeting report that "upwards of *Forty Mechanics*" signed a pledge to abide by the ten-hour rule (*Chicago American*, May 21, 1836; *Chicago Democrat*, May 18, 1836). Though the workers were initially unsuccessful, the "Clerks of Chicago" (i.e., cashiers) led by A.G. Burley, T.W. Goodrich, C.P. Bradley, E. Densmore, and C.R. Harmon would later win the ten-hour day in the fall of 1841 by signing up at least thirty-two local merchants on a petition that called on employers for an "early closing" of 8 o'clock in the evening (*Chicago Daily American*, September 13, 24, and 30, 1841). Unfortunately, we know very little about the clerks' ideological rationale for the ten-hour rule, but the party press reported the argument that "after a hard day's labor . . . the clerk is fairly entitled, at the very least, to a portion of the evening" (*Chicago American*, September 13, 1841). The latter sentiment echoes the cry of the wider ten-hour movement for some modicum of economic independence in a time when the competitive pressures of the new market economy were making a life of wage labor the rule rather than the exception.

Of course, Chicago Whigs also supported the ten-hour day, so more must be said to explain why the city's workers tended to support the Democrats instead. One clue is the Whigs' corporatist vision of interclass harmony. Indeed, the Whig *American* devoted at least as much, if not more, of its praise for the adoption of the new ten-hour system, to the merchants' "enlightened spirit and liberality," adding that the rule would not likely hurt employers, since "comparatively little business is done here after 8 o'clock" (*Chicago American*, September 13 and 24, 1841). The city's Democrats were not as likely to give economic elites much quarter especially in matters of banking and paper money, and we know from another example of collective protest that the attitude of Chicago workers and farmers was similar to that of the party.

Although wages and employment had gone into decline as early as the Panic of 1837, these indicators of worker prosperity went into free fall when construction of the Illinois and Michigan Canal, the city's main development project since 1836, was suspended in the fall of 1840. By the spring of 1841, wages had fallen 20 to 50 percent, such that the starting monthly wage for a common laborer slipped in the ensuing two years from approximately $30 (at $1 per day) to $16. Because workers and others had less money to spend and because lending and borrowing virtually ground to a halt, Chicago's local market collapsed, and with it, the state bank, whose notes had been the chief currency in use during the preceding years. By October 5, 1842, the currency had been discounted to 65 percent of its former value. Accordingly, the city was flooded with "wildcat currency," paper money backed ostensibly by solvent banks, "whose worthlessness resulted in a series of protests from farmers and workers victimized by merchants who used it in their operations" (*Chicago Democrat*, June 8, 29, 1842; Pierce 1937, 72, 72n162).

Whereas Chicago Whigs defended banks and paper money as critical to a sound financial system, the city's Democrats assailed these institutions. In the middle of the currency crisis, the *Chicago Democrat* wrote, using the familiar trope of aristocracy, "Citizens of Illinois! Have you not been swindled enough by these banking gentry from Michigan and Ohio?" Referring to the bankers' fallacious claims that their notes were as good as "specie" (i.e., gold and silver), the *Democrat*, which advocated a hard metal currency, wondered, "why do not these knaves take specie along with them?" (*Chicago Democrat*, June 29, 1842).

Chicago workers and farmers seemed to approve of the Democrats' oppositional rhetoric on this issue. In a letter to the editor of the *Democrat*, for example, a farmer wrote, "I am pleased to see . . . your paper, awake to this important subject," while a workingman commended the paper's "laudable efforts" to call attention to the subject of "a depreciated currency" (*Chicago Democrat*, June 8 and 29, 1842). The workingman, in particular, went on to add that the depreciation of the ten-cent denomination, which constituted a large portion of the

TABLE 2.1   Democratic share of Chicago's presidential returns in 1844 by precinct

PRECINCT	1844 (POLK)
North	62.3
Southwest	56.1
Southeast	52.5
West	62.7

Sources: For socioeconomic statistics, Einhorn (1991, 261); for 1844 electoral returns, *Chicago Democrat*, November 12, 1844.

money circulating among "tol-worn" laborers, is "swindling" 25 percent from those "whose small pittance is accumulated by the sweat of the brow" (*Chicago Democrat*, June 29, 1842). As precinct-level protest meetings were being organized, one letter to the editor by "THE VOICE OF MANY," reads, "I think the farmers and mechanics should feel themselves more interested than they have done formerly and get their own class appointed delegates to the conventions, and nominate honest farmers and mechanics. I think the Bank party have ruled long enough" (*Chicago Democrat*, June 8, 1842). This last letter is important for at least two reasons. First, the "Bank" or Whig party, which took power in 1840, is blamed for the present calamity. Second, the author views farmers and workers as a class, reflecting both the Democrats' political strategy and, as the research of Reeve Huston suggests, the widespread view on the ground of workers and farmers as a unified class of producers. Incidentally, all three of the foregoing letters supported the Democratic call for a hard specie-based currency.

Finally, there are the presidential returns of 1844. These are unfortunately the earliest available precinct-level data, but they are important as the last set of election results before the onset of the political crisis over slavery. The 1844 returns listed in table 2.1 were not reported by ward but by relatively sprawling precincts and are therefore less precise than the 1852 data. However, they point to an important divide between the north and west polls, on the one hand, and the southwest and southeast polls, on the other. The southeast or lakeshore precinct was by far the most affluent section of town (as it continues to be today). The southwest poll, located just inland from the lakeshore below the mouth of the Chicago River was the next most affluent. Table 2.1 shows that the Democrats were strongest in the west and north, which were immigrant majority-worker precincts, breaking the 60 percent barrier in both cases. By contrast, the Democrats were held to well below that mark in the wealthier more native-born precincts, doing worst of all in the southeast poll, where Chicago's Yankee elite resided.

The returns provide evidence of competing ethnic- and class-based electoral coalitions. Democrats performed better in precincts where German and Irish workers predominated, whereas the Whigs did better in precincts that contained middle- to upper-income native-born neighborhoods.

Conclusion

If the above data suggest anything, it is that Francis Scott Key's invocation of the hireling and slave was no offhand poetic flourish. It reflected a widely held assumption that wage labor was not free labor. The discourse of dependency emerged from a particular vision of republican civic virtue, which assigned to economic independence the peculiar role of preventing citizens and their representatives from enriching themselves at the expense of the republic as a whole. Accordingly, those who were imagined to live off the fruit of their own labor, especially farmers, became the icons of independence in this period, while those who were said to depend on others for their livelihood such as slaves and wage workers were stigmatized for their subjection to a master class.

In the Jacksonian era, the discourse of dependency became all the more salient as the economic independence of mechanics eroded under the pressure of the market revolution. The increasing influence of merchant capitalists, advances in transportation, and the emergence of the banking system for the provision of large capital outlays, together combined to give rise to the market economy. As that economy absorbed local spheres of production into its ambit, it compelled master mechanics to compete against their own kind for survival. Journeymen mechanics, in turn, saw their work subdivided into discrete tasks that were increasingly performed by women, children, and convicts. The artisan's shop gave way to sweat shops in the main, but both would soon become outmoded by the factory.

Such developments, however, did not preordain one politics over another. Economic context and interest are important to understanding party politics to be sure, but the former do not give rise to the latter in a linear manner. Rather workers' interpretation of their experience under early American capitalism was refracted through the prism of party politics. If the Democrats were successful in articulating urban workers together with farmers in the Jacksonian era, they did so in part by fastening the evocative tropes of the discourse of dependency onto commercial measures. For their part, the target audience experienced the reality of mounting dependency in their own lives and were moved to action not only by what we might call "labor republicanism," but also by the notion—articulated by the party—that their situation approximated that of the original patriots, who rose up against the impositions of the British aristocracy. For the Whigs, it was the Democratic Party that embodied the aristocracy, while the men of all classes played the patriots who were shackled by the political dependency inculcated by Democratic patronage.

In both cases, the major parties attempted to establish a circuit of recognition with would-be constituents. That is, each party tried to articulate workers as part of an overall vision of the fundamental cleavages of American society, though these actors tended to recognize themselves more consistently in the Democrats' economic populism than in the Whigs' antipartyism. The two ends of this diode must connect for political dominance to take hold. By extension the circuit must be broken and established anew with a different set of identities, interests, and constituents to generate lasting social and political change.

In this, the political identity of workers, as shaped by their own organizations and the major parties, turned simultaneously on class and race. The stigma of wage dependency derived in no small part from the frequent allusions in political discourse to the situation of southern slaves. To insult a peer, one needed only to insinuate that he was in the "pay and service" of a master (whether a bank or a party), and then it mattered little whether one was a hireling or a slave. One was akin to the other in Jacksonian parlance. Rather than resign themselves to degradation, antebellum workers struggled to obtain tokens and statuses that distinguished themselves from African bondsmen. They became farmers, appealed to employers for a ten-hour day, and elevated the Democratic Party to the halls of power. With respect to class identity, it bears repeating that Jacksonian era workers did not see themselves as the proletarianized mass of industrial capitalism, which was just beginning to emerge, but instead as one with farmers (the former aspiring to be the latter) in an electoral coalition of producers.

3

THE POLITICAL CRISIS OVER SLAVERY AND THE RISE OF FREE LABOR, 1844–1860

The last chapter illustrated that the critique of wage dependency permeated Jacksonian political discourse. It targeted the wage system directly, and it comprised the underlying framework of each party's economic policy. The assumption at the heart of the critique's Jacksonian usage was that wage dependency was tantamount to slavery; the black southern variant was condemned by an abolitionist few, but its white northern counterpart was widely stigmatized. If free wage labor is the central feature of capitalism as Marx, Weber, and many others have argued, then we might say that the antebellum polity was less than enthusiastic in its support. Accordingly, the question arises: Why did the critics of wage dependency reorganize in favor of a liberal capitalist democracy?

The answer I offer in this chapter is that partisan contention over the issue of slavery extension—that is, over whether slavery could rightfully exist in the western territories—shifted the terms of political debate away from a critique of dependency under industrial capitalism, toward a critique of dependency under slavery. Instead of arguing about the tyranny of banks and other economic institutions, the major parties argued about whether wealthy southern planters would monopolize western lands and thereby prevent workers from escaping wage dependency in the nation's cities. The anti-extension or Free Soil factions of the major parties bolted their respective organizations and established the Republican Party. Party factionalism, in turn, disrupted ethnic and class voting blocs on the ground, Irish and German workers being among the most prominent. A majority of the Irish remained loyal Democrats due to anti-Catholic sentiment in certain Republican quarters, but German workers, who were mostly Protestant and, by 1860, the largest foreign-born voting bloc in the country and in Chicago, resonated with the Free Soil critique and defected from the Democratic Party.

As the foregoing summary implies, the prime movers of this transformation were political parties, but not all parties are created equal. Because the Democratic Party was hegemonic just prior to the political crisis over slavery, and because Democratic hegemony was anchored in the critique of wage dependency, we must of necessity focus primarily on the factors that fractured that electoral coalition. By way of preview, I argue that the struggle over slavery extension overlapped with a largely intergenerational struggle for leadership succession in the Democratic Party. With the rise of the new leadership, territorial policy eclipsed economic policy as the central object of political debate; in time this shift would beg the divisive question of the status of slavery in the territories. Republicans were not merely the passive beneficiaries of Democratic disorganization, however. As I demonstrate toward the end of this chapter, the Republicans deftly suppressed anti-immigrant elements in their midst so as to secure the support of the vast majority of German voters, while retaining a specifically anti-Catholic posture that alienated the Irish and other Catholics, but in doing so further cemented their support among Protestants and secularists. The Republican Party also forged a distinct procapitalist synthesis of the discourse of dependency that polarized the electorate into pro- and antislavery coalitions and thereby made other political issues meaningless as positions.

As in the last chapter, I leave economic change and audience reception to the second half. The focus of that section will be on German workers, as the Irish remained in the Democratic coalition for the reasons just identified. The overarching implication of the second half of the chapter is that the partisan struggle over slavery extension shaped both German civil society and an incipient labor-centered public sphere. Where once workers and farmers came together to protest a sham paper currency, echoing the strains of Jacksonian Democratic rhetoric, in 1848 Chicago workers, led in part by German artisans, organized a land reform league to protest slavery extension as the major parties took up the issue. When the Compromise of 1850 settled that controversy temporarily, the city's workers organized unions for the first time and in 1853 participated in a national strike wave. Later, during the economic downturn of 1857, when unemployed workers appealed to city hall for relief, the Republican Party influenced the strategy of the largely German-led movement by tying local economic issues to the issue of slavery extension.

None of this is to say that workers merely do what parties tell them. Chicago workers continued to cultivate their own relatively autonomous grievances about the evolution of workshop production and the dimming prospects of economic independence. These grievances turned not only on the preexisting critique of wage dependency, but also on the ideologies that immigrant workers brought over with them from Europe. Many German Republicans, for example, were refugees of the 1848 revolutions; some of them were socialists and loose associates of Karl Marx. Yet immigrant workers did not bring these influences into a political vacuum. In their encounter with American politics, they either abandoned their earlier ideological commitments or, as was more often the case in the antebellum period, fused them creatively with partisan demands for land reform.

Neither does economic change or the business cycle turn at the behest of political parties. The 1850s saw a dramatic economic expansion, which inflated the price of staples beyond the pace at which it drove up workers' wages. This factor, too, which was at least partly unmediated by institutional politics, shaped workers' actions at the time, providing some of the impetus for the 1853 strike wave, for example. But partisan struggle cast a shadow even in this case, for the absence of antislavery agitation after the Compromise of 1850 created room for the contestation of other issues. This is demonstrated counterfactually both by workers' collective protest of slavery extension in the period immediately prior to 1850, and by workers' abrupt organizational return to the slavery issue in 1854 with the debate and passage of the Kansas-Nebraska bill. Of course, slavery was not the only factor that defused labor organization in this period. The successive economic downturns of 1854–1855 and 1857 also disempowered the strike wave unions, but hard times cannot explain why workers found the organizational strength and will to mobilize against slavery extension from 1854 through the Civil War. The "hard times" thesis also conceals the ways in which the economic crisis and the community response thereto fed back onto slavery extension politics as Republicans blamed the downturn on the Democrats' loyalty to the South.

The centrality of political parties in my account is therefore not some kind of partisan reductionism, where factors located "outside" of institutional politics are simply a reflection of what is going on "inside." Rather, I hope to foreground the complex interaction of parties, civil society, and economic change in this period. As I have argued time and again, economic change and social differences matter, but how they matter depends to some degree on the ways in which political parties use them as a basis for mass mobilization. In this period, that process unfolds with a fateful shift in political debate from economic to territorial policy.

Territorial Expansion and the Critique of Wage Dependency

A generational transition in Democratic Party leadership shifted the terms of political debate from economic to territorial policy, with the Democrats supporting aggressive territorial expansion and the Whigs counseling caution and the development of existing territory. In Illinois, the champions of territorial expansion were Democrats: Senators Sidney Breese and James Shields and Congressmen William A. Richardson, John Wentworth, and John A. McClernand. The leader of these so-called Young America or New Democrats both in Chicago and nationally was Congressman, and later Senator, Stephen A. Douglas (see figure 3.1) (Eyal 2007, 13; Kiper 1999, 7; Pierce 1937, 390).

Despite the pivot to territorial policy, New Democratic politics, like Jacksonian politics, were anchored in the critique of wage dependency. New territory

FIGURE 3.1.   Photographic print; ICHi-10086; Portrait of Stephen Douglas, probably taken before 1860. Photographer: unknown. Courtesy of the Chicago History Museum.

promised additional public domain, and that, in turn, allowed workers to move on from places where land had largely ended up in elite hands, to new ones where land was cheap and its use by squatters was essentially free (Eyal 2007, 148; Nelson and Sheriff 2008, 12). As one Democrat put it, the effect of cheap land in the west, "would be to invite a large number of individuals who had settled in eastern cities, who were half-starved and dependent on those who employed them, to go to the West, where with little funds, they could secure a small farm on which to subsist and . . . get rid of that feeling of dependence which made them slaves" (Morrison 1997, 17). The solution to wage dependency, then, was not the prostration of the "Monster Bank" as it was under Andrew Jackson, but instead a sprawling frontier to which factory and sweatshop operatives could escape and farm their own land.

Conversely, Democrats condemned Whig vacillation on territorial expansion as tacit support for the permanent enslavement of free white men in industrial servitude. By way of background, the Whigs opposed the taking of western lands like Texas and Oregon by force, largely out of fear that the maneuver would provoke a costly war with foreign powers like Great Britain. So as not to be on the wrong side of territorial expansion, which had become immensely popular with the electorate, the Whigs urged caution instead of outright intransigence. As a brief discussion of Whig territorial policy will show below, the focus of their attacks remained Democratic demagoguery, but to the extent that they offered substantive policy alternatives, they generally favored peaceful solutions to territorial disputes. For example, whereas the Democrats vowed to make war with Great Britain over Oregon (most famously in the slogan, "54°40′ or fight!"), the Whigs advocated a treaty with the mother country and an exchange of "equivalents"—a piece of American soil for British soil.

In response, the Chicago Democrats redeployed the discourse of dependency in two ways. First, because the Whig presidential nominee, Henry Clay, opposed the immediate annexation of Texas, and because this then forestalled settler migration to the West, the Democrats insinuated that he favored the enslavement of his fellow citizens. Thus, on June 19, 1844 at the height of the Texas controversy, the editor of the *Chicago Democrat* wrote sardonically of Clay that "if he cannot have BLACK slaves, [he] is determined to turn his fellow men into WHITE ones."

Second, the Democrats claimed that the Whigs were secretly in cahoots with the British crown. For example, as the 1844 presidential election drew to a close, the *Democrat* posted the official returns from across the country. Over the states that gave their electoral votes to the Whigs, the editor affixed the image of a crown that echoed the third verse of "The Star Spangled Banner." Like the "hireling and slave" who were bound to the will of King George III, the inscription on the lower band of the crown signified the Whigs' subservience to British interests: "ENGLAND EXPECTS EVERY WHIG TO DO HIS DUTY" (*Chicago Democrat*, Nov. 27, 1844).

Chicago Whigs offered a two-point reply. The first was policy-centered. The annexation of Texas, the Whigs predicted, would involve the United States in "a war with Mexico, probably with other foreign powers" that would be not only "dangerous to the integrity of the Union," but also "inexpedient in the present financial condition of the country" (*Chicago Daily Journal*, September 2, 1844).

Beyond a sober assessment of the cost and geopolitical risk of territorial expansion, the Whigs once again turned back the charge of aristocracy by framing the Democrats' uncritical loyalty to party as the disposition of hirelings and slaves. Moreover, because many Chicago Whigs had abolitionist leanings, the annexation of Texas to the southern part of the Union took on added meaning: Democratic support for that initiative signified subservience both to the party and to the South. Accordingly, in the heat of the 1844 presidential campaign season, the Whigs argued that the Texas issue was "forced upon" "the better portion" of the Democratic Party by "its slaveholding leaders" and that "multitudes" of the latter's rank-and-file were "striving to burst the party shackles, and regain a mental independence" (*Chicago Daily Journal*, September 2, 1844). Later that year, when U.S. congressman John Wentworth cast a prosouthern vote despite his stated abhorrence of slavery, the Whigs invoked the image of the hireling by calling Wentworth "a white slave," whose "taste might incline him to remain in ignoble servitude" (*Chicago Daily Journal*, December 26, 1844).

The Free Soil Revolt

Thus, while the policy issues had changed, the critique of wage dependency remained central to the parties' appeal to workers, with Democrats framing the West as an escape hatch from industrial servitude and the Whigs framing adherence to Democratic demagoguery as political servitude. The pivot to territorial policy might have continued to integrate seamlessly with Jacksonian rhetoric in this way had the status of slavery in the new territories not bedeviled its boosters and played on preexisting resentments.

Internal tension had already been brewing since the unanticipated defeat of Martin Van Buren for the 1844 Democratic presidential nomination. A majority of Democratic powerbrokers viewed the 1844 campaign cycle as a chance to avenge Van Buren's defeat in the 1840 presidential election. The incoming Democratic-controlled Congress had elected a Van Buren lieutenant, John W. Jones, speaker of the House, to push through his legislative agenda, and the majority of delegates going into the national convention were pledged to Van Buren. But Young America Democrats had national leadership aspirations and were eager to replace their party's populist opposition to a national bank and other commercial measures with a policy of aggressive territorial expansion. Thus, after Van Buren announced his opposition to the annexation of Texas in April 1844, the Young America faction pounced and at the national convention called the now infamous "two-thirds rule," which required that the presidential nominee have the support of at least two-thirds of those assembled. Having organized just enough delegates to deny Van Buren a supermajority through eight ballots, they forced the nomination of a compromise candidate, James K. Polk of Tennessee, who at the time was a washed-up politician but had the backing of fellow Tennessean and former Democratic president Andrew Jackson. In a sign of the rancor to come, Silas Wright, one of Van Buren's closest allies, declined the nomination for the vice-presidency, the first ever vice-presidential nominee to do so (Eyal 2007, 127; Feller 2001, 65; Johannsen [1973] 1997, 127, 143–145; Leonard 2002, 253; Merry 2009, 1; Morrison 1997, 13–14, 28–31; Seigenthaler 2003, 3).

Though nearly all Democratic cadres dutifully supported Polk in the 1844 presidential election, the party was splitting into two great factions: the "hunkers," mostly midwestern and southern Democrats who aligned with the new Young America leadership, and the "barnburners," mainly northern Van Buren Democrats. The latter would later oppose the expansion of slavery into the western territories, a position that earned them the additional moniker, Free Soil. Some Democrats emerged from the 1844 convention as full-fledged barnburners, but many others had to arrive at that conclusion. One such Democrat was David Wilmot of Pennsylvania.

When Congress took up debate in 1846 on payment for territories acquired in the settlement of the U.S.-Mexican War, Wilmot attached a proviso to the appropriations bill that slavery be prohibited from any such territory. Wilmot, it is important to note, was no fringe abolitionist. Prior to the debate over slavery in the Mexican cession, he had been the most regular of regular Democrats. But after President Polk vetoed federal funding for northern infrastructural improvements and negotiated half of Oregon away to Britain after insisting on annexing all of Texas, Wilmot and other party stalwarts began to connect the dots from the betrayal of Van Buren at the last Democratic convention to a "slave power conspiracy," in which a southern minority schemed to thwart the will of the northern majority. If the slave power could impose Texas annexation as a litmus test for the 1844 presidential nomination, then Wilmot and his colleagues wanted to show them that two can play at that game. During the 1848 presidential election, the barnburners mounted a third-party challenge to bar slavery from the western territories, on the grounds that a monopoly of the land by wealthy planters would prevent free white men from escaping wage dependency in the nation's cities. Southern Rights Democrats charged that the prohibition would make them second-class citizens, while the Young America leadership tried to quell dissension with a middle-of-the-road policy called "popular sovereignty" that would have allowed settlers to decide by referendum whether their territory should be free or slave (Feller 2001, 67–68; Leonard 2002, 253–254; Merry 2009, 286–287; Morrison 1997, 39–41).

In Illinois, Wilmot's proviso pit the Chicago Democratic machine led by Congressman John Wentworth, who was Free Soil, against the state party led by Senator Stephen A. Douglas, who favored popular sovereignty. Wentworth was the only member of the Illinois congressional delegation to vote in favor of the proviso. Further, he explicitly justified his position both as a defense against the slave power conspiracy and as retribution for the Texas controversy of 1844 (Fehrenbacher 1957, 63 passim).[1] Although Wentworth did not officially leave the party, the 1844 and 1848 presidential returns nevertheless point to an unprecedented division in the local Democratic organization and a defection of once reliable Democratic precincts (see table 3.1).

Early Worker Opposition to Slavery Extension

Recall that the southeast and southwest polls were Chicago's most affluent precincts, while immigrant workers tended to cluster in the north and west precincts. Table 3.1 reminds us that in 1844 the Democrats carried the city with a comfortable majority and did best in lower-income immigrant precincts. By 1848, voting patterns had shifted dramatically. That Democratic support fell precipitously in the southeast and southwest is not particularly surprising as these were Whig-heavy precincts; of greater interest is the fact that Democratic support dropped by double digits throughout the city, including the north and

TABLE 3.1 Democratic share of Chicago's presidential returns in 1844 and 1848 by precinct

PRECINCT	1844 (POLK)	1848 (CASS)
North	62.3	41.7
Southwest	56.1	16.6
Southeast	52.5	30.4
West	62.7	28.6

Sources: For socioeconomic statistics, Einhorn (1991, 261); for 1844 electoral returns, *Chicago Democrat*, November 12, 1844; for 1848 electoral returns, *Chicago Daily Journal*, November 8, 1848.

west. According to official returns published in the November 11, 1848 issue of the *Democrat*, Van Buren, now running as the presidential nominee of the Free Soil Party, carried Chicago with just over 40 percent of the vote, whereas Cass, the regular Democratic nominee, came not in second place, but in third behind the Whig nominee, Zachary Taylor.

The surviving statements of Chicago workers on the issue of slavery extension explain why the Free Soil message gained traction among less affluent voters. In March 1848, a group of artisans organized the Chicago auxiliary of the National Reform Association (NRA), which sought to make land an entitlement of free white men (Bronstein 1999, 169; Lause 2005, 99, 100, 102). In the December 8, 1848 issue of the NRA organ, the *Gem of the Prairie*,[2] the Chicago land reformers framed their "protest against the further extension of the area of chattel slavery and monopoly of the soil" in this way:

> A denial to the mass of mankind of their equal right to a portion of the earth, must, in the course of events, build up a state of society in which the monopolists of the earth will accumulate all the wealth of the country while the toiling millions, who are the producers of that wealth, must become wage slaves, and sink into hopeless destitution and famine.

The terms of the NRA's opposition to slavery extension are palpably similar to Free Soil and earlier Democratic rhetoric, suggesting that the party's attempt to bind the critique of wage dependency to the policy of territorial expansion was shaping not only how workers voted, but also how they understood the prerequisites of freedom and citizenship. Indeed, Wentworth had fulminated against the "monopoly of the soil" in the columns of the *Chicago Democrat* as early as January 11, 1848, two months before the founding of the Chicago NRA (see also Fehrenbacher 1957, 74).

The backstory to the establishment of the auxiliary provides still further evidence of the effect of Free Soil organization on the course of worker opposition to slavery extension. A leading figure in the German-American land reform movement was one Hermann Kriege, who, before sailing for the United States, had been a dyed-in-the-wool socialist, a student of Ludwig Feuerbach, and a member of the League of the Just, which later fused with the communist organization headed by none other than Marx and Engels. Upon immersing himself in American politics, however, Kriege abandoned communism in favor of a "democracy of the land," establishing the Association der Social-Reformer (the Social Reform Association, or SRA), which was aligned with the English-speaking NRA. Kriege worked with Carl Hellmuth, a physician, printer, and early editor of Chicago's

German-language Democratic organ, the *Illinois Staats-Zeitung*. Hellmuth was a founding member and vice president of the Chicago NRA, and it was Hellmuth who helped mobilize German voters in the city's North Side for the Free Soil Party in 1848 (*Gem of the Prairie*, May 20, 1848; Levine 1992, 105, 150). The city's NRA auxiliary worked so closely with Free Soilers that they formally amalgamated at the Chicago Court House on November 30, 1848, resolving, "That we, as National Reformers, will discontinue our regular public meetings, and unite with the Free Democracy" (*Gem of the Prairie*, December 9 1848; see also Lause 2005, 100, 102). Like the Jacksonian labor organizations we encountered in chapter 2, then, the Chicago land reformers borrowed from Free Soil discourse and aligned with that faction of the Democratic Party organizationally.

The Compromise of 1850 and Democratic Détente

In the shadow of their defeat, the Democratic leadership predicted correctly that if they could put the issue of slavery extension behind them, cadres like John Wentworth would fall back into line, and with them, the immigrant worker base. Thus, when a compromise bill seemed doomed, Senator Stephen A. Douglas resuscitated the deal by shepherding a series of votes on its individual components until the whole compromise was passed. The Democrats thus settled the debate over Wilmot's proviso by making California free, pledging "noninterference" in New Mexico and Utah, and referring all future disputes over slavery in the territories to the U.S. Supreme Court (Morrison 1997, 124).

TABLE 3.2 Democratic share of Chicago's presidential returns by ward and class, 1852–1860

WARD	1852 (PIERCE)	1856 (BUCHANAN)	1860 (DOUGLAS)
1	48.7	28.3	36.5
2	In ward 1 count	37.0	42.1
3	65.1	39.1	46.3
4	74.9	48.2	50.05
5	**56.1**	**38.7**	**731 short of majority**
6	**73.2**	**40.6**	**34.8**
7	**86.8**	**55.2**	**48.2**
8	**63.5**	**51.1**	**44.2**
9	in ward 8 count	51.4	49.1
10	n/a	n/a	57.8

Sources: For socioeconomic statistics, Einhorn (1991, 261, 263); for electoral returns, *Chicago Democrat*, November 9, 1852; *Chicago Tribune*, November 7, 1860; de Leon (2008, 54).

Note: Boldface indicates majority worker wards.

With everyone committed to "finality" (the concept that the controversy over slavery extension had been settled), the hunker and barnburner wings of the Illinois Democratic party reunited. Douglas and Wentworth, who had been at odds over the proviso, buried the hatchet at a closed-door conference on May 21, 1851 (Fehrenbacher 1957, 117–118).

The 1852 presidential returns reported in the second column of table 3.2 suggest that the Democratic Party had reabsorbed the defecting precincts of 1848. Since the proportion of skilled workers throughout the city remained stable at about 25 percent in the 1850s, majority worker wards (signified in boldface) are those in which unskilled workers comprised at least an additional one-third of the male labor

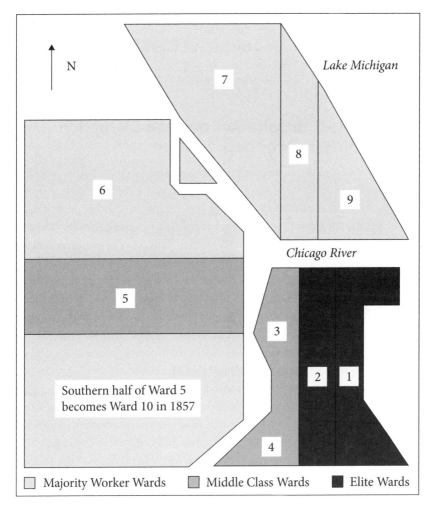

FIGURE 3.2. Chicago Ward Map, 1847–1863. Reproduced with permission from Emerald Group Publishing.

force, giving skilled and unskilled workers together a comfortable voting majority. The resulting ward designations reflect the natural break between Chicago's affluent lakeshore communities represented by wards 1 and 2 where unskilled workers comprised less than one-quarter of the labor force, and the interior of the city where the proportion of unskilled workers ranged from just over one-third (wards 5, 6, 8, and 9) to one-half (ward 7) (see figure 3.2) (Einhorn 1991, 249, 261).

Only the most affluent wards (1 and 2), which are located on today's Magnificent Mile corridor, cast a majority of their ballots for the Whigs. In contrast, all five of the city's majority worker wards and the two middle-class wards (3 and 4) gave the Democratic presidential candidate Franklin Pierce convincing majorities ranging from 56 to 86 percent. The Democratic wards consisted mainly of immigrant workers: a) the North side's seventh through ninth wards were ones in which German workers predominated; b) the West side sixth was evenly split between German and Irish workers; and c) the lower portion of the South side's fifth ward and increasingly the fourth were Irish majority worker neighborhoods.

The Kansas-Nebraska Act and the Disruption of the Chicago Two-Party System

The Democrats had therefore reforged their winning electoral coalition in Chicago by settling the status of slavery in the western territories. But rather than turn to economic or other issues that might have avoided slavery agitation, the Democrats doubled down on territorial expansion believing that the Compromise of 1850 spelled out the terms under which their party might take credit for annexing future territories. Indeed, even as the debate over the proviso raged, Douglas and other Young America leaders had been quietly moving to annex Cuba (Johannsen [1973] 1997, 326). Once the compromise had been finalized, the Democratic leadership was supremely confident that they would once again return to dominance on the twin strength of their appeal for more territories and Douglas's role in securing the passage of the compromise. As one Democrat put it, victory was assured "with Douglas and Cuba inscribed on our flag, as in 1844 we had Polk, Dallas, and Texas" (Morrison 1997, 125).

The Democrats thus renewed the country's march westward, and in a fateful move that put Chicago and the nation on a course toward crisis, Stephen A. Douglas authored the Kansas-Nebraska Act of 1854 to occupy the large Indian reservation just west of the Missouri River and link it to the lands of the Mexican cession (Douglas [1853] 1961, 270). By leaving the question of slavery in Kansas and Nebraska to a vote of the people (i.e., popular sovereignty), the act abrogated the Missouri Compromise of 1820, which prohibited slavery north of the

Mason-Dixon Line. As slavery could now conceivably be established in the North by popular referendum, the act resurrected the twin specter of the monopoly of northern lands by southern planters and the enslavement of free white men in the nation's sweatshops and factories. The Democrats' subsequent mismanagement of Kansas statehood then spelled the end of Democratic hegemony in Chicago and throughout the North. By attempting to force the proslavery Lecompton Constitution on the people of Kansas, the majority of whom were free soilers, the Democratic administration, then led by President James Buchanan, effectively reversed itself on the doctrine of popular sovereignty.

Wentworth was loath to break his truce with Douglas over the Kansas-Nebraska bill, but he denounced the measure nonetheless. He did so tentatively at first by voting with other Free Soil congressmen to postpone the vote on Douglas's bill and by authoring mild editorials in the *Chicago Democrat* in February and early March 1854 reaffirming his long-standing opposition to the doctrine of popular sovereignty. His tentativeness, however, gave way to outright mutiny after Douglas gave instructions to his henchman, Ike Cook, to establish an anti-Wentworth Democratic newspaper, the *Chicago Times*, and dismiss all postmasters who refused to promote its circulation. By late May 1856, Wentworth had rejoined his Free Soil colleagues from both major parties in a "fusion" movement that became the Illinois Republican Party; in 1857, he became Chicago's first Republican mayor (Fehrenbacher 1957, 128–135, 138–141).

The bill also divided the opposition. Chicago Whigs split in two with the Silver Gray establishment faction urging compromise with the southern planter wing of their party and the Republican faction calling for fusion with Free Soil Democrats. The feud culminated in the Congressional elections of 1854 when the Republican faction nominated a Free Soil candidate, Chicago mayor James Woodworth, while the Silver Grays, who found the nomination of their sworn enemy intolerable, nominated the more conservative Whig stalwart Robert S. Blackwell. Woodworth's Republican coalition won a clear majority, but Blackwell, who mustered only one-fifth of the popular vote, took 40 percent of the Whig base with him. As Holt notes, with the Republican faction in the ascendant, "the Chicago Whig organization had not been completely supplanted, but it had been ripped apart" (1999, 870).

The 1856 electoral returns reflect the renewed split between the Douglas and Wentworth wings of the Democratic Party and the rise of the Republicans. Recall that in 1852, just two years prior to the passage of the Kansas-Nebraska bill, the Democrats had carried Chicago overwhelmingly, capturing all five of the city's majority worker wards (5 through 9) and the two middle-class wards (3 and 4). The third column of table 3 shows that the Democrats retained only three of these in the 1856 presidential election, and witnessed a steep erosion of their base even in the wards they still carried. The Democratic Party's share of the popular vote dropped by double digits throughout Chicago, but the decline was most precipitous in the seventh ward, which housed the highest percentage of workers in the city.

Newspaper reports confirm that the defection took place principally among the majority-German wards of the city. In the lead-up to the 1856 election, those voters filled Chicago's imposing German Theatre and then marched in a torchlight procession in support of the Republican presidential ticket of John C. Frémont and William L. Dayton. The theme throughout the night's speeches was a "determination to battle zealously and untiringly for free labor." Significantly, the Turnverein, which was one of Chicago's earliest and most radical German-American labor organizations, was a prominent guest and presence at the event (*Chicago Tribune*, August 26, 1856, 2). Commenting on the German Democratic exodus with approbation, the editors of the *Chicago Tribune* wrote in terms reminiscent of Barrington Moore's account of realigning class fractions: "We are glad to notice this movement, as it betokens the final separation of the liberal German element from the intolerant Pro-Slavery Democracy" (July 15, 1856, 2).

Later, as local politics became consumed with the battle over Kansas statehood, the imposition of the proslavery Lecompton Constitution on that state's Free Soil majority pit President Buchanan, who supported Lecompton, against Stephen A. Douglas, who had come out in opposition to it in late 1857, because it had not been put to a vote of the people (Douglas [1857a] 1961, 403; [1857b] 1961, 405; Johannsen [1973] 1997, 678; Nichols 1948, 211–212). The somewhat paradoxical results of the 1860 presidential election reflect the all-out defection of Wentworth's Free Soil faction and a lukewarm satisfaction among the rump of the Democratic wards with Douglas's belated defense of northern sentiment. The Democrats bounced back modestly in wards 3 and 4 and carried the lower half of the old fifth ward, now the new tenth ward, where the Irish were the majority.

The foregoing resurgence notwithstanding, the Kansas-Nebraska Act had forced John Wentworth, the leader of the Chicago Democratic machine, to establish the Illinois Republican Party. This was quickly followed by a defection among once reliably Democratic wards whose electoral support of Free Soil candidates seemed to only deepen with the Buchanan administration's subsequent vacillation on Kansas statehood. Table 3.2 reports that in the 1860 presidential election the Republicans captured all but two wards in the entire city much as the Democrats had done in 1852, but with one crucial difference: the Republicans had united the Yankee elite wards of the lakeshore (1 and 2) with the German majority-worker wards of the North and upper West sides (6 through 9) in a cross-class interethnic sectional coalition. These returns reflect broader trends throughout Illinois. One study of statewide Illinois politics in this period reports that 90 percent of Germans gave their ballots to the Democratic nominee Franklin Pierce in 1852, whereas in 1860 only 30 percent of Germans in Illinois voted for Douglas (Hansen 1980; Levine 1983, 181n30).

Chicago Workers and the Onset of the Civil War: A Case Study of the German Experience

German workers' support for the Democratic Party, like that of other immigrant workers, was built on the latter's openness to foreigners, its resistance to the temperance movement (which sought the prohibition of alcohol), and its initial enthusiasm for territorial expansion and land reform relative to the Whig Party. But slavery had long been a political sticking point in the Chicago German community as Carl Hellmuth's defection to the Free Soil cause in 1848 makes clear. In the end, it was the reintroduction of the slavery question during the Kansas-Nebraska debacle that precipitated the last and decisive defection of German voters, and particularly German workers, out of the Democratic Party (Levine 1983, 168–169).

The German community in Chicago split into three factions over the Kansas-Nebraska Act—factions that reflected both ideological and class divisions. The weakening of these divisions resulted from the growing interclass and interethnic opposition to slavery extension in the wider city, cultivated by Free Soil political elites. The first such faction was what we might call "conservative." Its leader was Michael Diversey, co-owner of the Chicago Brewery and reputedly the wealthiest German in the city. Diversey was Stephen Douglas's most reliable German cadre and stuck by him through the lean years of the Kansas-Nebraska controversy. On Douglas's urging, he established the *National Demokrat*, the German-language equivalent of the *Times* to push the pro-Nebraska agenda of the mainstream Democratic Party. It was only after Douglas broke with President Buchanan over the Lecompton Constitution that Diversey at last abandoned his longtime ally. Just to the left of Diversey were the liberals, led downstate by Gustav Koerner and in Chicago by Francis A. Hoffmann. Koerner was a prominent southern Illinois lawyer who rose through the ranks of the Democratic Party, becoming a justice in the Illinois Supreme Court in 1845 and lieutenant governor in 1852. A former Lutheran minister, Hoffmann also took up the law and then turned to real estate and banking. He, too, rose through the political ranks, starting as a postmaster for rural Schaumburg Township in Cook County, continuing as a county clerk and then councilman representing Chicago's Eighth Ward, and eventually becoming lieutenant governor (as a Republican) during the war. The liberals opposed the Kansas-Nebraska Act, but remained unwilling to exit the Democratic Party in 1854. Koerner and Hoffman also refused to interfere with slavery where it already existed, though they personally abhorred the institution and would not countenance its expansion to the West. The far left included Carl Hellmuth but were led principally by Eduard Schlaeger and Teodor Hielscher, who were Forty-Eighters, veterans and refugees of the European Revolutions of 1848. Schlaeger and Hielscher were socialist artisans who perceived in the extension of slavery the prospect not only of permanent industrial servitude but also of the oppression they fled after the defeat of the revolution. The socialist faction of the Chicago German community was more amenable to an immediate break with the Democratic Party and had a history of flirting with abolitionism (Levine 1992, 201–203).

It bears mention here that of these, Diversey was the lone Catholic, who—like Chicago Irish Catholic Democrats—was suspicious of nativist anti-Nebraskans in the nascent Republican Party. Consequently, as James M. Bergquist's (1971) careful study of immigrant voting behavior in Illinois suggests, German Catholics—like their Irish counterparts—predominantly remained in the Democratic Party. Bergquist estimates that 70 to 80 percent of Catholic German communities remained Democratic in this period. This is probably why Gustav Koerner made a special effort to forge inroads in this voting bloc when he finally decamped to the Republican Party in 1856. There is some evidence that German Catholics in Chicago were somewhat more likely to vote Republican than those in other parts of Illinois, because local skirmishes between German Republicans and Irish Democrats made ethnic rivalries increasingly identified with the parties. However, the exception proves the larger rule of the Democrats' enduring influence among Catholics (Bergquist 1971, 209 passim).

This is an important data point, because after Irish immigration reached its peak in 1851, Germans replaced them as the largest foreign-born voting bloc. Between 1850 and 1860, the German-born population increased from 584,720 to 1.3 million. One-eighth of that increase took place in Illinois alone, and the city of Chicago was home to one-sixth of the state's total (Bergquist 1971, 197). If Irish and German workers together comprised the base of the Democratic Party before 1854, and if the Irish remained the Democrats' most valuable and reliable immigrant constituency, then it is critical to examine the dynamics of the single largest mass defection to the Republican Party, which took place among the majority of German voters, most of whom were skilled and unskilled workers.

The first dataset that speaks to this question is a petition from Chicago residents filed with the Illinois state legislature immediately after the introduction of the Kansas-Nebraska bill in January 1854. The petition, which opposed the bill, had 765 signatories, all but 64 of whom had German surnames. Cross-checked against Chicago city directories, the data reveal that over 60 percent of German signatories were skilled workers in trades dominated by immigrants such as shoemaking, carpentry, cabinet making, and stone work. An additional 10.4 percent were unskilled workers, suggesting that some three-quarters of German anti-Nebraska petitioners were workers of one kind or another. Of the 64 non-German signatories, 57.7 percent were craftsmen and 7.7 percent were unskilled laborers (Levine 1992, 201).

The next dataset results from the first mass German protest against the Kansas-Nebraska bill, which occurred at Chicago's North Market Hall on March 16, 1854. The meeting reflected both the aforementioned tension within German civil society as well as the potential for unity. The organizer of the meeting was the socialist Eduard Schlaeger but its keynote speaker was the liberal Francis A. Hoffmann. Of Mr. Douglas, Hoffmann said, "we weep for the fall of a great man of Israel. Henceforth we cannot acknowledge his claims to our esteem." Whatever his feelings for Douglas, however, Hoffmann notably stopped short of urging Germans to break with the Democratic Party, cautiously predicting that there might come a time when it would be necessary to "break the chains that fetter us to that party." Schlaeger, by contrast, was more impatient. He said, "The time has gone by . . . when it was only necessary to play the fiddle to make the Germans dance to any given tune," adding that it was "high time the German population ceased being led by the nose by the demagogues of the Democratic Party" (Levine 1992, 205).

The significance of these contrasting statements is threefold. First, they corroborate, albeit in different ways, the argument that German immigrants had been reliable rank-and-file Democrats before Douglas authored the Kansas-Nebraska bill. Hoffmann's reluctance to urge a full-scale break implies that old political loyalties die hard, while Schlaeger's appeal, though more strident, intimates that Germans "dance" to the tune of the Democratic Party. Second, both dissident Democrats take a page out of the Whig playbook by using the stigma of political dependency to mobilize their fellow countrymen against the Kansas-Nebraska bill. Hoffmann goes so far as to use the imagery of "the chains that fetter us to that party," just as Schlaeger means to agitate his listeners by suggesting that they were "being led by the nose" like beasts of burden. Third, although there are some differences in Schlaeger's and Hoffmann's attitudes toward the Democratic Party, there is quite a bit of overlap as well, particularly in their repudiation of Stephen A. Douglas, the leading Democrat of his time, both statewide and nationally. There was, in other words, considerable potential for a rapprochement at least between the liberal and socialist wings of German civil society.

Indeed, as a body, the attendants of the meeting united on strong language, echoing the Free Soil claim that the migration of southern planters to western lands would prevent Germans of lesser socioeconomic stature from becoming farmers and thereby effectively enslave them. The official minutes of the meeting state that the bill was roundly condemned for "reducing the free foreigner to the position now occupied by the slave, who is politically without any rights, depriving him of all influence against the phalanx of slaveholders." The residents further resolved, "we have lost our confidence in, and must look with distrust upon, the leaders of the Democratic party, to whom, hitherto, we had confidence enough to think that they paid some regard to our interests" (*Chicago Tribune*, March 20, 1854). Afterward, the members of the meeting marched from North Market Hall to Court House Square in the center of Chicago. Along the way they picked up crowds of supporters and burned Douglas's image in effigy. As Douglas himself was to write of the Nebraska debacle, "I could travel from Boston to Chicago by the light of my effigy on every tree we passed" (Levine 1992, 206).

In the weeks following the North Market Hall meeting, Germans organized a May convention in Peoria, Illinois to unify Germans across the state against slavery extension. This is the third dataset that suggests that Chicago's German workers provided both the vanguard and the main body of the exodus out of the Democratic Party. Because attendance from downstate residents was light, the sentiment of the convention reflected the dominance of the Chicago delegation, which consisted primarily of unions of journeymen carpenters and tailors founded during the strike wave of 1853 as well as other radical labor organizations like the Turnverein. Note that whereas the unions were engaged in industrial action just months before, they now mobilized against slavery extension, an issue brought to the fore by a matter of partisan contention, namely, the Kansas-Nebraska bill.[3]

To repeat, Germans were not uniformly anti-Nebraska. German Catholics were at least suspicious of, if not downright hostile toward, the incipient Republican organization. For example, in 1856 German Pro-Nebraska forces disrupted a Republican meeting, publicly burned the newly Republican *Illinois Staats-Zeitung* editor George Schneider in effigy, and marched on the paper's offices, threatening to seize the premises and set it ablaze until the Turnverein arrived on the scene to thwart the attack (Levine 1983, 174).

In any case, demonstrating unity is not necessary for analytical purposes. More important for the arguments posed in this book is that German civil society was notably convulsed by the context of partisan struggle. Preexisting class and ideological differences in and of themselves did not animate the preeminent issues of German public discourse in this period. Instead, the prime mover of political sentiment was the Democratic Party's disastrous miscalculation that after the Compromise of 1850, territorial expansion could provide the foundation for an enduring Democratic hegemony.

Nor was the Republican Party merely the passive recipient of Democratic missteps. Among the gravest threats to Republican ascendancy were the extreme nativist elements in their ranks, who were liable to repel German voters, the largest immigrant voting bloc not only in Chicago and Illinois, but in the country as a whole. Accordingly, the Republicans worked to cultivate a proimmigrant ethos in the face of Democratic attempts to brand their organization as irretrievably nativist.[4] For example, when Chicago anti-Nebraska newspaper editors, Charles Ray of the *Chicago Tribune* and George Schneider of the *Illinois Staats-Zeitung*, met in Decatur in February 1856 to draft a Republican platform, Abraham Lincoln himself intervened to include an antinativist plank. At the state party convention in May of that year, Orville H. Browning, who served as platform committee chairman, won the adoption of a similar plank. Then at the 1856 national convention in Philadelphia, western Republicans secured the election of Henry Lane of Indiana as convention president to thwart their nativist eastern colleagues (Bergquist 1971, 204–206).

If the Free Soil critique was the foundation on which a German home in the Republican Party could be built, then the repudiation of nativism was its threshold. The nomination of Lincoln for president in 1860 went a long way in this endeavor, for a requirement of both the liberal and socialist wings of German civil society was that the nominee have no history or taint of nativism in his past. Lincoln not only fit the bill, but was also conspicuous in his advocacy of the antinativist party platform. The most likely prospect of a nativist nominee was Edward Bates of Missouri, who was put forward as a galvanizer of moderate to conservative Whig voters, but the party in its wisdom declined. This being satisfied, local German liberals required additional assurance that the party would not be overtaken by hotheads like Hielscher and Schlaeger. In this the prominence of former moderate Whigs like Lincoln and Browning in the leadership of the new party was an important signal, as was Hoffmann's nomination to the post of Illinois lieutenant governor. Though radical Republicans like William H. Seward and John C. Frémont were more to the taste of Hielscher and Schlaeger, they evidently accepted the moderate Republican leadership. Indeed, the Republicans received their strongest organizational support in the radical wing of the German community from the popular Arbeiterverein, Chicago's German workers' mutual aid society.

The Politics of Economic Distress

None of this is to suggest that workers had become oblivious to their economic plight. As in the Jacksonian era, Chicago workers built their own organizations in this period based on their unrequited expectations of craft production. However, they continued to interpret their ongoing encounter with the market economy through the prism of dependency, which remained the grist of political discourse throughout the debate over territorial expansion. The strike wave of 1853 is a case in point.

That series of job actions resulted from at least three concurrent processes. The first was primarily structural in nature: a prolonged economic expansion in the early 1850s led to inflation in the price of staples even as wages failed to keep step. Accordingly, the principal demand of the strike wave was a pay increase of at least 10 percent and as much as 25 percent. Another was partisan in provenance, namely, the absence of slavery extension as a lightning rod for mass mobilization. If the Wilmot Proviso prompted Chicago artisans to mobilize against the usurpations of southern planters, then conversely the Compromise of 1850 put the issue of slavery extension to rest for the time being and thereby generated space for the articulation of different cleavages and grievances. Still another factor facilitating the strike wave of 1853 was the eclipse of cooperative self-employment (e.g., worker-owned shops) as a strategy for enabling workers' economic independence and the attendant rise of labor militancy as an alternative. That is, instead of scraping up enough capital to start and run their own joint enterprises, some insisted that workers should remain employees, but push their employers around through strike activity and effectively set the terms of their own employment. The spark giving expression to these longer-term processes was a railroad workers' strike in Baltimore beginning in February, which prompted some three thousand workers in other trades to call work stoppages throughout that city. The conflagration then spread to New York, Philadelphia, Pittsburgh, Cincinnati, and Chicago. Though Chicago workers had struck in the 1840s, this was the first time that they did so as formal trade unions. The bulk of strike activity in Chicago was concentrated among tailors, plasterers, and carpenters. Predictably the ideological frame for the action was once again economic independence. As one triumphant tailor put it, "The call to independence sounded by the oppressed workers of the East has found a thousand-fold echo in the hearts of the western workers, who share their lot" (*Chicago Tribune*, October 4, 1851, 2; April 23, 1853, 2; May 4, 1853, 2; and November 16, 1853, 3; Levine 1992, 137, 139–140; Pierce 1940, 160, 165, 166; Schneirov 1991, 385).

The economic downturn of 1857 put the strike wave unions on their heels as employers slashed wages and staffing levels to stay afloat. In a city whose total population numbered 93,000, the panic left 20,000 workers unemployed (Huston 1987; Pierce 1940, 156; Skogan 1976). Accordingly, the locus of labor politics shifted away from the work place and the demand for higher wages to the conditions of the unemployed.

Here the surviving letters of one Nikolaus Schwenk comprise a window onto the way in which the discourse of dependency colored interpretations of the panic. Schwenk was a German coppersmith who immigrated to the United States in March 1854 and arrived in Chicago in 1855. In a letter to his brother, dated November 15, 1856, Schwenk wrote, "to work for others as a journeyman, dear brother don't blame me, but that's not really what I want . . . I would like to try something else, and finally to take a step which, if luck would have it, could lead to independence." Accordingly, he saved a "respectable bit of capital and . . . bought land with it" in the hopes of settling there the following spring. By November 17, 1857, at the nadir of the economic downturn, Schwenk had become far less hopeful. Though he himself had a job, "Thousands of workers," he wrote, "are unemployed and look with fearful hearts towards the approaching winter." What was worse for these workers, however, "most criminal of all," Schwenk continued, was that they were robbed of their seed money—money that they hoped, as he hoped, "could lead to independence." "What little they had put aside with the sweat of their brows and invested in savings banks—is gone," Schwenk wrote, adding, "the worker who thought his well-invested money to be his only consolation and hope now finds himself without anything" (Schwenk [1856] 1988, 27; [1857] 1988, 28–29).

In addition to Schwenk's personal account of dreams deferred, protests for rent control and unemployment relief also suggest that Chicago workers were neither disoriented by the slavery question nor numb to the economic consequences of the panic. In the first week of November, with the local economy bottoming out, the North Side's tenants banded together to demand, and ultimately win, a reduction in rent (*Chicago Tribune*, November 5–7, 1857). A few days later, workers in the North side and the West side's sixth ward began holding mass meetings to assist the ranks of the unemployed, inspired in part by similar efforts in New York where workers were calling on city hall to deliver "bread or work" (*Chicago Tribune*, November 17, 1857, 1).

Such examples of autonomous labor action notwithstanding, Republicans successfully discouraged working class-based political appeals in this period by counterspinning the critique of dependency. When the unemployed were laying plans to march on city hall for relief, for instance, the Republican Party deployed a city clerk and 48er named Herman Kriesmann who convinced an audience of roughly 400 workers that they could not treat the government like a "nursing mother." In response, the workers cancelled their march and established the Arbeiterverein instead (Schneirov 1991, 384).

Moreover, community mobilizations fed more directly back onto party politics as Republican elites insinuated that the Democratic Party had been compelled by their southern masters to adopt a low-tariff trade policy to the economic ruin of workers and farmers in the West. If the partisan controversy over Kansas had done the crucial work of splitting German majority-worker wards off from the Democrats and dividing the Whigs' native-born middle- to upper-income base, then the subsequent politicization of the Panic of 1857 constituted the last straw in that process, since it helped to move the North side into the Republican column and thereby unite renegade elite and nonelite wards.

Local and state elections from 1856 to 1858 reveal that the economic crisis had a dual significance. On the one hand, a north-side majority had eluded the Republicans as late as March 1857 when former Democrat John Wentworth became the first Republican mayor of Chicago, just five months before the downturn (*Chicago Tribune*, March 9, 1857, 1). The results of the 1858 mid-term election for state treasurer show that after the panic, the Republicans had at last begun posting majorities in every North Side ward (*Chicago Tribune*, November 5, 1858, 1). On the other hand, the shift in the popular vote was relatively minor compared to that of 1856. Thus, while workers' unmediated economic interests during the panic may have issued the final blow to Democratic hegemony, it is well to remember that the economic crisis was itself politicized as an outcome of the slave power's hold on the Democratic Party. Moreover, it was primarily an artifact of institutional politics—the Kansas-Nebraska Act of 1854—that emptied the ranks of the Democratic bloc, in effect setting the panic up to seal the revolutionary cross-class inter-ethnic sectional coalition one year later.

Here, Joseph Weydemeyer's ill-fated socialist agenda of the 1850s is illustrative of the influence of mainstream party politics on workers' political identity. Weydemeyer, who was a friend to Marx and a committed socialist, exhorted his fellow German workmen to pursue a course of political independence from the major parties. However, nationally and in New York City, where Weydemeyer first built his political organization, the Arbeiterbund, he was outnumbered by those in his very own membership who sought to reform the Democratic Party from within (Levine 1992, 142). The pattern repeated itself in Chicago, where Weydemeyer relocated in 1859. There the movement failed to carry its founder's program beyond moving the organization from New York and sending a Chicago delegation to assorted socialist conventions. The Chicago Turnverein, which had been an allied socialist organization, officially withdrew its support of the socialist position in 1859 and six years later changed its name from the "socialist" to the "North American" Turners. Even Weydemeyer dropped what he was doing to fight slavery extension in the run up to the Civil War (Pierce 1940, 187).

Free Labor or Slave Power: The Republicans' Delicate Dance with the Critique of Wage Dependency

The Republicans' hold over even the most class conscious Chicago workers had at least as much to do with the party's rhetorical finesse as it had with workers' ongoing concern with economic independence. In some ways, the Republican Party picked up where the Free Soilers had left off, namely, by suggesting that a slave power conspiracy to monopolize western lands would permanently confine white men to industrial servitude. In 1854, for example, the Republican *Chicago Tribune* ridiculed the national Democratic administration, charging that they "cry 'the people, the people'" for election purposes, but in allowing the expansion of slavery into the western territories "degrade every poor white man below even the slave himself." The "grand aim" of the South and its northern collaborators, the *Tribune* added, was "centered in the accomplishment of one object—the degradation of all free labor, and as an inevitable necessity, the mental and physical enslavement of the great mass of the people" (July 11, 2). Accordingly, a territory's brave refusal to accept the status of a slave state was described as "a preference for white men and white labor" (*Chicago Tribune*, April 30, 1858, 2), while the insistence to remain a slave state was derided as a preference for "intense 'niggerism'" (*Chicago Tribune*, April 23, 1857, 1).

The starkest evidence of this southern conspiracy, the Republicans contended, was the Dred Scott case of 1857, in which the U.S. Supreme Court ruled that neither territorial governments nor the federal government could ban slavery in the territories. Because no one had the authority to outlaw slavery, the latter could exist anywhere in America with impunity. This decision supplemented existing proslavery acts, including the Fugitive Slave Law of 1850, which stipulated that anyone suspected of being a runaway slave could be arrested and returned to any white man who swore that he owned the black person in question. Adding insult to injury, the expansion of slavery would not only condemn northern workers to a life of wage dependency, but also deputize them in the menial task of returning southern "property" to their rightful owners. Thus, Chicago Republicans argued that the law "compulsorily puts every man in the North on the level in the moral scale, with a nigger-catcher's blood hounds" (*Chicago Tribune*, June 14, 1859, 2).

Far from intending to free the slaves, then, the Republicans exploited pre-existing anxieties about the attainability of economic independence by deploying racist imagery that foreshadowed the descent of white men into slavery. A vote for the Democrats was a vote for a future in which white men would eventually be no better than black men. Thus, the *Tribune* would describe Democratic plans to win the mayoral contest of 1859 as a "Scheme for Africanizing Chicago" (*Chicago Tribune*, January 5, 1859, 1). Similarly, the Republicans used the supposed appearance of Democratic support for interracial sexual relations and equality as evidence of that party's intention to blacken and thereby enslave whites. The *Tribune* wrote that among the Democratic rank-and-file, "were half a million fathers of mullato children," adding that "Nearly every Southern leader in that party, is a blood relation of Negroes, either as parent, brother, uncle, cousin or nephew . . . Is not a party this mixed with and related to people of African descent, practically in favor of negro equality? . . . The Republicans wish to keep the black and white races separate and unmixed" (September 1, 1857, 2).

With racial amalgamation and white enslavement apparently near at hand, it was difficult to resist the Republicans' insistence that the slave power had to be defeated at all costs, even at the cost of party loyalty. For instance, northern Know-Nothings, who comprised the nativist faction of the old Whig Party, were persuaded that their nemesis, the Roman Catholic Church, was in cahoots with the slave power, since the Democratic Party—whose urban base was largely Irish Catholic—was very clearly the party of the South.[5] Thus, though the *Tribune* generally kept a proimmigrant policy to articulate German Protestants and secularists to the Republican Party, they nevertheless, on occasion, made specifically anti-Catholic statements. One *Tribune* editor insinuated that "There is not a Catholic journal within our knowledge, in this country, that is not intensely Pro-Slavery" (February 11, 1856, 2). The majority of Illinois Know-Nothings, for their part, like other state affiliates in the North, "avowed to have no Slavery outside the Slave States," and thus, repudiated the popular sovereignty platform of their national party (*Chicago Tribune*, July 13, 1855, 2). Hopelessly divided, northern nativists' only hope of defeating the "Papal Power" seemed to be in joining the Republican coalition. This, perhaps more than any other factor, explains the resistance of Irish majority-worker wards to the Republican Party in 1856 and 1860.

Other national movements and parties met a similar fate. Having crossed Stephen A. Douglas and his followers in the national and state party, anti-Nebraska Democrats like John Wentworth had nowhere to turn but the Republican Party (*Chicago Tribune*, May 1, 1855, 1). The only major contender for national power not vulnerable to such a split was the Republican Party itself, whose base was almost entirely northern. Of the 1856 Republican National Convention, the Democratic *Times* remarked, "few, if any, of the Southern States will have a representative in the Convention. Their object is to array the North against the South" (*Chicago Times*, June 19, 1856, 2). The Republicans embraced a strict dichotomizing logic that forced Chicagoans to choose between what they claimed were the only possible alternatives at play: free labor or slave power. An article entitled,

"Logic in Politics," published in the Republican *Tribune*, exemplifies this point nicely:

> The Republicans believe that Slavery is wrong; that they are under such obligations to the Constitution and the laws that they may not interfere with it where it legally exists; that, however, they have the right to prevent its extension to the parts of the public domain now free, and this right they openly declare that they will exercise; that they will discourage the influence of Slavery in the national councils, and in diplomacy and legislation; and that it is their duty in all conflicts between Freedom and Slavery to aid and favor the former to the limit of their constitutional obligation. The National Democracy (we mean the party in which Breckinridge stands at the head) believe that slavery is right; that it extends by force of the Constitution to all the Territories; that it is their duty to plant it wherever it will flourish, and that it is the duty of Congress to protect. (July 16, 1860, 2)

Here, the *Tribune* conveniently ignores the fact that the official Democratic presidential nominee was Stephen A. Douglas and insists instead that the sentiment of the true Democratic Party is embodied in its southern rights wing, led by Vice President John C. Breckinridge. Having made this leap in logic, the *Tribune* then reasons that all other parties, that of Douglas and John C. Bell and Edward Everett (southern Whigs, hoping to avoid secession by forming the Constitution Union Party) were meaningless as positions between the two dominant positions, and predicted that the pressure of this dichotomizing logic would lead the Bell and Douglas factions to one of the dominant poles.

In a context where the free labor or capitalist system was framed as the antithesis to slavery, the discourse of dependency paradoxically worked to undermine the once potent distinction between hirelings on the one hand, and farmers and artisans on the other. Republicans increasingly referred to wage labor as "free" merely by its differentiation from slavery. In the words of one historian, "Preoccupation with the overriding issue of expanding slavery blurred the earlier distinctions and made freedom a term as broad and inclusive as middle-class America" (Wilson 1974, 14). A Republican parade just a few months prior to Lincoln's election indicates that wage workers had snuck into what was once a more exclusive club. The following is a description of the various floats and banners on display:

> There was a huge frame on wheels . . . filled, below and on top, with machines . . . On this . . . was a four-horse-power portable engine, driving turning lathes, and furnishing power for various machinists. There

were blacksmithing, planing, sawing, boring and hammering, and fifty other things a doing . . . 49 men from the corn planter factory for Lincoln! . . . On wheels was a blacksmith shop and forge; five grim smiths sledge-hammered a bar of iron, striking in time . . . There were three or four more blacksmiths' shops on wheels. Other wagons bore along loads of cabinetmakers, house builders, carpenters, brick layers, stone cutters, tinners, shoe-makers, dusty millers, harness-makers . . . A platform on wheels had a farm in miniature on it. There was a small log cabin, worm fence, corn field, wheat, oats, meadow, all kinds of fruits in the orchard, a grape vine climbing the side of the house loaded with luscious grapes. (*Chicago Tribune*, August 23, 1860, 1)

The scene is an admixture of occupational categories that would have been curious in the Jacksonian era when farmers and mechanics were distinguished in sharp opposition to hirelings. In addition to showcasing the support of farmers and tradesmen, the parade also included the floats of wage workers from "a corn planter factory" and a model factory, "filled, below and on top, with machines."

The sudden inclusion of factory operatives into the sacred circle of independent men spelled the beginning of the end for the two-party system's critique of wage dependency. For if white male wage earners were no longer understood as a dependent population, then the only dependent men left were black slaves. And if the Civil War was to be a war between free labor and slave power, then the defense of freedom would necessarily include the defense of a system whose survival relied on wage work. As a result, the Civil War inadvertently became a struggle against capitalism's detractors, rather than a struggle of free labor against both capitalism and the extension of slavery.

Southerners had done their own part in casting themselves as the enemies of capital, providing limitless copy to the *Tribune*, which was more than eager to reprint southern anticapitalist sentiment. Proclaiming that the secessionist threat was a mere bluff, for example, the *Tribune*'s editors took the occasion to steel their readers' Republican resolve by reminding them that a southern paper had once dismissed northerners as crude "capitalists, money makers and money seekers" (January 8, 1857, 2). When southern states passed "non-intercourse laws" to cease all trade with the North and encourage reliance on their own manufacturing, the *Chicago Tribune* cast doubt on the wisdom of the policy in this way: "Because, manufacturing in competition with the North and with Europe, requires skilled free labor; and to obtain and retain in the slave States a million of intelligent artizans [*sic*] and capitalists, it will be necessary to repeal all laws suppressing free discussion, free newspapers, and free political action . . . Unless these privileges are accorded, the 'greasy mechanics' will stay on the North side of Mason and Dixon" (January 4, 1860, 2). The editors thus make two noteworthy moves in reimagining the discourse of dependency. First, the *Tribune* employs yet another moniker supposedly given to northern laborers by their southern neighbors, "greasy mechanics," to stir resentment among the Republican rank-and-file. Second, irrespective of their ongoing battle over the labor process, artisans and capitalists are partnered here in opposition to the South by virtue of their allegedly ingrained preference for freedom.

Eventually the *Tribune* took to identifying any attack on capitalism with the insidious machinations of the slave power. After the death of several factory workers at Pemberton Mills in New England, for example, the paper dismissed southern charges that the North was keeping "white slaves," and in doing so, both justified its ability to call New England operatives free, and discredited the critique of capitalist production as a cynical attempt to defend slavery. "The 'white slaves of the North,'" the *Tribune* wrote, "are used everyday, in and out of Congress, to illustrate the disadvantages of free society and the blessings of the [peculiar] institution" (February 9, 1860, 2).

Republicans also used the slave power conspiracy to discredit the Democrats' long-standing opposition to banks. "In looking over the vote by counties, one is struck by the heavy majorities cast 'against banks' in all the present Pro-Slavery counties, and the opposing heavy vote 'for banks' in the Republican counties ... The same spirit of servile submission to the orders of party leaders that caused them to oppose a Banking system, caused them to oppose Freedom in Kansas" (*Chicago Tribune*, June 6, 1857, 2). In this passage, the Republicans, many of them former Whigs, advance a variant of the discourse of dependency that punched up their once monotonous carping about political dependency. Dependency has two meanings here: uncritical submission to party leaders, its traditional Whig usage, fused powerfully with northern servility to southern slave masters.

Finally, when Chicago's unemployed were hatching the aforementioned plan to demand "bread or work" from city hall during the Panic of 1857, the Republicans drew the improbable relationship between European socialism and the slave power. "When the Slave Power is dominant and the doctrines . . . that it is the duty of the upper classes to enslave all men who are not capable of taking care of themselves . . . are fully established, then will be the time in which the claims of the poor and unfortunate upon the authorities, for what they eat, drink and wear can be maintained . . . Let us have no European socialism here" (*Chicago Tribune*, November 16, 1857, 1). Taking advantage of the familiar preoccupation with white male economic independence, then, the Republican Party attempted to stigmatize socialism as the political program of an enslaved people, who are "not capable of taking care of themselves." Defeating the slave power, on this account, was one and the same with creating the conditions under which socialism could never arise. To oppose the slave power was quite simply to oppose socialism.

Conclusion

Why then did the critics of wage dependency reorganize in favor of a liberal capitalist democracy? The present chapter addresses this question by examining two sets of critics—political elites and workers. The politicians' story began in 1844 with the unexpected defeat of Martin Van Buren for the Democratic presidential nomination. Van Buren had sought to keep the attention of parties and voters squarely on putatively tyrannical economic institutions like the Second Bank of the United States. His defeat was the fulcrum upon which the pivot to territorial policy was achieved. That pivot might still well have carried the Jacksonian critique of wage dependency seamlessly into the debate over territorial expansion had the latter's sectional logistics not combined so explosively with the leftover resentments of the 1844 Democratic leadership fight. As it happened, however, the critique of dependency shifted targets: with the defection of Free Soil cadres like John Wentworth from the Democratic Party, politicians began discussing the prospect of permanent industrial servitude as if the latter hinged solely on the expansion of slavery to the western territories. Though the new Democratic leadership, including Stephen A. Douglas, brought the likes of Wentworth back into the fold with the Compromise of 1850, they squandered any good will they had acquired by renewing the country's march westward and reopening for discussion the status of slavery in the West. When that happened, the Democrats' Free Soil cadres left for good and worked with like-minded dissident Whigs to establish the Republican Party. From there, the Republicans used the issue of slavery extension to reframe the capitalist free labor system as the consummate symbol of American freedom, where once its central feature—the individual wage contract—had symbolized moral degradation and abject servility.

The land reform dimension of these politics resonated with workers because of their own critique of wage dependency and their corresponding dream of economic independence as self-sufficient farmers. A monopoly of the soil by wealthy southern planters threatened to defer that dream indefinitely. Accordingly, Chicago workers organized a land reform league in 1848 (eventually amalgamating with Free Soilers) and mobilized as anti-Nebraska Democrats and later as Republicans. Worker support for the Republican Party was not uniform, however: Protestant and secular native-born and German workers embraced the free labor cause, whereas Catholics, both Irish and German, were skeptical due largely to the Republicans' unremitting hostility toward the Pope and Roman Catholic Church.

Indeed, the role of race and ethnic relations in general cannot be underestimated, for the critique of wage dependency as it was deployed during the onset of the Civil War retained the racist elements of its Jacksonian usage. Republicans, for example, framed the prospect of slavery extension (and by association Democratic victory) as a scheme for "Africanizing" Chicago; that is, for condemning white workers to a life of industrial servitude that would make them no better than black slaves. Beyond workers' racialized anxiety over wage dependency (which the Republicans strategically heightened), workers understood land reform as an entitlement not of all men, but of white men in particular. The political crisis over slavery and the liberal democracy to which it gave birth were animated by distinctly white supremacist notions of who deserved to be enslaved and who did not.

But it is important to stress that this is only half the answer, for worker support of the free labor cause begs a follow-up question: why did Chicago workers shortly thereafter reject the social order they brought into being? In the following chapters, I build the case for the argument that Chicago politicians used the northern victory in the Civil War to assail collective bargaining as a new form of slavery.

In fairness to the political parties who take the brunt of scrutiny in the next two chapters, Chicago workers assisted, halfway unwittingly, in laying the politicians' trap. Chicago workers bought, and Republicans happily sold, the plainly false dichotomy between capitalism and slavery. For years and in plain sight, incipient northern industrialists relied on southern slavery for the raw materials they processed in their sweatshops and early factories. Slavery was, in other words, part and parcel of the capitalist system; black bonded slavery and white wage dependency, complementary forms of labor control. That antebellum workers failed to point out that stunning hypocrisy was understandable given the heated politics of the time. Karl Marx himself uncritically celebrated these spurious Republican claims from across the Atlantic. However, the American polity had by this point just passed through an extended period of Jacksonian populism, when politicians and workers alike publicly fulminated against banks, paper money, and the wage system. Moreover, the Republican Party had shown early signs of impatience with criticisms of capitalism, especially during the Panic of 1857 and during the war itself. In this, workers bear some responsibility for turning a blind eye to the writing on the wall. We might therefore say that they conspired in their own subordination, but not for long.

THE WAR YEARS, OR THE TRIUMPHS AND REVERSALS OF FREE LABOR IDEOLOGY, 1861–1865

The Republican free labor coalition had begun to fray well before the end of the Civil War. By the fall of 1864, when inflation for basic necessities had for two years outpaced wage increases for most workers, Andrew Cameron, editor of Chicago's English-language trade union paper, the *Workingman's Advocate*, published this attack on the party of Lincoln:

> When it can do nothing else it can bleat about "slave-drivers." Alas! gentlemen (?) of the *Tribune*, your old demagoguecial [*sic*] cry is worn out. We are no longer going to permit you to make dupes of us by your false statements and past hypocritical catch-words, nor mislead us from protecting our own interests and rights. You have already made yourselves rich by bleating about the Negro, for whom you cared not a fig . . . This is a white man's question. Our brave soldiers in the field are taking good care of the "slave owners and slave drivers." To them we leave them . . . We are determined to prevent a wholly unscrupulous set of scoundrelly and hypocritical politicians and purse-proud, moneyed aristocrats from bringing want and slavery to the doors of the FREE LABORING MEN OF THE NORTH. (*Workingman's Advocate*, September 17, 1864, 2)

Chicago workers had subscribed to the slave power conspiracy, Cameron writes, but as the war drew to a close the contradiction between their defense of the free labor system and the belt tightening of their daily existence had become inescapable. That Northern workers felt robbed of the promise of the Civil War, which they understood to be nothing less than the emancipation of free white labor from industrial servitude, presented the party system with an entirely new set of challenges. Chief among these was the task of reassuring workers that capital and labor—erstwhile partners in the Grand Army of the Republic—remained free and equal after the war, even as the deprivation of the times tended to undermine that assurance. The two-party system's solution to this dilemma would eventually be a combination of persuasion and domination: the rhetoric of free contract and right to work, backed by the threat of state violence. In the meantime, though the outlines of an antilabor democracy were taking shape (e.g., in the LaSalle Black Law of 1863), the political establishment vacillated unsystematically between outreach and attack. The Republicans praised immigrant workers when they volunteered in droves to fight the Confederacy, but whenever the incipient labor movement resisted the party line on economic policy or the conduct of the war, the Republicans publicly condemned labor's resistance as treason. In contrast, the Democrats were more consistent in their appeal to organized labor in Chicago, but when the politician and workingman were at odds, most notably in the September 1864 strike at the *Chicago Times*, the party responded with mass firings and union busting. Not surprising, by war's end, the leadership of the city's labor movement had vowed to become politically independent from the major parties.

Cameron's editorial offers three additional lessons as we prepare to digest the triumphs and reversals of free labor ideology in this period. The first is that nothing in politics is forever. When parties fail to do the work of articulation, their coalitions threaten to come apart (de Leon et al. 2009). This chapter is a transition point—not just chronologically in between the political crisis over slavery and postbellum Reconstruction, but also analytically—from the Republicans' successful articulation of workers and employers as a northern or sectional alliance against the South to the disarticulation of workers from that alliance. The chapter also highlights the explanatory power of the political articulation framework relative to other theories of party system change such as those of the realignment tradition in political science. Though the latter employ competing metaphors (e.g., "flash points," "evolution") to describe the rise and fall of political regimes, most theories assume that power shifts rhythmically from one party to another over time (de Leon 2014; Pierson 2004). This sense of time, or "temporality" as academics call it, has a mechanical feel in stark contrast to the rough-and-tumble temporality of partisan struggle in practice that the concept of political articulation seeks to capture. "Hegemony," or the acquisition of mass consent to rule, is by definition always incomplete: parties may unite groups formerly articulated as sworn enemies, then fail to keep them together, and then recover, bringing defectors back into the fold.

Second, as a lesson to the many scholars who look exclusively to the development of unions and other labor organizations for the origins and character of American working class identity, Cameron directs his fire not at "employers" or "bosses," but to "scoundrelly and hypocritical politicians" and "purse-proud, moneyed aristocrats." These appellations allude to political parties, directly in the case of politicians, and indirectly in the case of aristocrats. The latter, as we have seen, was the pejorative used by the Jacksonian Democratic Party to brush certain capitalists with the taint of British monarchy; Cameron uses the term here to evoke the same associations. Chicago workers were, in other words, trying on a new collective identity during the war, separate and apart from their shared identity with all northerners, as the "free laboring men of the North." This analysis was anchored both in disputes with their employers *and* in their sense of betrayal at the hands of the Republican Party, which had sworn (or so they thought) to safeguard their economic independence.

Third, one must take care not to assume that "free laboring men" is exclusively an economic or class category, for as Cameron's editorial implies, Chicago workers' identity was simultaneously racialized. The labor question, he writes, "is a white man's question." For Cameron, and it is fair to say for many of Chicago's early labor leaders, the Civil War was only a partial victory, one that overcame the southern rebellion and African slavery, but not the underlying tyranny that spurred white workers' support for the free labor cause in the first place. What remained—what was promised—was a solution to the specter of permanent wage dependency, which, if left to the tender mercies of politicians and aristocrats, would undoubtedly bring "want and slavery to the doors" of the workingman. That emerging disjuncture, between workers' unrequited economic and racial ambitions, on the one hand, and the city's inconsistent political response, on the other, is the story of this chapter.

Triumph, Part I: War Fever

It must have been difficult, looking forward from November 1860, to imagine that the Democrats' political fortunes could dim any further than they had when they lost the White House to an upstart third party and a largely unheard-of politician in Abraham Lincoln, but dim further they did. On April 12, 1861, the South Carolina militia fired on a U.S. military installation called Fort Sumter. The following day, U.S. Army major Robert Anderson, who had command of the fort, surrendered. The attack vindicated Republican warnings of a slave power conspiracy and hung the albatross of treachery around the necks of the Democrats, whose Southern Rights wing was the vanguard of the secessionist cause.

As soon as the news hit Chicago on April 13, a war fever took hold. The newly elected Republican governor of Illinois, Richard Yates, immediately called for six regiments of volunteers. Among the most enthusiastic were Chicago's immigrant workers. What they could not donate in cash to the war effort, they more than made up in enlistments. Hungarians, Bohemians, and Slavs formed one company. French-Canadians, Belgians, and Swiss comprised the French Battalion. The Scots organized the Highland Guards. Chicago Scandinavians joined the Wisconsin Scandinavian Regiment. Even the Irish, under the influence of Fenian nationalists, who opposed slavery and condemned the Catholic Church's alliance with the Democratic Party, established the Irish Brigade in the 23rd Illinois under Colonel James A. Mulligan. Organized German workers supplied the most recruits. For example, the German Turnverein organized the Turner Union Cadets, who were in the first regiment to muster in southern Illinois on the governor's order. Nationally, the Turners became a giant recruiting agency: three-quarters of its members enlisted in the army and comprised the core regiments not only in Illinois, but also in Missouri, Indiana, and most famously in Washington, where the Turnverein organized the first battalion to respond to the national crisis (*Chicago Tribune*, April 18, 19, 1861; Montgomery 1967, 94; Pierce 1940, 256, 258, 260).

It has been said that the early American labor movement "was the child of civil war" (Montgomery 1967, 91). In this, the attack on Fort Sumter was formative. The future leaders of the National Labor Union (NLU), the first countrywide labor federation, responded enthusiastically to the call to arms. For example, William H. Sylvis, who would become the most famous of the NLU's presidents, had initially urged compromise with the South; but after the attack on Fort Sumter, he raised a company for the war effort and eventually enlisted in the Pennsylvania militia. So fervent was labor's response to the muster that unions were depleted of their members and dues. The National Typographical Union (NTU), which would play an important role in the Chicago labor movement toward the end of the war, held no convention in 1861; in 1862 John M. Farquhar, the NTU's president, joined the army. One study estimates that 42 percent of all U.S soldiers were either mechanics or laborers (Montgomery 1967, 92–94).

The South's attack on Fort Sumter and the attendant upsurge in nationalist sentiment left Democrats little room to maneuver. This is at least partly why Stephen A. Douglas moved quickly to distinguish himself as a Union man. Douglas would die in Chicago on June 3, 1861, but in his remaining time, he volunteered his services to President Lincoln. The president was especially grateful for Douglas's offer to organize southern Illinois, which was known to contain enclaves of strong proslavery sympathy. Thus, on April 25, 1861, Douglas spoke at the Illinois statehouse in Springfield to crowds of legislators and local citizens. There he echoed the rhetoric of the Republican Party by warning of "a wide-spread conspiracy" and "a war of aggression and extermination . . . against the government established by our fathers." Further north, he whipped his fellow Chicagoans into a war frenzy. In one notable stem-winder, he again warned of "an enormous conspiracy," formed long before Lincoln's election and declared, "There are only two sides to the question . . . Every man must be for the United States or against it. There can be no neutrals in this way, *only patriots—or traitors*" (Johannsen [1973] 1997, 864–866, 868; Nichols 1948, 510–511; Pierce 1940, 260–261).

Douglas's performance notwithstanding, Chicago Democrats were so stigmatized that they were loath to nominate an official ticket for even the municipal elections of that year. Instead, a group of private citizens organized the People's Union ticket under the tacit leadership of known Democrats—Cyrus H. McCormick and Melville W. Fuller. During the campaign, the Democrats trod carefully, discussing only the importance of keeping government spending in check. In stark contrast, the Republicans sought to focus the electorate on Fort Sumter. Observing that the Democratic *Times* had been silent on the late attack, the *Tribune* exhorted the public to "Remember that in all that the Chicago *Times* has said of the secession movement, the taking of Sumter and the minor acts of the great treason, not one word has yet been uttered in condemnation of the traitors and rebels—not a word" (*Chicago Tribune*, April 15, 1861). In the contest between economic retrenchment and patriotism, the latter, advanced by the Republican mayoral nominee, Julian S. Rumsey, prevailed. The time for compromise had passed, the Republicans argued, and a vote for them was now everyone's solemn duty (*Chicago Tribune*, April 15 and 18, 1861; Pierce 1940, 254).

Reversal, Part I: War Weariness

No sooner had the war fever begun than dissatisfaction set in regarding the conduct of the war. In response, the party of Lincoln went so far as to support the city council's effort to administer a loyalty oath to Chicago residents (Pierce 1940, 261). After the passage of the loyalty ordinance, the *Tribune*'s editor warned,

> Now let us see whether these Chicago sympathizers with rebellion who have been seeking safe occasions to talk treason, will purchase a continued residence here by an oath of allegiance, or go at once to the ranks of their friends. Let them do one or the other. Treason must be dumb in Chicago. (*Chicago Tribune*, August 28, 1861)

Though perhaps this passage may appear to suggest that the Republicans were simply pressing their advantage, in fact, its manifest coerciveness signals an awareness on the part of the local Republican leadership that their hegemony was failing.

As the military conflict wore on, the polity split into four great political tendencies. David Montgomery (1967) usefully categorizes them according to their respective positions on the four war measures. The war measures consisted of the legal tender acts (1862, 1863), which established the greenback as the national paper currency and thus required creditors to accept the bills at face value; slave emancipation (various Congressional acts and the presidential proclamation itself, 1862–1863); conscription (1863); and direct taxation (1861–1862), which was designed to fund the war and simultaneously cool the inflationary pressures created by the greenback. "Old-line" or "Peace" Democrats opposed the war and the war measures. "Conservatives" of both parties (such Democrats were also known as "War" or "Union" Democrats) accepted the war measures but wanted to limit their reach. "Radical" Republicans were the war measures' chief sponsors in Congress and tended to push their implications well beyond the comfort zone of Conservatives and Peace Democrats. Radicals, for example, took emancipation to imply black enfranchisement, whereas their counterparts denied that assertion. Finally, the labor-reform movement, which included workers, their unions, and middle-class reformers, most notably from the abolitionist movement, predominantly accepted the war measures but resented their unforeseen effects and loopholes. For instance, labor movement activists had been among the first and most enthusiastic enlisted men as we have seen, but they grew mutinous when they discovered that one could avoid the draft by paying the government $300, an amount well out of the reach of most workingmen (Montgomery 1967, 45–46).

The fourth tendency was consistent with the emergent tensions among workers on the ground not only in Illinois, but also across the country. The adoption of the greenback resulted in high inflation for necessities from foodstuffs to rent, but the rise in wages failed to keep pace. The *Chicago Tribune* estimated that whereas the cost of living increased an average of 82 percent between 1861 and 1864, the wages of mechanics had increased only 55 percent. Contemporary scholarship on national wage rates corroborates the *Tribune*'s impressionistic data. In contrast to nominal wage data, which suggest that the hourly compensation of U.S. production workers in manufacturing increased by 38 percent during the war, Lawrence H. Officer argues that real average hourly compensation (i.e., accounting for inflation) declined sharply from $0.95 in 1861 to a wartime low of $0.69 in 1864, a mere penny above the real wage of workers in 1841. The

demand for higher wages was therefore the marquee demand of the labor movement in this period, with calls of pay hikes of as much as 30 percent (Jentz and
Schneirov 2012, 68; Montgomery 1967, 96–97; Officer 2009, 166, 170; Pierce
1940, 155, 157–158, 500).

The resulting strikes prompted two innovations that further stoked workers'
resentment of their employers and the political establishment. First, employers
used the wartime labor shortage as a strategy for pressuring the federal government into both recruiting southern freedmen to loosen up high wage conditions in
the North and providing military support to break strikes. Second, state legislatures
passed conspiracy laws to bar unions from interfering with wage rates. For example, the LaSalle Black Law of 1863 in Illinois was a political response to the coal
strikes of that year (Montgomery 1967, 97–99; see also chapter 5 in this volume).

Illinois Democrats played on racial and class sentiments to great effect in this
context. The remaining Douglasites galvanized support for their once mighty
party by campaigning on new state constitutional provisions, one forbidding
the immigration and settlement of blacks and another forbidding black suffrage.
The majority voting in favor of a ban on black immigration was 100,590 in the
state and 1,604 in Chicago; the other, forbidding black suffrage, passed with even
larger majorities: 176,271 statewide and 8,397 in Chicago. Though they also ran
on other issues (e.g., successive military defeats, economic uncertainty, President Lincoln's suspension of habeas corpus for suspected rebels), the Democrats'
principal strategy during the referenda was to take a page out of the Republican playbook by arguing that the influx of untrained black workers would flood
the labor market and thereby "Africanize" the state (*Chicago Tribune*, June 23,
1862; Pierce 1940, 267). In 1862, the Democrats took control of the state General
Assembly and, with War Democrat Francis C. Sherman as their nominee, the
mayoralty of Chicago (*Chicago Tribune*, April 16, 1862; Pierce 1940, 266–269).

Though overall the city remained prosperous due to government contracts
for the war, prosperity by itself was no guarantee against mounting war fatigue.
Dissatisfaction with the conduct of the war set in not only among War and Peace
Democrats, but also among the GOP itself (Pierce 1940, 272). Resistance to the
draft did not take the form of large-scale riots as it did in New York, but it did find
expression in a booming informal market for "substitutes," men who offered to
fight in place of those who could not or would not fight in exchange for a special
cash consideration. War weariness was a central theme of partisan agitation as
well, especially as it concerned Chicago's draft quota (i.e., the number of con-
scripts Washington expected from the city). Even the hawkish Republican editor
Joseph Medill led a delegation to the nation's capital to ask President Lincoln
to reduce the quota (Pierce 1940, 273–275; see also the *Workingman's Advocate*,
November 5, 1864).[1]

Reversal, Part II: The Labor Movement Lobby

Despite the obvious lack of political consensus even in the first half of the war, David Montgomery, in his canonical work, *Beyond Equality*, maintains that northern workers did not go "coppery" or Democratic in this period. He writes that in Illinois in particular, a majority of workers voted for Abraham Lincoln in 1864. Workers' wartime grievances did not make them Democrats, he concluded, but activists in the labor movement (Montgomery 1967, 101 passim).

At least one problem with Montgomery's conclusion is that the Democrats carried most of Chicago's majority worker wards in the 1864 presidential election (see table 4.1 below).

As the table indicates, the number of wards grew after the 1860 presidential election. In addition, the ward map was redrawn so that wards 6 through 9 were located in the South Side where Irish workers predominated, while wards 15 and 16 were in the Near North Side where German workers remained the majority. Recall that in 1860, the Republicans carried four out of six majority worker wards. Table 4.1 reports that by 1864 the Republicans controlled only two such wards.

What explains this outcome? Is Montgomery wrong? In fact, the data gesture toward a more complicated story. The 1864 presidential returns were the culmination of twin processes. On the one hand, Chicago workers came to approximate a force that we might today call "organized labor." In this sense, workers' wartime grievances made them activists in the labor movement as Montgomery contends. On the other hand, organized labor experimented with "lobbying," understood here as a strategy whereby labor resolved to endorse prolabor candidates regardless of party affiliation. In this light, Montgomery's claim that

TABLE 4.1 Lincoln's share of Chicago's popular vote in majority worker wards, 1864

WARD	1864 (LINCOLN)
6	32.3
7	42.5
8	38.0
9	72.6
15	52.7
16	45.9

Sources: For socioeconomic statistics, Einhorn ([1991] 2001, 265); for ethnic settlement patterns, Hirsch (1990, 101); for electoral returns, *Chicago Tribune*, November 9, 1864.

workers' grievances did not make them Democrats requires some clarification. The Democrats carried majority worker wards when they pledged to support prolabor measures and when Republicans refused to do so, which is to say that the Democrats carried such wards often in this period. Yet Chicago workers were not "traitors," so-called copperheads, though certainly that is what the Republican *Tribune* charged. Their flirtation with the opposition in 1864 grew out of the discovery that their first citywide labor federation, the General Trades Assembly, afforded them political muscle, and that the muscle could be flexed. To borrow a concept from the political scientist Paul Frymer (1999), Chicago workers sought to avoid being a taken-for-granted or "captured" constituency in either party by endorsing whichever candidate worked harder to court their support. As such, workers' disaffection from the Republican Party passed from a general war weariness to a phase of organizational experimentation with political independence. Their guiding ideological compass in this experiment, as with each passing phase of nineteenth-century party-worker interaction, was labor's variant of the Jacksonian critique of wage dependency.

The rapid development of the labor movement lobby was punctuated by four episodes in 1864: the founding of the General Trades Assembly in April; Radical German support of Frémont against Lincoln for the Republican presidential nomination in May; the Chicago Typographical Union's strike at the *Chicago Times* in September; and the Trades Assembly's endorsement of the Democrat and industrialist Cyrus McCormick against Chicago mayor John Wentworth in the 1864 Congressional election.

Background

Before going into great detail about 1864, however, we would do well to pause a moment and discuss the context for the rise of the city's wartime labor unions. I have noted above that Chicago workers suffered through mounting inflation, but they were also emboldened by the labor shortage that resulted from enlistments to the army. Employers, they reasoned, would have no choice but to accede to their demands in a tight labor market and with the military in need of supplies. Accordingly, a spike in industrial conflict occurred in 1863 when bakers, carpenters, cigar makers, coopers, painters, sailors, and tailors organized and struck. In 1864 musicians, dockhands, stonecutters, and sewing women followed suit, while harness makers and bricklayers established their own organizations in 1865. These unions were different from the labor organizations of the antebellum period, which were benevolent societies in the main and struck only rarely, most notably in the strike wave of 1853 (Jentz and Schneirov 2012, 66–67; Schneirov 1998, 32).

The case of the carpenters' union is emblematic of these wider trends. Prior to the American Revolution, carpentry had been organized according to the old apprenticeship to master system. The shift to wage dependency occurred with large-scale commercial building as journeymen were unable to save or front the necessary capital to become builders themselves. In time, master carpenters grew dependent on speculators, promoters, and other middlemen who possessed the means to finance construction. By the eve of the revolution, masters' associations had largely collapsed and building prices and journeymen wages became subject to the market forces of supply and demand instead of custom (Schneirov and Suhrbur 1988, 2, 3).

Thus, the artisan system was defunct by the time Chicago carpenters organized, but organization was spurred by further changes, namely, the advent of piecework and the industrialization of journeyman carpentry. Balloon framing was invented in Chicago in 1833 by Augustine Taylor. It involved the use of studs held together by nails instead of the older and more onerous "post and beam" method, in which wood was held together with joints; in balloon framing the dead weight of the house was carried straight to the ground by vertical studs instead of being transferred to distant corner posts. The new method made construction easier overall, but in the early nineteenth century the journeyman carpenter remained a multiskilled craftsman. The true test of skill was "trimming," the ability to turn out window and door casings, moldings, stairs, doors, and other kinds of wood finishing (Schneirov and Suhrbur 1988, 3–5).

This all changed when Chicago factories began taking over the trimming process in 1839. Mechanization turned the mid-nineteenth-century carpenter into an installer of factory-made woodwork and enabled the piecework system to undercut the trade. In piecework, speculators bypassed the master and his skilled journeymen to contract out specific tasks like hanging doors and laying floors to firms devoted solely to that purpose. Carpentry thus became fragmented such that fewer and fewer people who called themselves carpenters were actually multiskilled craftsmen. Skill fragmentation was further exacerbated by the advent of railroads and travel along the Great Lakes, which flooded Chicago with unskilled labor. Eventually the wages of a carpenter were comparable to those of laborers and sweated workers (Schneirov and Suhrbur 1988, 5–7).

The modern carpenters' union emerged in response to these changes in the labor process and the corresponding decline in real wages. Though the union had two antebellum precursors, the German Schreiner Verein (1855) and the Carpenters, Ship Carpenters, Caulkers, and Ship Joiners Union of Chicago (1857), "The first citywide attempt of journeymen house carpenters to protect their trade interests came during the Civil War as a response to rising prices." The union's organizing message recalled the antebellum critique of wage dependency as slavery. A German carpenter, for example, published this appeal to his fellow carpenters in the *Illinois Staats Zeitung*: "with these prices we can't hold out, can't think of a better future, if we don't earn more. Should we then be eternal slaves of capital? Can't we also stand on our own?" Thus, although the carpenter's demand was at one level purely monetary (the ratio of inflation to wages), his ideological motivation, as Schneirov and Suhrbur rightly observe, consisted of the "values held in common by the vast majority of nineteenth-century Americans: personal autonomy and dignity, economic and social independence, and pride in one's labor." The watchwords of the carpenters' union were "manhood and slavery," in that the advent of the piecework system robbed the journeyman of his manhood and reduced him to wage slavery "not unlike that which had been recently abolished in the Southern states" (Schneirov and Suhrbur 1988, 8, 9, 13).

Episode 1: The General Trades Assembly

It was in this highly charged atmosphere that eighteen unions met to organize Chicago's first labor federation. George K. Hazlitt, president of the Chicago Typographical Union, gave the keynote address at the April 26, 1864 gathering, insisting that the General Trades Assembly was necessary to protect workers "against the present aggressive attitude of capital." A fellow member of the typographical union, James Tracy, echoed Hazlitt, adding, in terms also reminiscent of the Jacksonian discourse of dependency, that the present conditions threatened to reduce workers "to a condition of servitude." Jentz and Schneirov note that "Such comparisons of white labor to slavery had been revived late in the war," due to the fact that "a war to emancipate the slaves freed up labor leaders to use the volatile and powerful imagery of servitude to describe labor's plight" (Jentz and Schneirov 2012, 74–75; Pierce 1940, 168).

Three other facts about the establishment of the Trades Assembly bear mention. To begin, in addition to forming the organization, the member unions agreed to establish and support a newspaper, the *Workingman's Advocate*, which was not only the Assembly's organ, but in time became an influential organ of the national labor movement. Andrew Cameron, who was editor of the *Advocate* as we have seen, recruited the socialist 48er and sometime Republican Eduard Schlaeger to edit the paper's German-language edition. Second, as Cameron's partnership with Schlaeger suggests, the wartime Chicago labor movement was multiethnic, bringing together the city's English- and German-speaking workers among others. Third, the Democratic Party played an important role in these early days. Solicitous of labor's support as they and other organizations were, the Democrats deployed Edward W. McComas, former lieutenant governor of

Virginia and ex-editor of the *Chicago Times*, to speak at the Assembly's inaugural meeting. McComas would become an important figure in the Trades Assembly's adoption of the lobbying strategy and in the organization's support of the Democratic Party in the 1864 Congressional elections (Jentz and Schneirov 2012, 4–5, 74–75; Schneirov 1998, 32; *Workingman's Advocate*, September 17, 1864).

It was, however, a mass meeting of 2,000 workers on August 20 that marked the Assembly's entrance into the political arena as a bona fide lobby. The overarching theme of the meeting was a refusal to accept the dictates of any political party. For example, George Hazlitt, now president of the Assembly, opened the meeting by railing against an unnamed newspaper that presumed to instruct the city's workingmen on the party line. He said, "The workingmen of this city could not be dictated to by any man or men on the face of the earth, and could not be used by any party or any press." Likewise, Eduard Schlaeger spoke of "the uselessness of falling back upon the old political parties . . . who must be made to obey the sovereign will of the people." He added that workingmen must do this work "and change the laws to the interest of the working classes." The resolutions of the meeting were carried unanimously by those in attendance, including one which read, "*Resolved*, That we will at present put no candidates on our Presidential ticket, but shall organize and run upon our platform, until we can ascertain who will prove most loyal to our interests" (*Chicago Tribune*, August 21, 1864; Jentz and Schneirov 2012, 75–76).

Here the Republican and Democratic parties' respective attitudes toward the August meeting are instructive. The Republican *Tribune* referred to the meeting at turns as a "copperhead gathering," calling into question the workers' patriotism, and a "convocation of soreheads," minimizing the workers' grievances. By contrast, though McComas made several comments about the war that would have seemed heretical to the erstwhile ranks of the free labor coalition, many of whom were veterans themselves, he nevertheless spoke their language on economic questions. For example, consistent with Andrew Jackson's attack on the "Monster Bank," he theorized the present condition of the workingman, saying, "The everlasting Moloch of aristocracy—Money—takes hold of the Government, and through it the people were ground to powder." Referring to the specter of permanent wage dependency, McComas intoned, "The country was in revolution, and the people, the working men, must take it in hand themselves, or they and their children were slaves for all time to come" (*Chicago Tribune*, August 21, 1864). It is probable, as Montgomery held, that McComas's presence at this and other meetings of the General Trades Assembly did not make Chicago workers dyed-in-the-wool Democrats, but neither did the Republicans' dismissiveness and condescension assure workers that the party of Lincoln was on their side. Accordingly, between the Scylla of the Democrats' damaging association with the

South and the Charybdis of Republican scorn, the city's labor leaders began to chart a course of political independence.

Episode 2: Frémont

The lobby thesis is further borne out by another episode of party-worker inter-action, for the city's workingmen did not just consort with Democrats like McComas, but with a competing faction of the Republican Party as well. From the Left, a narrow majority of German workers mobilized to deny Lincoln the 1864 Republican nomination and divert it to the more reliably abolitionist John C. Frémont, the party's first presidential nominee and, during the war, the com-mander of the Western armies.

German disaffection with Lincoln began in the summer of 1861 when the president reversed Frémont's "August order," emancipating all rebel-owned slaves in Missouri. When Lincoln then removed Frémont from his command a few months later, the organized German Left in Chicago staged mass protests. In September, a meeting of the Chicagoer Arbeiterverein declared, "slavery existing in the southern states of the Union is the cause of the present war" and accord-ingly, "the peace of the Union cannot be restored unless this infamous institution is completely abolished." The tenth ward's more radical Socialer Arbeiterverein went further, calling "Lincoln's mutilation of General Frémont's proclamation" an act of "treason against our country" (Levine 1992, 260; Pierce 1940, 261).

Given the lackluster prosecution of the war and the reversal of the August order, the president's emancipation proclamation in 1863 was, for many of Chi-cago's more progressive German workers, too little and too late. The Arbeiterver-ein, then led by Teodor Hielscher and Caspar Butz, approved of the proclamation and were "perfectly willing to acknowledge the good personal qualities of our present Executive," but they remained dissatisfied with the Lincoln administra-tion, which they characterized as "a vacillating one, without any system." Iden-tifying an alternative candidate, they continued, "no one has such a deep hold upon the sympathies of the majority of German citizens as John C. Frémont." Nor was this tendency confined to Chicago. On May 17, 1864, the Arbeiterver-ein membership voted to send a three-person delegation, including Hielscher, to the Radical Republican convention in Cleveland, Ohio to formally nominate Frémont for the presidency. The movement to ditch Lincoln was so pervasive in fact that the president himself privately despaired of a split in the German vote, for such dissension would hand Illinois, Wisconsin, and New York to the Democratic nominee, George B. McClellan. Mr. Lincoln's concern was not with-out merit. After the May meeting in Chicago, 102 Arbeiterverein members who voted against sending a delegation to the Frémont convention registered their dissent by publishing their names in the pages of the *Chicago Tribune* (May 26, 1864; Levine 1992, 261–262; Pierce 1940, 261, 270).

Episode 3: The *Times* Strike, the *Tribune*'s Support

The decisive turning point in the development of the labor movement lobby was the Typographical Union's strike at the *Chicago Times* in September 1864. That conflict hardened organized labor's antagonistic posture toward the major parties. The dispute was touched off by the mass firing of striking union compositors at the *Times*, owned by Wilbur F. Storey, a member of the National Democratic Executive Committee. Storey further humiliated the union by training and hiring female compositors as replacement workers to break the strike and then, after defending the right of women to work, summarily replaced the women with nonunion male compositors once the strike was defeated. The *Tribune*'s approval of its adversary's course later distanced the labor movement from the political establishment as a whole (*Chicago Tribune*, September. 11–12, 1864; Jentz and Schneirov 2012, 78; Pierce 1940, 162–163).

That the *Times* strike hardened labor's attitude toward the two-party system is evident from the bitterness of the resolutions passed at a mass meeting of the Trades Assembly held on September 10, 1864. "It is a direct insult," one resolution read, "to ask us to give our suffrages and support to any publisher or candidate either directly or indirectly, who is not in practice a friend of labor." In another resolution, the Assembly declared, "we hereby mutually pledge ourselves to lay aside our party ties and predilections . . . and vote only for the known friends of the laboring man and, if deemed advisable, that we will nominate and elect to office men from our own ranks in whom we have confidence" (*Chicago Tribune*, September 11, 1864; *Workingman's Advocate*, September 17, 1864).

It is important to note that the resolutions were not an all out repudiation of institutional politics, as the Democratic operative Edward McComas remained a behind-the-scenes force at these meetings. For example, the Assembly stopped short of denouncing the Democratic Party tout court, calling instead upon the Democratic leadership "to remove Wilbur F. Storey from [the national executive] committee as being totally unworthy to represent the Democratic Party in such an important position." The body also urged party elders "to repudiate the Chicago *Times* as the organ of the party, and establish a new Democratic organ in this city," to which they pledged to give their "hearty and earnest support." But true to the obvious sting of the *Times*' betrayal and the growing support for a course of political independence, the organization warned that "unless such a course is adopted, the Democratic Party stands in danger of losing both prestige and support with the masses of laboring men." As for the Republican Party, the workers had this to say: "The Chicago *Tribune* has been at all times the prompt and ready enemy of both the labor organizations and their friends, and a leader of even the *Times* in such opposition." They added, "we include the *Tribune* in our denunciations against the enemies of labor" (*Workingman's Advocate*, September 17, 1864).

Episode 4: The Congressional Election of 1864

The Trades Assembly, in turn, applied the lessons learned in the *Times* debacle to their strategy in the 1864 Congressional elections, in which the labor movement endorsed the conservative Democrat Cyrus McCormick against Republican mayor John Wentworth. Taken out of context, one might be tempted to interpret this move as evidence that the Trades Assembly had officially gone Democratic. It would be closer to the mark, however, to suggest that the labor movement had adopted a candidate-centered endorsement policy.

On October 22, 1864, the Assembly published a letter to candidates, whose title and preamble made clear that it was written "without distinction of party." In it, the labor federation asked several questions and requested the candidates' "unequivocal answers to them through our organ, THE WORKINGMAN'S ADVOCATE." Among the questions were, "Will you endeavor to procure the repeal of the "*La Salle Black Laws*" and "Will you agree to introduce and advocate the passage of a bill to *shorten the hours of labor*?" The questions thus amount to a labor litmus test akin to *Roe v. Wade* in contemporary American politics. Cyrus McCormick, whose response appears in the November 5, 1864 issue of the *Advocate*, replied, "Looking over the measures and principles proposed in the interrogatories passed by the 'Trades' Assembly,' I find nothing to disapprove, but, on the contrary, regard their demands just and correct in principle." In contrast, John Wentworth refused to supply answers either way. In an editorial on Wentworth, Andrew Cameron then asked Chicago workingmen what they thought of the competing candidates' responses. He wrote, implying support for McCormick, "Will you vote for a man who refused to answer the questions propounded by the Trades' Assembly under the plea that 'they are unworthy of notice [?]'" (Jentz and Schneirov 2012, 79; Pierce 1940, 169, 281–283; *Workingman's Advocate*, November 5, 1864). In sum, Cameron's reaction suggests that the federation endorsed McCormick not because they were a Democratic or "copperhead" body, but because the Democratic nominee was the only candidate in the field who passed their test.[2]

Triumph, Part II: Victory and Martyrdom

Had it not been for a dramatic turnaround in the progress of the war, there is no telling how the sum total of these burgeoning defections would have shaped the fortunes of the Republican Party or the North's position vis-à-vis the South as the military conflict wore on. As it happened, Union General William T. Sherman captured the southern stronghold of Atlanta on September 2, 1864. From there, the Republican Party went from strength to strength. Public opinion both in Chicago and across the North turned sharply in favor of Abraham Lincoln, who took on the aura of one who now was able and willing to crush his foe. With the fall of Atlanta came the collapse of Frémont's campaign for the Republican nomination. On September 22, 1864, he withdrew his candidacy. President Lincoln was reelected, while labor was brushed with treason for their overt association with the Democratic Party. It bears mention, however, that in Chicago, the president's margin of victory was less than 2,000 out of 27,000 votes cast: Lincoln received 14,388 ballots to McClellan's 12,691. This was hardly a rout given the Democrats' vulnerable position after Atlanta, a fact that speaks to the lingering effects of wartime dissension in the free labor coalition (Jentz and Schneirov 2012, 78; Levine 1992, 262; Pierce 1940, 280).

McCormick lost his challenge to the perennial Chicago politician Long John Wentworth. In the full flush of military victory, McCormick, Democrat that he was, could do nothing but bleed from the taint of copper. The reaper magnate lost badly, and labor lost, too, by association. The movement's first turn as a bona fide lobby had gone terribly awry (Jentz and Schneirov 2012, 79; Pierce 1940, 283).

The political noose around all remaining alternatives tightened further still with a paradoxical mix of triumph and tragedy. On April 3, 1865, the capital of the Confederacy, Richmond, Virginia, fell to Union forces, and on April 9, General Robert E. Lee surrendered to General Ulysses S. Grant at Appomattox. These two victories signaled the end of the war, and Chicago erupted in a days-long street celebration. But consistent with the triumphs and reversals of the Civil War, celebration all too quickly gave way to sadness on April 15 as Chicagoans heard the news that President Lincoln had been assassinated (Pierce 1940, 283). Though it is undoubtedly crass for a scholar such as myself to dwell even briefly on the political implications of this event, it is an inescapable fact of the shooting's aftermath that the Republicans politicized the assassination. Ahead of the 1865 municipal election, the GOP felt it necessary to remind Chicagoans that the choice was between the friends of "the martyred Abraham Lincoln" and his enemies, warning that a victory for the opposition would cover Chicago "with ignominy." Republican mayor John B. Rice prevailed (*Chicago Tribune*, April 18, 19, 1865; Pierce 1940, 284).

Conclusion

There is a pervasive assumption among social theorists that wartime politics are not "politics-as-usual." The oxygen, they imply, gets sucked out of the room of possible alternatives, where reason and compromise normally reside. For example, Anthony Downs (1957), whose economic theory of democracy is the dominant paradigm in the study of political behavior, argues that once a typically centrist polity becomes polarized, the distribution of voters goes from "normal" (where the majority cluster around the ideological center) to bimodal (where the community gathers at either extreme of the political spectrum). Such a polity is unstable and teeters on the edge of, or descends precipitously into, civil war. There is no incentive for politicians to appeal to the center where a resolution can be sought, because no voters can be found there. Even Antonio Gramsci, upon whose work I base my theoretical framework, implies that the people cross a point of no return when they pass from pluralist democracy into revolution (Riley 2011). Under pluralist democracy, parties vie with one another to articulate social classes to their respective organizations, but in a time of revolution, the different progressive social fractions coalesce into a single class under one party against another class under an opposing party.

This chapter has shown that the binary of peacetime and wartime does not hold up as well as we might think. "Politics-as-usual" do persist in times of war after a fashion, and to the degree that they do, the golden rule of political articulation applies, namely, that parties must actively work to naturalize social divisions, otherwise their coalitions, however once hegemonic, threaten to fall apart. This became evident as early as the summer of 1861, when the Republicans felt it necessary, amid whispers of dissent, to administer a loyalty oath to Chicago residents. From there, the political position of Mr. Lincoln's party went from bad to worse as the Democrats capitalized on the people's war weariness, racial anxieties, and economic grievances.

Of course, the Republicans were not defeated in the end, and here some attention must be given to the causal impact of unexpected events or "contingencies" as historical sociologists call them. If the unforeseen defeat of Martin Van Buren for the 1844 Democratic presidential nomination was at least partly responsible for the subsequent political crisis over slavery, then during the war, military victories beginning with the capture of Atlanta in 1864 played a corresponding role, each working to restore the Republican Party to power and snatching victory from the jaws of probable defeat.

It would be a mistake, however, to presume that events in and of themselves are able to have such impact, for both the meaning and shock value of events are resolved within preexisting power relations. In each case—1844 and 1864—there was both a discredited party, vulnerable to blame, and a vindicated one, ready to interpret the course of events in terms favorable to them. In the case of 1864, the Republicans seized upon Atlanta as a vindication of Abraham Lincoln's leadership and a repudiation of every living Democrat, whether he questioned the president's leadership or not. The dynamic is similar to that of other crises. According to Michael Mann (2012, 241–242), for example, some states lurched leftward during the Great Depression, because the incumbent party had been conservative, whereas other states moved to the right, because the incumbents had been liberal, labor, or socialist. Wars, like other crises, have no natural ideological valence: their political meaning depends on the context of partisan struggle.

It is also within this context that the relatively autonomous politics of Chicago workers must be interpreted. The arc of the narrative in this chapter begins with workers thoroughly articulated as enthusiastic partners in the Grand Army of the Republic. As their economic position on the home front deteriorated and as the Democrats emerged early on to give expression to their corresponding doubts, Chicago workers began to defect from the free labor coalition. But the strike at the Democratic *Times* in September 1864 and the Republican *Tribune*'s support of their rival paper's course in that dispute, left the labor movement disaffected from both major parties and preferring to occupy the position of a politically independent lobby—one that was ready to do business with any candidate who pledged to support prolabor policies. This remained the strategy of organized labor as it entered the postbellum period, and it met with some success, not least, the passage of the first eight-hour day law in the country. However, the political establishment's withdrawal of support for that legislation, justified by the right to work and backed by state violence, would lead the labor movement from the lobby and into the streets.

ANTILABOR DEMOCRACY AND THE WORKING CLASS, 1865–1887

Republican usage of the discourse of dependency had already begun to undermine the once potent distinction between hirelings, on the one hand, and farmers and artisans, on the other. However, no coherent alternative had yet emerged to define the civic standing of free white men in an era now formally without slavery. If the latter's freedom was once understood in terms of self-sufficiency—that is, in terms of one's escape from wage dependency—for most of the antebellum period, then it was not yet clear as the country emerged from civil war whether freedom now entailed the opposite, namely, one's subordination to wage dependency. As John B. Jentz and Richard Schneirov (2012) correctly point out in their analysis of postbellum Chicago politics, the Republicans had hedged on the issue of wage dependency: capitalism was framed as the antithesis of slavery for the purpose of prosecuting the war (even though slavery had been central to American capitalism), yet it seemed politically important to keep western lands cheap and accessible for white workers seeking to escape industrial work in the nation's cities.

Free labor ideology, in other words, was a transitional discourse on the way to what was then still an emerging political language of civic standing: the freedom of contract. In the postbellum period, civic standing came to be understood in terms of an individual's ability to enter into contractual relations with another individual. Chief among such contracts (for it addressed the specter of mounting labor unrest and the vexing status of hirelings) was the wage bargain. According to the contractual vision of a free society, the wage worker was free, because instead of being coerced into relinquishing labor to his master, he negotiated the wages and other conditions under which he would willingly exchange his labor. Because collective agreements prohibited the "right to work" below (or theoretically above) union scale, collective bargaining was said to obstruct the wage bargain and enslave one or both side(s) of the agreement. Thus, unions and other labor organizations became subject to state repression, up to and including incarceration and violent force, very much as southern secessionists had been just a few years earlier.

At the heart of the contractual vision of civic standing, then, was a double standard that turned on the question of "corporate personhood," the right of a collective to claim the freedoms of an individual citizen under the law. Employers and workers alike established "combinations" to cope with the changing economic terrain of the mid- to late-nineteenth century United States. As Richard Schneirov writes, "In the course of competition business proprietors began to combine or associate in such organizations as trusts, employers' groups, and corporations to consciously regulate market competition. The new organizations were an inescapable reaction to the need to accumulate large sums of capital and labor and to protect them in an unpredictable marketplace" (1998, 8). Workers were doing the same, but whereas an employer combination enjoyed the standing of a free rights-bearing individual, a worker who combined in a union with other workers was construed as a conspiracy to undermine the freedom of contract.

It bears mention that other scholars have discussed the contradictions of free labor ideology and free contract, especially in inaugurating the notably unforgiving economic order of the late nineteenth-century United States. These scholars suggest that jurists were the prime movers of this transformation (see, for example, Hattam 1993; Steinfeld 1991; Tomlins 1992). Though such research has contributed mightily to our understanding of the U.S. labor movement, it has largely sidestepped or downplayed the importance of political parties in this process. Victoria Hattam, for instance, holds that it was "a strong judiciary . . . rather than the consequence of the party system" that "created a politically weak labor movement in the United States," especially in its broad application of the doctrine of criminal conspiracy to include trade unionism (1993, ix, 30–75). In this chapter, I argue that beyond being a legal doctrine or a convenient justification for employers to stonewall workers' demands, free contract was also a rhetorical and policy device of party leaders, who, in the American system of "party government," controlled the means of state violence (i.e., the military, police) and impinged upon legal decisions made from the bench by, for example, becoming judges themselves. The political establishment had conceived of free contract as a rhetorical tool for rearticulating workers and employers together in a postbellum version of the wartime free labor coalition. When workers rejected it as a glorified version of wage dependency, politicians followed the doctrine of free contract to its antilabor conclusion: the right to work.

The right to work became a tool for enlisting the support of all those terrified of labor's successive mass protests against economic inequality under capitalism, from the first May Day strikes for an eight-hour-day in 1867 to the nationwide strikes of 1886 known as the Great Upheaval. Because the right to work eviscerated any preexisting legitimacy for collective bargaining, while simultaneously upholding the prerogative of the state to suppress labor "conspiracies" in the name of victimized employers and employees, America's transition out of slavery was not toward just any kind democracy, but rather toward a specifically antilabor democracy.

The Politics of Labor Conspiracy

The notion that free contract, right to work, and labor conspiracy were exclusively legal in provenance is incomplete for several reasons. First, scholars have identified numerous factors giving rise to, and subsequently shaping, the meaning and use of these concepts. Perhaps the best known of these is Amy Dru Stanley's *From Bondage to Contract* (1998), according to which social scientists, abolitionists, labor reformers, and jurists together placed freedom of contract at the center of the postbellum social order. In doing so, however, Stanley largely omits the role played by political leaders in achieving this monumental transformation. By contrast, Johann Neem (2008) and Daniel Ernst (1995) offer important clues about the role of party politics in shaping key legal precedents.

Consider the famous case of *Commonwealth v. Hunt* (1842), which is often (though incorrectly)[1] taken to spell the end of labor conspiracy cases in the United States. Decided initially by the Boston municipal court in 1840 and then on appeal by the Massachusetts supreme court in 1842, the case concerned the Boston Journeymen Bootmakers' Society, which fined one of its members, Jeremiah Horne, for doing extra work without pay. When Horne refused to pay the fine, the union insisted that he be fired, because the union's constitution pledged all members to work only for employers whose employees abided by union regulations. Judge Thacher, speaking for the municipal court, told the jurors that unions were usurping the state's authority to tax. As such, unions unlawfully coerced others to agree to their terms and, in addition, effectively comprised "a new power in the state, unknown to its constitution and laws, and subversive of their equal spirit." Thacher's logic was the colonial-era doctrine that no association could exist without being authorized by the state as one operating in the public interest. Robert Rantoul, representing the union, appealed the case to the state supreme court. Chief Justice Lemuel Shaw, speaking for the court, agreed with Rantoul that while the journeymen could not "form closed shops that fostered class antagonism and violated market freedom," they could rightfully form their own associations. The court's holding has a twofold significance. To begin, "the state would no longer condemn citizens for organizing without the state's sanction." However, although workers could associate, "they could not act as a class but simply as a voluntary association of free individuals." In effect, Rantoul and Shaw worked to expand workers' freedom of association even as they refused to protect "the objects of their association" (Neem 2008, 161–163).

This partial concession to the labor movement, though seemingly legal in nature, is in fact empirically political. According to Neem (2008), the United States had not always been a "nation of joiners," forming voluntary associations as a countervailing force to the power of the state, as Tocqueville famously argued. Such associations had once been permitted only if they were viewed as representing the interests of the community as a whole (Harvard College, for instance, was originally chartered as a state school) and were incorporated as agencies of the state. The gradual separation of voluntary associations from the state was accomplished primarily by groups for whom state authorization was out of reach such as nonestablishment churches and opposition parties. Thus, Jeffersonian Republicans insisted on, and were implicitly accorded, the right to associate, though they opposed the policies of Federalists, who controlled the reins of state power in Massachusetts. Likewise, when Democrats were in the ascendant, Whigs went "underground" to build an oppositional power base in associations like Atheneums and other learned societies, which they were able to shield from Democrats seeking to undermine them. Accordingly, by the 1840s, "the number of voluntary associations had expanded dramatically." Judge Shaw's decision in *Hunt* was therefore a response to the prevailing political context of the time. "To prevent laborers the right to form a voluntary association when everyone else was doing so," Neem writes, "would be indefensible," for "to find the laborers guilty would mean finding almost every voluntary association guilty of conspiracy" (2008, 162). In short, organized political dissent, notably among parties, shaped even these earlier and seemingly legalistic court holdings on labor conspiracy.[2]

The *Danbury Hatters* case (1908) is another example of the difficulty in separating party politics from the judiciary in matters of free contract, right to work, and labor conspiracy. In that instance, Chief Justice Melville W. Fuller, writing for the U.S. Supreme Court, ruled against the United Hatters of North America for boycotting the hats of an employer, Dietrich Eduard Loewe, because he refused to unionize. Employing the doctrine of free contract, Fuller held, "The boycott of Loewe's hats was an unlawful breach of individual dealing in the marketplace—an intolerable violation of 'the liberty of the trader'" (Ernst 1995, 5, 7). The backstory of this case and a convenient segue into the political origins of early Illinois labor law is that Melville W. Fuller was a leading Chicago Douglas Democrat, who was instrumental in shaping that party's antilabor posture after the Civil War.

Fuller's involvement in declaring unions conspiracies in restraint of trade might plausibly be divorced from party politics if Illinois politicians had little to no role in writing labor law in this period, but in fact the opposite is true. Thus, the second reason that free contract, right to work, and labor conspiracy cannot be treated as the sole province of the courts is that much of early Illinois labor law was not handed down by judges on the basis of English common law, but by party politicians in the state General Assembly. Earl Beckner's (1929) still widely cited study states that though "the First Illinois General Assembly, meeting in 1819, declared English common law and all acts of Parliament in aid thereof" to be "in full force and effect in Illinois," the question of labor conspiracy "did not come before the Illinois courts until comparatively recent times." "In the meantime," he added, "the General Assembly passed a number of laws relating to the problem of conspiracy and the right to organize" (Beckner 1929, 9). In short, Illinois conspiracy laws were statutory laws made by politicians, not legal precedents established by jurists. Such laws articulate perfectly the contractual vision of a free society and the double standard of corporate personhood for employer combinations and conspiracy for labor combinations. Significantly, the three most important laws of the nineteenth century were passed during and immediately after the Civil War, suggesting that the relationship between parties and workers became increasingly strained as the labor question eclipsed the slavery question in political discourse.

The first of these was the LaSalle Black Law. Passed by the General Assembly in 1863, the law was a response to a series of strikes in the coal mines of LaSalle, Illinois, one of which, the Illinois Valley Coal Company, was owned in part by Joseph Medill and Horace White, editors of the *Chicago Tribune* and powerbrokers in the Chicago Republican Party. Section 1 of the law, which established the right to work and applied to the general workforce, prohibited "any person from seeking to prevent, by threat, intimidation, or otherwise, any other person from working at any lawful business on any terms that he might see fit." Violation of this section was punishable by a fine of up to $100. Section 2 prohibited "any two or more persons from combining for the purpose of depriving the owner or possessor of property of its lawful use and management of any person or persons from being employed by such owner or possessor of property." Violation of this section was punishable by a fine of up to $500 or six months imprisonment. In sum, Section 1 prevented interference with the individual wage bargain, and

Section 2 declared striking workers unlawful conspiracies, while simultaneously constructing combinations of capitalists (e.g., the Illinois Valley Coal Company) as individuals bearing inviolable property rights (Beckner 1929, 9–10; David 1936, 43–44; Montgomery 1967, 427; Schneirov 1998, 30–31).[3]

After the LaSalle Black Law, the next such bill passed by the General Assembly was the Merritt Conspiracy Law of 1887. Like Melville Fuller, Thomas E. Merritt, the law's primary sponsor, hailed from a family of staunch Douglas Democrats: his father and brother were editors of the state Democratic organ, the *Illinois State Register*, and Tom Merritt himself had been the leader of that party on the floor of the House (Dorris 1919, 631, 633). The bill cleared the General Assembly in 1887 by a large bipartisan majority—a political response to the Haymarket bombing of 1886. The law rendered any act injurious to "human life, person, or property" an unlawful conspiracy and made it possible to convict without evidence connecting the alleged conspirator to the crime. For example, under Section 2 of the law the state could convict "every person who, by public utterance, or by writing, publishing, or circulating any written or printed matter should advise, encourage, aid, abet, or incite other persons to revolution, riot, violence, or resistance to law." However, in that event, "the prosecution was not required to show that the speaking was heard or that the written or printed matter aforesaid was read or communicated to the person actually committing the crime, if such speaking, writing, or publishing was shown to have been done in a public manner in Illinois." Nor was it necessary to "prove that the parties on trial had ever come together and entered into any agreement to accomplish the unlawful purpose" (Beckner 1929, 14–15; see also *Chicago Tribune*, May 5, 1887). Merritt went well beyond the LaSalle Black Law, for even the speaker of a "public utterance" could be convicted as a labor conspirator. At the same time, the law protected any individual whose life, person, or property could be construed as being injured in said conspiracy.[4]

The last such law passed by the Illinois General Assembly in this period was the Cole Anti-Boycott Law, so named because it was introduced by Charles E. Cole, a Democrat from the forty-eighth senatorial district. The law specifically made boycotts a conspiracy, such that "if two or more persons conspired together, or the officers or executive committee of any society or organization uttered or issued any circular or edict instructing its members to institute a boycott or blacklist, they should be deemed guilty of conspiracy and be imprisoned in the penitentiary not exceeding five years, or fined not exceeding $2,000, or both" (Beckner 1929, 35). Whereas boycotts urged union members to avoid buying nonunion-made goods, blacklisting urged employers to avoid hiring union members. According to Beckner and contemporary observers, however, the employer practice of blacklisting was included in the law only for appearance's sake to pass constitutional muster. In practice, as the Democratic *Chicago Times* itself noted, the law enforced the aforementioned double standard, whereby the work of "strike societies" would be frustrated, while blacklisting would remain unchecked (Beckner 1929, 36; *Chicago Times*, June 16, 1887).

Thus, in Illinois, political parties were equally central to the establishment of conspiracy laws, if not more so than the courts, whose job was to adjudicate cases on their basis. The widely held claim that the judiciary was mostly or exclusively responsible for framing unions as conspiracies in restraint of trade (thus sending the U.S. labor movement on a more conservative political trajectory than their European counterparts) is therefore incomplete. Still the partisan origins of early conspiracy statutes take us only part of the way to the broader argument of the book as they tell us little about the evolving relationship between parties and workers between 1863 and 1887. For that we must turn to a content analysis of party newspapers.

Initial Support

Another reason that the legal thesis is only a partial explanation is that the character of working class militancy in this period was shaped by the political establishment's initial offer, and subsequent withdrawal, of support for the labor movement's signature postbellum demand: the eight-hour day. The Radicals in particular, who became the Republicans' ruling faction immediately after the war, briefly reversed their party's wartime aloofness and welcomed the protests of Chicago's workingmen. For example, when workers organized an "imposing" torchlight procession to reduce the workday from ten to eight hours, the *Tribune* (then an organ of the Radical wing of the party), referred to a banner that read, "Eight hours for labor, eight hours for sleep, eight hours for rest and mental improvements," by calling it "a most excellent division of time." Where once the *Tribune* detected treason in the political strategy of the Chicago labor movement, the paper now found it "natural" for these men to prefer working eight hours over ten hours, adding that "This country is now free from Maine to Texas, and involuntary labor is not permitted." The editor then ended on an encouraging note, saying, "Let the eight hour system be tried" (*Chicago Tribune*, December 11, 1865, 4).

There were, however, limits to Radical support, and these limits presaged the response of both major parties to subsequent labor protests, which tended to take the form of strikes and boycotts. In the same article, the *Tribune* voiced a single complaint: that a rumor was circulating to the effect that the workers wanted "ten hours' pay for eight hours work." Alluding to the laws of political economy, they warned that "the higher the wages, the dearer the goods." They could accomplish such a goal not by forcing employers to submit to the demand, but rather by clubbing "together and [forming] co-operative establishments," for only then would they be able to "secure both the wages of labor and the profits of capital." Thus, Radical support for the labor movement rested on the false hope that labor's foremost demand could be met without industrial antagonism. As Montgomery famously observed, the Radical Republican agenda eventually "foundered on the shoals of class conflict" (1967, x).

The Democratic Party recognized perhaps more than the Radicals themselves did that GOP-led Reconstruction consisted of both black suffrage in the South and rapid economic development nationwide, managed principally by northeastern capital. That the Civil War was a ruse perpetrated by Yankee speculators to protect their financial interests has long been disproved, but that Reconstruction advanced an economic agenda as well as a civil rights agenda is an established fact, confirmed to varying degrees by historians as far apart on this subject as C. Vann Woodward—for whom Reconstruction represented the consolidation of capitalist hegemony, and Eric Foner—for whom Reconstruction was primarily about civil rights (Foner 1988; Montgomery 1967; Unger 1964; Woodward 1951). It was on the overweening influence of Yankee capital that the Democrats relied for what seemed to be their prolabor stance immediately after the war.

The Democratic *Chicago Times*, for example, took regular aim at the Republicans' support of a protective tariff, because it could only mean that a hidden cost would be passed on to workers through higher consumer prices. When "the tariff bill passed the senate in Washington . . . by a vote of twenty-seven to ten," the *Times* railed against the measure, quoting the *New York Post*'s characterization of it as "an enormous and cold-blooded swindle upon the workingmen of America." The *Times* continued, "The prices of almost all commodities now are double what they were in 1860 . . . they will be further increased at least a third" (*Chicago Times*, February 2, 1867, 4). The Democrats were therefore no longer critical of factories or the wage system, but of legislation that shielded manufacturers from foreign competition while doing nothing to shield workers from manufacturers.

Eventually, the appeal of both major parties to workers would become limited to arguments for and against the tariff, with the Republicans insisting that import taxes would protect domestic manufacturing jobs from foreign competition, and the Democrats countering that the tariff made the necessities of life too expensive for regular working people (Jentz and Schneirov 2012, 4, 7). This was a convenient turn in more ways than one: the tariff had been a familiar and long-standing dispute between the parties, and it had the potential to organize future debate as the end of the slavery extension issue threatened to leave a political vacuum.

But the major parties' posture toward the incipient labor movement did not solely consist of this subtle shift in policy. In addition, and more important for our purposes, political elites advanced the rhetoric of free contract and the right to work to counter workers' attempts at recuperating the Jacksonian critique of wage dependency. Before we examine the political uses of free contract in detail, however, we discuss what I call the "structural supports" that undermined claims that the wage bargain was in reality a lopsided one, in which employers dictated the terms of employment and workers had little to no power. This was a critical rhetorical move, for the contractual vision of the postbellum republic rested on the assumption that individual workers and employers were free and equal partners to the wage bargain. Pushing back against the labor movement's critique of this assumption, party leaders worked to construct employer and employee as standing face-to-face on the level ground of the market. This fact, too, puts meat on the bones of the aforementioned legal thesis, for these ideological supports originated in not only jurisprudence, but also the partisan appropriation of political economy among other discourses.

Structural Supports: Economics, Meritocracy, and the Defeated South

The first such support was classical economics or as it was known then, "political economy." The impersonal law of supply and demand served to exonerate employers for layoffs and low wages. The implication was that employers do not actually "dictate" workforce size or wage rates but are instead bound by the labor supply; the wage bargain thus takes place within these constraints—constraints for which the employer holds no responsibility. For example, Chicago's first ever strike for an eight-hour day was a movement in 1867 to force employers to abide by an act of the Republican-controlled state legislature, which made eight hours a legal day's work for all those paid by the day. The law itself was made deliberately weak, in that it provided for no means of enforcement and allowed employers to evade the law by paying workers by the hour or the week. Though legislators might easily have made the law more stringent by closing such loopholes, the *Chicago Times* predicted that the strike was doomed to fail, because "The law of supply and demand is a 'higher law' than legislators can make" (May 8, 1867, 4). The allusion here to the divine may have been overstating the point, but the basic claim is clear, namely, that wages and the hours of work were a mechanical effect of natural laws that could not be legislated or protested away. The very next day, the *Times* condemned the eight-hour strike as "an attempt to amend the natural law of supply and demand, by creating an artificial scarcity where a natural scarcity is not found" (*Chicago Times*, May 9, 1867, 4).

The invocation of political economy was further strengthened by the claim of meritocracy, in which capital and labor were said to be equal because most capitalists were at one point as poor as any workingman. This cult of the self-made man also undercut the old Jacksonian claim that wage workers were in danger of permanent industrial servitude. In one instance, the *Tribune* assailed a series of letters to the editor penned by one "Mechanic" that urged the redistribution of wealth in Chicago. The editors held that capital and labor in the United States were equal and free since neither was "afflicted with an hereditary nobility and a law of primogeniture." On the contrary, "the acquisition of property is entirely open to all, and . . . the sons of the poor oftener attain great wealth and high station [than] those of the rich" (*Chicago Tribune*, April 20, 1867, 2). Unlike Europe, then, where social mobility was virtually impossible under the law, the *Tribune* here holds that American workers and employers occupied different positions on a more or less fluid continuum.

A slightly more extreme version of this argument was a perversion of antebellum producerism, which, to repeat, held that farmers and workers belonged to the same class by virtue of the fact that they transformed raw materials into useful commodities. Free labor producerism, by contrast, included elites in the class of producers. The Democratic *Times*, for example, argued that capitalists and workers held equal claim to free labor identity: "The capitalist who employs a half-hundred workingmen is engaged just as much in the interests of labor as the men who work for him." In such a case, the editor wrote, "All capitalists are workmen" (*Chicago Times*, April 22, 1867, 4). By this logic, to say that employer and employee were free and equal was almost superfluous, for they were more than that to each other—they were one and the same thing.

But if the motif of the self-made man or boss-worker was a powerful structural support to the freedom of contract, then it was due in part to another motif that was often deployed in tandem with it, namely, the comparison of Europe and the defeated South with the United States. The implication was that capital and labor were equal and free, because workers were neither serfs nor slaves. The image of the South was an especially popular foil in this regard as the memory of the war remained fresh in the minds of Chicagoans. In the midst of the Depression of 1873, for instance, when Chicago workers were demanding that the state support them when capitalists would not, the *Tribune* responded, "the denunciation of the rich and of the middle class of citizens was simply absurd. We have no privileged class in this country. The wealthy man of to-day may be the poor to-morrow . . . Ninety-nine per cent of the rich of this country began life in poverty" (*Chicago Tribune*, December 23, 1873, 4). Here the editors employ the familiar trope of meritocracy, which, as we have seen constructed workers and their bosses as two positions on a fluid continuum. But the *Tribune* did not stop there as the editors then anchored their invocation of the self-made man in a comparison of the United States and the Old South:

> Ours is not a paternal Government which takes the earnings of the
> labor of the people, and, in return engages to feed, clothe, and house

them . . . That was the system which prevailed at the South before the War, when the entire product of human labor was taken by the few, who in return fed, clothed, housed, and in the end, buried the laborer. The American Government repudiated the whole system of feudal slavery . . . The duty of the Government to the citizen begins and ends with securing him equality, and entire freedom in the exercise of his abilities, and full protection and security in the possession of the fruits of his labor. The citizen to be free must be self-dependent, and this is the precise difference between the citizen of the United States and the citizens of other countries. (*Chicago Tribune*, December 23, 1873, 4)

Using the free labor rhetoric of wartime in this way, the Republican Party sought to discredit depression-era appeals to the state for bread or work as a plan to reintroduce the slave power—in the guise of socialism—into the same republican institutions that Chicago workingmen had recently risked their lives to protect. Turning the tables, the *Tribune* cast the party's rejection of the workers' pleas for relief as a defense of workers' freedom. Note, too, that though the civic standing of workers is grounded in being "self-dependent," there is nothing here to suggest that earning a wage disqualified them from citizenship. Vaguely being "in the possession of the fruits of his labor" was enough.

Even Democrats, many of whom were uncomfortable with Republican swipes at the South, pointed to the end of slavery as sufficient proof that workers and their employers were equal and free. On one occasion, the *Chicago Times* wrote, "It is only in a condition of slavery that the interests of labor are antagonistic to the interests of capital. Where men are free, having the right to dispose of their labor to the best buyer and to enjoy the proceeds themselves, the interests of labor and capital are and always will be mutual" (May 3, 1867, 4). Contrary to the vision of class antagonism increasingly embraced in labor circles, then, postbellum political elites held that in the absence of slavery, no such antagonism existed. The passage of bonded servitude from the Republic left a free and open marketplace, where the only permissible and indeed logical practice was the mutual exchange of labor for wages—the freedom of contract.

The Right to Work, Corporate Personhood, and Labor Conspiracy

Having established that employer and employee were equal and free, the above structural supports enabled the political establishment to advance a clear alternative to a civic standing based on the escape from wage dependency. That alternative was a civic standing based on the freedom of individuals to enter into contracts with one another. As the previous example suggests, workers met their potential employers in a non-coercive environment where both sides could strike a bargain that was mutually agreeable. Because either one could freely walk away from the deal, neither could be a slave to the other. And far from engendering class conflict, it was imagined that the wage contract bound capitalist and worker to the same fate such that their interests were fundamentally identical. This notion proved an elegant way to undercut any claims to power based on the antebellum critique of wage labor as slave labor.

Ironically, the Democrats were particularly fond of using the wage contract to debunk their once populist critique of wage dependency. Countering the claim that capital and labor were intrinsically antagonistic, the *Times* wrote in tones reminiscent of Whig corporatism, "It does not explain any antagonism that exists, or that can be supposed to exist, between the *interests* of capital and labor. It explains only the antagonism that may rise between two individuals in the act of exchanging commodities." Thus, the Democrats begin by denying the very existence of class (a reversal of their erstwhile project to articulate farmers and workers as a class of producers against nonproducers) and reducing the moment of exchange to a transaction between free-floating individuals. The *Times* continued by saying that even the interests of the individuals are the same: "The interests of both parties are that the commodities shall be exchanged. Their interests, therefore, are mutual . . . The whole system of what is called commercial exchange, whether the exchangeable commodities be labor or money or groceries, or anything else, rests upon mutuality of interests. No such thing as antagonism of interests can exist . . . The true interests of all men who have commodities to exchange is the liberty to exchange them in an open and free market. Any restriction of this freedom . . . is detrimental to the general interests of both parties" (*Chicago Times*, May 10, 1867, 4).

The antagonism, then, is not between labor and capital, which are, in any case, artificial constructs masking what are really individuals interested in consummating an exchange. Rather, the antagonists are individual employers and employees united in opposition to any "restriction" to their freedom to exchange commodities on the open market. This guiding assumption is significant for three reasons. First, present in its infancy here is the right to work: the principle that nothing should impede the individual employer and employee from exchanging wages for labor, least of all the requirement to join a union or abide by union rules. Second, there is a crucial double standard at work. The buyer of labor (i.e., the "employer") may in practice be a collective like a partnership, company, or corporation, yet they enjoy the status of a rights-bearing individual or corporate person. By contrast, the seller of labor who forms a collective or union with other sellers (i.e., workers) is a conspiracy to restrict the freedom of both parties to consummate a wage bargain. Third, the right to work, corporate personhood, and labor conspiracy all turn on a deeper transformation, in which parties and other actors were redefining civic standing in a free society from one based on the escape from wage dependency to one based on unfettered market exchange in general and the once stigmatized wage contract in particular.

The Republicans likewise employed the freedom of contract to undermine the Jacksonian critique of wage dependency. This may be glimpsed in the *Tribune*'s duel with the aforementioned subscriber "Mechanic." The journal might be credited for even publishing these letters to begin with, but its editors seemed to be using them as a vehicle for expounding on free contract, sometimes with multiple editorials on the same letter. In the following passage, the editors reject the argument that the free labor system is equivalent to slavery:

> We deny utterly that the "master owns the mechanic" during the hours of labor. It is a libel on both the employer and the employe [*sic*] to assert it, and he is no friend of the laboring man who makes such an assertion. The mechanic's skill and labor constitute his capital. He 'owns' the employer as much as the employer owns him. He works on *shares*. He says to the capitalist, "I will go into your shop and take charge of your engine, lathe, forge, tools or machinery. I will take the raw material you have provided and shape and fashion it according to your wishes, for a specific cash consideration. I will work by the "piece" or by the day. You will take all the chances of fire, of loss and depreciation. You shall pay all the public taxes and assessments; and in lieu thereof shall have what the fabric will bring to the market—assuming all the risks yourself." A bargain is struck; the service is performed; the stipulated wages are paid. If the employer finds a favorable market for the product of his shop, he makes a profit. (*Chicago Tribune*, March 26, 1867, 2)

There are several notable dimensions to this passage. To begin, the Republicans are able to suggest that capital and labor are equal by assuming that the worker owns his own capital. The worker is not a slave because—contrary to the Jacksonian critique of wage dependency—he does not actually sell himself, but a tradable commodity that is disembodied, namely, his own labor, which is his capital and property. Both parties to the bargain are therefore equal, because both are capitalists. Furthermore, the editors take pains to paint a vivid picture of the wage bargain, describing in detail, step-by-step, how the conversation between the worker and his employer might take place in the open market. Significantly, the employer does not dictate the terms of the bargain—a frequent critique of the freedom of contract within the labor movement. It is instead the worker who lays out the conditions under which he will exchange his labor, while the employer passively consents and, moreover, bears the heavier burdens of risk, fire, loss, and depreciation. Nor does the employer make a profit by exploiting his employee by either paying subsistence wages or overworking him: the editors are careful to say that profit originates with a favorable market for his product. Third, though the seller of his labor in this context is properly referred to in the singular as the "mechanic," the "employe," and the "laboring man," it is unclear whether the employer is an individual or collective. Nevertheless, the latter is described in the language of corporate personhood as "the capitalist."

From here, the freedom of contract became the basis on which Chicago political elites hung the familiar albatross of aristocracy (described at turns as "tyranny," "despotism," and "slavery") around the necks of trade unions. Among the more eloquent practitioners of this rhetorical turn was Joseph Medill, a Radical Republican and editor of the *Chicago Tribune* from 1856 to 1865. For Medill, the wage contract was a form of insurance against slavery. At a workingmen's parade in 1872, for example, he said this:

> Rights of persons are exactly equal. The rule works both ways. The employer is not bound to offer more wages than he pleases, nor to accept the services of those he does not see fit to engage. He is under no obligation to pay any attention to the rules of labor-unions. He can determine the number of men he desires to employ, the hours of labor per day . . . and the wages he is willing to pay therefore. It is his privilege to propose and yours to accept or decline; and yours to offer terms and his to accede or refuse. Neither party can dictate *both sides of the bargain*, for that would be tyranny and submission to it slavery." (*Chicago Tribune*, May 16, 1872, 4)

Perfect freedom of action thus entails the ability of individuals to enter into one-on-one exchange relations, in which each party to the bargain is at liberty to offer terms and either accept or reject them. Any combination or mechanism such as "the rules of labor-unions," whose purpose is to obstruct unfettered exchange, is a conspiracy to "dictate *both sides of the bargain*" and thus is tantamount to slavery itself. To ignore union rules is therefore to act freely. By this ingenious maneuver, Medill not only shifts the locus of dependency from wage work to the obstruction of the wage contract, but also provides the justification for the violent suppression of labor unions by equating them with the proslavery South. In this, we see once again the implicit double standard animating the contractual vision of the postbellum republic: whereas the employer, though possibly a collective, is constructed as a rights-bearing individual citizen, the worker, by combining with others into "labor-unions," conspires to tyrannize and enslave employer and employee alike. Conversely, the "right to work"—that is, to exchange one's labor at whatever price he is able to fetch on his own in the open market—is framed as the worker's ultimate freedom.

Not to be outdone, the Democrats likewise charged unions with scheming to dictate both sides of the wage bargain. Unions "undertook to regulate both the supply and the price of labor," the *Times* editorialized, by creating "an artificial scarcity of some article," and in doing so "rob employers by obliging them to pay as much for poor as for good workmen." Of unions, they added, "If they can be removed, labor will then be free, will have the advantages of competition in an open market . . . Let employers determine to no longer submit to the dictation and tyranny of trades organizations . . . Let capitalists at once assert their independence" (*Chicago Times*, May 8, 1867, 4). This passage represents a dramatic reversal of the Democrats' erstwhile critique of wage dependency: here it is the capitalist who is the victimized constituent, while the worker, by daring in combination with others to regulate the price of labor and thus tilt the once reviled wage contract in their favor, has become the tyrant. The abolition of unions, it followed, would amount to an assertion of "independence" on the part of employers. Note, however, that the employer is not the only one freed by the removal of unions, for labor, too, is emancipated by the right to work, framed here as "the advantages of competition in an open market."

Thus, both major parties defended the employee's right to work with the tone and tenacity of a crusading abolitionist. The *Tribune* wrote, "The right of each man to labor as much or as little as he chooses and to enjoy his own earnings, is the very foundation stone of free government . . . Take this right from the workingman and he is as completely enslaved as the Negro was five years ago" (May 3, 1867, 2). Accordingly, Republicans framed the eight-hour strike of 1867 as "an effort to prevent men from selling their own property (their labor) on such terms as were agreeable to both seller and purchaser. It was the voice of the slave power crying out—You shall work only when, where and on such terms as we dictate" (May 3, 1867, 4). Similarly, the Democrats, eliding their party's complicity in the southern rebellion, held that "the attempt of trades' organizations to compel men to shorten their hours" would inaugurate a world in which "The workingman would be at liberty to seize the capitalists' money, and the capitalist would have the corresponding liberty to seize the other's labor by reducing him to the condition of slavery" (*Chicago Times*, May 17, 1867, 4).

The Right to Work and the Logic of Antilabor State Violence

Having thus equated trade unionism and collective bargaining with slavery, Chicago political elites moved to crush labor's uprising just as the North had crushed the southern rebellion. In each instance of state violence below, I document the political establishment's military and rhetorical response to three episodes of labor protest: the 1867 strike for an eight-hour day, the Great Railroad Strike of 1877, and the Great Upheaval of 1886, and, by association, the Haymarket Affair.

We begin with Chicago's first strike for an eight-hour day, which took place in the spring of 1867. Two dimensions of the prelude to the strike bear mention here. First, between 1863 and 1866, Chicago workers had organized a total of nineteen new unions. Unlike their antebellum forebears, these unions were multiethnic and oriented towards conflict; like antebellum unions, however, they organized skilled tradesmen almost exclusively. The second dimension of the strike's prelude entails the initial bipartisan support mentioned above for eight-hour legislation. Radical Republicans had been hopeful that advocacy for the eight-hour day would revive the free labor coalition. Meanwhile Illinois Democrats sought to capitalize on their gains among working class voters during the war, but did so by distinguishing themselves as a more moderate voice on the labor question. Yet for all their stratagems, the parties ultimately failed to cultivate mass consent for a meaningful eight-hour law. Instead they drafted a weak bill in an attempt to appease both employers and workers and in the end appeased neither. Thus, the law applied only to workers who were paid by the day and provided for no mechanism of enforcement, as noted above. Significantly, it also contained a free contract proviso, whereby individual employees could contract to work for longer hours with individual employers if they so chose. Despite the toothlessness of the law, employers remained intransigent, due in part to the onset of a mild recession immediately following the war. By May 1, 1867 when the law was scheduled to take effect, seventy Chicago manufacturers had already started paying workers by the hour to circumvent the law, with the railroads following suit. Meanwhile several unions, lacking confidence in their employers, planned to take the law into their own hands by enforcing it with strike action beginning on May 2. Thus, although eight-hour legislation sailed nearly unopposed past the city council in April 1866 and the Illinois General Assembly in March 1867 (making it the first such law in the nation), the legitimacy of the law was ultimately decided in the streets (Montgomery 1967, 306–308; Schneirov 1998, 32–33).

The protest itself began peaceably enough on May 1 with a parade of some 6,000 workers in forty-four unions marching from the Back of the Yards to the Lakeshore, but the tone changed as the strike spread across the city on May 2. Perhaps the most important aspect of the strike was that it was not "general" per se. Among skilled tradesmen, the strike was concentrated in the building trades (especially among plumbers, gasfitters, and painters) and in the metal trades (primarily among machinists, iron molders, blacksmiths, and boilermakers). The centers of the conflict were the large metalworking factories of P.W. Gates and R.T. Crane and the railroad car shops. But the strike among skilled workers, who were union members and experienced in mounting disciplined job actions, was distinct from the strike as it expanded to outdoor workers and unskilled factory operatives, who tended not to be in unions but who struck anyway, particularly in the brickyards, lumberyards, planing mills, and furniture factories of working-class communities like the Irish neighborhood of Bridgeport. There, workers used a strategy that scholars sometimes call "crowd action" or "the bandwagon effect," whereby striking workers went from workplace to workplace sometimes recruiting workers to strike and at other times chasing workers off the job (Montgomery 1967, 309; Schneirov 1998, 35).

The political establishment's rhetorical response to the strike was to urge violent force and to frame the job action as a conspiracy against free contract and right to work. For instance, in an article titled, "Shall Mobs Rule Chicago?" the *Times* wrote, "The right of every man in Chicago to work as many or as few hours as he pleases, and to be secure in the enjoyment of that right, must and will be protected. The right of every employer in Chicago to manage and control his own property and to make and carry out such bargains with his employes [*sic*] as he and they may agree to, must and will also be protected . . . rioters should be swept out of existence by a discharge of artillery" (*Chicago Times*, May 4, 1867, 4). Here again the ability of individuals to work and contract with one another is framed as an inviolable right, whereas the workers' collective project to shape the workday is framed as the insolence of "mobs" and "riots" that should be "swept out of existence" with "artillery." Accordingly, when one crowd action swelled to 5,000 workers in Bridgeport, Conservative Republican mayor John Rice invoked the LaSalle Black Law, which protected the right to work, and deployed the Dearborn light artillery to put the crowd action down. Though many workers took up arms in defense, they were ultimately outmatched by the mayor's forces, who dispersed the Bridgeport workers and placed the entire city under martial law (Montgomery 1967, 310; Schneirov 1998, 35).

The next episode of state violence occurred during the Great Railroad Strike of 1877. The immediate causes of that conflict were twofold. The first was a rate-cutting war among railroad companies, the losses of which were passed on to their employees by slashing wages by as much as 30 percent in the spring of 1877. The prime mover of the strike in Chicago was the local chapter of the Workingman's Party of the United States (WPUS), which was then led by a young cadre of English speakers, most prominent among them, Albert Parsons, an American-born printer and fiery public speaker, recently arrived to Chicago with his African American wife, Lucy Parsons, from Texas where they had been Radical Republicans. Parsons and his associates were then primarily Lasallean socialists, meaning that they favored an electoral path to working class power, in contrast to Marxists, who favored strike action. The second precipitating cause was the passage on July 2, 1877 of city vagrancy laws that permitted the arrest of unemployed workers on the streets without warrant. The key advocates of the laws were Republican mayor Monroe Heath and his base in the affluent and virulently antilabor Citizens' Association (Schneirov 2008, 81–83).

Strike pressure began to mount on Tuesday, July 24 with a crowd action, touched off by a small group of striking Michigan Central railroad switchmen. Again, roving gangs called workers out to strike and shut down factories in their wake. In immediate response, the city and allied employers had Albert Parsons fired from his job at the *Times* and threatened him with arrest, while police broke up a peaceful WPUS meeting by clubbing workers and firing revolvers into the air (see an artist's rendering in figure 5.1).

Overnight, a private militia (organized by property owners), police, and several companies of the United States armed forces were assembled on the orders of the mayor, governor, the secretary of war, and the president of the United States. In total, over 20,000 men were under arms. The confluence of the crowd action and the mustering of troops precipitated what is now known as the "Battle of Halsted," which was a series of armed confrontations from Wednesday evening, July 25 through Thursday (see figure 5.2). Two communities suffered the most

FIGURE 5.1.   Lithograph; ICHi-14018; "Driving the Rioters from Turner Hall," from *Harper's Weekly*, August 18, 1877, Chicago, Ill. Artist: unknown. Courtesy of the Chicago History Museum.

FIGURE 5.2. Engraving (prints); ICHi-04893; "Fight between the military and the rioters at the Halsted Street Viaduct" from *Harper's Weekly*, August 18, 1877, Chicago, Ill. Artists: C. and A.T. Sears. Courtesy of the Chicago History Museum.

casualties: the sixth ward Bohemian fourth precinct, also known as Pilsen, and the fifth ward Irish community of Bridgeport, which housed the three fastest growing industries in the city: brick making, iron and steel making, and slaughtering and meat packing. Of the many confrontations in the battle, perhaps the most egregious took place on Thursday when police and others descended upon 300 unarmed journeymen cabinetmakers peaceably assembled to negotiate with their employers, shooting and clubbing workers, killing one carpenter, Carl Tessman, and wounding dozens of others. In all, approximately 30 men and boys were killed, many of whom were buried anonymously in lime pits, while another 200 were wounded, the largest number of casualties of any city in the nationwide strike. Among police, none were killed and eighteen suffered minor injuries (Schneirov 2008, 86–89, 92–95). In contrast to the workers of Pilsen and Bridgeport who mourned their dead in the days following, Republican elder Joseph Medill unapologetically urged the enforcement of the law against labor's interference with trade, writing, "A few lives taken at the first saves human life in the end . . . A little powder, used to teach the dangerous classes a needful lesson, is well burned, provided there are bullets in front of it" (Foner 1970, 151; Schneirov 2008, 95).

But of course the most infamous of Chicago's industrial conflicts of this or any other period is the Great Upheaval of 1886 and, by association, the Haymarket bombing of May 4, 1886. Infamy has its drawbacks, not least for scholars seeking to revisit the narrative and mythology of Haymarket, much of which involves police brutality, worker radicalism, employer intransigence, and political corruption, leading to a bombing, the public execution of four anarchists on the flimsiest of evidence, and the prostration of the U.S. labor movement, some say for the short term, others say for the long term.[5]

Scholars have cited numerous causes of the Haymarket Affair. Schneirov (1998), for example, cites the withdrawal of business support from the labor-friendly administration of Mayor Carter Harrison; the fastest period of per capital economic growth in the country's history; the simultaneous growth of the Knights of Labor (K of L) from a union umbrella of 100,000 members to 725,000 mostly in the span of a year; and the disjuncture of the K of L leadership from its local assemblies in Chicago and elsewhere, where rank-and-file activists organized the militant boycott and eight-hour strikes leading up to the Haymarket bombing. The immediate cause (and on this most scholars agree) was a violent confrontation at the McCormick Reaper Works on May 3, 1886, in which police killed two workers and wounded several others. In response, August Spies, who witnessed the McCormick killings, organized a workers' rally the next evening. The police had begun to break that demonstration up, too, when someone, who to this day remains unknown, threw a dynamite bomb, killing one officer instantly and injuring many others; the police, numbering 176 in strength, then began shooting into the crowd indiscriminately, leaving many workers and fellow officers dead or wounded (see figure 5.3 below) (David 1936, 204; Hirsch 1990, 73–74; Schneirov 1998, 201).

Though reports vary on the extent to which the labor movement suffered in the bombing's aftermath (see, for example, Schneirov 1998, 202–204), it is probably fair to say, as Eric Hirsch (1990) suggests, that what followed was the first widely prosecuted "red scare" in American history. On Mayor Harrison's order, labor meetings in Chicago were disrupted; infantry regiments and citizens' neighborhood patrols were put on ready alert; some 50 socialist and anarchist gathering places were raided; over 200 suspects were apprehended without warrant and held without charge; and all anarchist newspapers, including the *Alarm* and German-language *Arbeiter Zeitung*, were shut down. An artist's rendering of the Haymarket raids is pictured in figure 5.4 below. A year and a half later, on November 11, 1887, August Spies, Adolph Fischer, George Engel, and Albert Parsons were hanged; Louis Lingg, who had also been sentenced to death, committed suicide, while Michael Schwab's and Samuel Fielden's sentences were commuted to life in prison (David 1936, 221–230, 454–460; Hirsch 1990, 76–78; Schneirov 1998, 201–202).

FIGURE 5.3. "Illinois—the anarchist-labor troubles in Chicago—the police charging the murderous rioters in old Haymarket Square on the night of May 4th," from *Frank Leslie's Illustrated Newspaper*, May 15, 1886, 200–201. Courtesy of the Newberry Library.

The purpose of this chapter, however, is not to document the blow-by-blow of the Haymarket Affair, but to theorize the major parties' disavowal, and the workers' recuperation, of the critique of wage dependency. In this, the rationale of Chicago party elites for the Haymarket crackdown was emblematic of the wider discourse of free contract. Beyond writing laws based on such principles, they continued in the arena of public debate to frame trade unionism (to say nothing of revolutionary anarchism) as a violation of the right to work. On the day after the Haymarket bombing, the Democratic *Times*, for example, sounded a familiar tune: "those who desire to work" should be "assured of protection in the exercise of their unquestionable right to contract their services upon such terms as they see fit" (*Chicago Times*, May 5, 1886). Further, any contravention

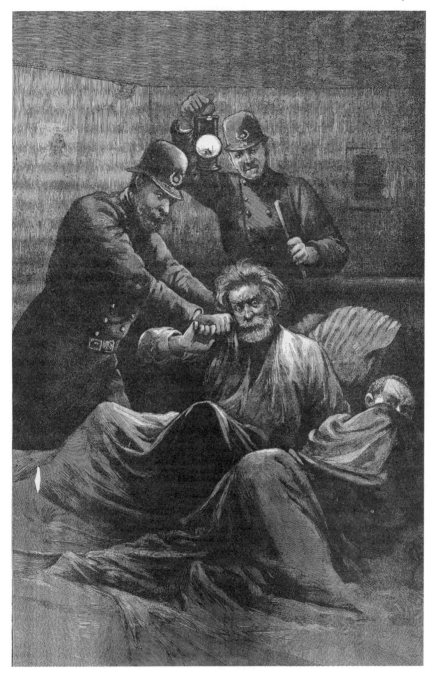

FIGURE 5.4. "Illinois—the recent troubles in Chicago—the police capturing leading anarchists at one of their dens, no. 616 Centre Avenue," from *Frank Leslie's Illustrated Newspaper*, May 22, 1886, 217. Courtesy of the Newberry Library.

of that unquestionable right must be met with state violence. "Mobs that make war against individual rights," the Democratic journal intoned, "must be made objects of war by all men that would maintain their rights" (*Chicago Times*, May 4, 1886).

There can be no mistake, then, of the link between elite ideology and antilabor state violence. The liberal doctrine of free contract, and its core implication, the right to work, was the chief justification for the city's use of force against striking workers. We have just seen an example of this linkage in the Haymarket Affair, but it was just as much in evidence in 1867 and 1877. In ordering the police to put down the 1867 strike, Mayor John B. Rice invoked Illinois's right to work law, the LaSalle Black Law, which, to repeat, "prohibited any person from seeking to prevent . . . any other person from working at any lawful business on any terms he might see fit" (Jentz and Schneirov 2012, 131). Elites echoed the ideological justification for antilabor state violence during the 1877 railroad strike. At a July 25 meeting of Chicago employers and elected officials in the Moody and Sankey Tabernacle, Carter Harrison, then U.S. congressman and later mayor of Chicago during the Haymarket Affair, made plain the rationale for the use of force. After endorsing Mayor Monroe Heath's call for 5,000 armed volunteers, Mr. Harrison said,

> It stands us in hand here to determine that men shall work,—and that . no crowd of a dozen, or of a hundred, or a thousand, shall keep honest labor from the privileges of work. [Cheers.] Sir, work is worship. Every one has a right to work. Let every man that wants to work have the privilege, and let the remainder of us see that the muscle that wants to labor shall be protected. (*Chicago Tribune*, July 26, 1877)

Economic Change and Audience Reception
A Major Industrial Power

As the competing political projects of workers and parties in the postbellum period suggest, economic change has no natural political valence, tending to one ideology or another. Nor is the nature of economic change so self-evident that it is obvious to one and all what it means and whether it should be accelerated, slowed down, or reversed altogether. Economic conditions are forever being interpreted and politicized by competing actors. Yet there can be no doubt that something is being interpreted—some reference point to which political elites and workers among others are gesturing as they attempt to acquire power and reorganize society according to their respective agendas. It is for this reason that we turn now to the economic context out of which the freedom of contract and working class identity both grew.

While other midwestern cities were crippled during the Civil War by the obstruction of steamboat traffic to the South, Chicago flourished due to government contracts for shoes, clothing, and meat. By 1880 Chicago had become the major industrial power west of the Appalachians (Jentz 1991, 231). The city's fastest growing industries were brick making, iron and steel making, and slaughtering and meatpacking, with meatpacking the largest of them all, accounting for one-quarter of the city's manufacturing output (Schneirov 2008, 77). From 1860 to 1880 capital investment increased by some thirteen times from $5,571,025 to $72,401,453 as gross product grew eighteenfold from $13,555,671 to an unprecedented $253,910,548 (U.S. Census Office 1860 (3), 87; 1883b, 960).[6] This was probably helped in no small part by the 4,649 miles of railroad added to Illinois's already formidable 2,912-mile system (U.S. Census Office 1860 (3), 330, 333; 1883c, 307). In that same interval, immigrants from Europe and the rest of the United States swelled Chicago's population from 109,260 to 503,185 (U.S. Census Office 1860 (1), 90; U 1883a, 382, 546). Moreover, Chicago was a working class city: wage laborers and their families comprised 38 percent of the population; of these 69 percent were foreign-born (Schneirov 2008, 77).

Ironically, the watershed in this growth period was the Great Fire of 1871, which destroyed most of the industrial infrastructure that had been built up since the town's incorporation. Between 1870 and 1880, the number of workers in the city jumped from 31,105 to 79,414, up fourteen times from the 5,593 workers employed in all of Cook County just twenty years earlier (Schneirov 1991, 394; U.S. Census Office 1860 (3), 87; 1883b, 1047).

Workers shared very little in this prosperity, however. The workingmen of Chicago were worse off in general by 1880 than they had been just prior to the war. Between 1860 and 1880, a day's wages for a "common laborer" either declined (from $1.05 to $1.00) as in furniture woodwork or slightly increased (to $1.50) as in agricultural implements, but in either case their weekly board, for example, would have jumped over 60 percent. In real dollars these wage rates were equal to, or only pennies higher than, those that prevailed before the failure of the Illinois State Bank in 1841 (Pierce 1937, 72, 72n162; U.S. Census Office 1860 (1), 512; 1886, 108, 544, 561).[7] Workers therefore spent a larger share of their wages on board in 1880 than they did in 1860: whereas skilled and unskilled workers paid an average of 20.5 percent and 34.4 percent of their wages to board respectively in 1860, they would have paid as much as 26.5 percent and 58.8 percent in 1880. These conditions worsened with a series of downturns after the war culminating in a depression that bottomed out between the fall of 1873 and late 1874 when

20 percent of manufacturing workers became unemployed (Jentz 1991, 245; Schneirov 1991, 396; U.S. Census Office 1860 (1), 512; 1886, 108, 535, 544, 561).

German workers, who constituted just over 24 percent of those employed in manufacturing, mechanics, and mining in 1880, continued to feel the pinch more than other workers, as the share of skilled workmen in the German community fell by 13 percent between 1850 and 1870 (Schneirov 1991, 394; U.S. Census Office 1883b, 1398–1399). This figure dropped still further after the Great Fire of 1871 when thousands of unskilled German workers flooded the labor market during the rebuilding of Chicago (Jentz 1991, 242).

For postbellum workers, Chicago was awash as much with want as with opportunity. Periodic assessments of economic conditions found in the *Tribune*, Chicago's paper of record, offer eyewitness accounts of the situation on the ground. As early as the end of 1865, the *Tribune* observed that "Hundreds of families in the city" were "starving in a land of plenty. Men willing to work, are obliged to remain idle, and hear their children beg for that bread, which they have not to give" (December 11, 4). By 1869, not much appeared to have changed: "The cities are overcrowded by men, with families and without, seeking employment in any and every capacity. Some manage to secure situations, at wages depreciated by reason of the superabundance of persons out of place, and willing to be employed at any rate which will insure them against starvation, while others gain a precarious, and sometimes insufficient subsistence by such jobs as chance throws their way" (*Chicago Tribune*, April 26, 2). By 1877, at the end of Reconstruction and beyond the worst of the 1873 depression, the *Tribune* would report, "there is no employment, and consequently no wages, for one-third of the workmen" (*Chicago Tribune*, October 7, 4).

The Chicago Working Class, 1864–1886

The Republican wartime coalition no doubt crumbled under the weight of these deteriorating conditions. Presidential electoral returns from 1864 to 1876 suggest that Chicago's majority worker wards defected from the Republican Party in this period. Recall that the number of wards grew after the 1860 election, and the ward map was redrawn so that wards 6 through 9 were located in the predominantly Irish South Side, while wards 15, 16 and 18 were in the largely German Near North Side. In 1860, the Republicans carried four out of six majority worker wards. Table 5.1 reports that with the exception of 1872 when two factions of the Republican Party were on the ballot, the GOP did not carry more than two out of six such wards after 1860. In 1876, the party captured just one out of seven majority worker wards, though in that year their lackluster performance was due also to the resurgence of the Democratic Party nationally and the weakness of

TABLE 5.1 Republican share of Chicago's presidential returns in majority worker wards, 1864–1876

WARD	1864 (LINCOLN)	1868 (GRANT)	1872 (GRANT)	1876 (HAYES)
6	32.3	36.4	54.6	34.0
7	42.5	45.4	58.4	28.8
8	38.0	41.1	47.0	31.9
9	72.6	74.3	41.9	53.8
15	52.7	46.5	68.8	40.2
16	45.9	50.1	68.5	37.4
18	n/a	n/a	46.3	45.7

Sources: For socioeconomic statistics, Einhorn ([1991] 2001, 265); for ethnic settlement patterns, Hirsch (1990, 101); for electoral returns, *Chicago Tribune*, November 9, 1864; November 5, 1868; November 16, 1872; November 9, 1876.

Rutherford B. Hayes as a candidate (Foner 1988, 567; Klinghard 2010, 207; Skowronek 1982, 56; Woodward 1951, 16). The Republican bloc, in other words, had become a coalition of middle and upper class wards after the war.

But economic deprivation and electoral returns tell only part of the story. A content analysis of period newspapers reveals that Chicago workers came to understand themselves as a multiethnic class in this period, principally by way of three interlocking claims. First, the parties' embrace of free contract and the antilabor violence it permitted comprised a betrayal of workers' military service to the nation and the very promise of the war, which they understood to be nothing less than their emancipation from wage dependency. In this, the laws of political economy and their putative right to work counted for little against their structurally subordinate position as a class in the open market. Second, it was now the duty of workingmen to finish what they started. That is, the new conflict between labor and capital was a logical next step after the war between free labor and slavery. Third, because they could no longer trust either of the major parties to advocate on their behalf, it was necessary for workers to look elsewhere for relief, initially in their own party, and later in revolution.

Having risked their lives on behalf of the Republic, Chicago workers, now war veterans, viewed their meager existence and the major parties' high-handedness as a betrayal of their military service and the promise of the war. It was through this fundamentally political affront that workers came to see themselves as a class in opposition to another. At the May Day festivities inaugurating the 1867 eight-hour strike, one union representative made these remarks:

> Who conquered the late rebellion? Was it the man who fought against them today? [Cries of "No."] Then that man was a traitor to their cause.

It was the laborer that had defended the country through war . . . But a few years have passed away since the emancipation of our country. Yet look at us now. See the factory operatives in Massachusetts, one third of whom die at an early age because [of being] overworked . . . Workingmen have their rights, which are acknowledged when the capitalist wants their vote, or their services on the battle-field, but on the questions of labor they have no rights. Is it the right of the workingman to work forever, night and day, to pay a debt contracted while he was fighting for sixteen dollars a month?" (*Chicago Tribune*, May 2, 1867, 4)

The speaker begins by calling those who attempted to repress the strike "traitors," no more worthy of their respect than the architects of the "late rebellion." Then, in a direct challenge to the right to work, he scoffs at the notion that Chicago's workers possess any "rights" other than "the right of the workingman to work forever" to pay off debts he acquired while fighting the war for roughly half the pay of a common laborer. It is important to note that the union official identifies the major parties with the "capitalist" who "want their vote" and distinguishes him from "the workingman" and "the laborer."

Reflecting on the right to work, workers often wondered what freedom such a right afforded, given the state's violent hostility toward them and the mass unemployment of the 1873–1874 depression. At a celebration of the anniversary of the Paris Commune in which 1,000 were in attendance, Carl Klings, a spokesman for the unemployed, connected the contradictions of postwar American freedom to the massacre of workers in the French Revolution. "The only liberty workingmen now had was to starve," he said, urging his compatriots to "remember the thousands of innocent men and women killed at Paris," as "their fate would be the same if they neglected their duty" (*Chicago Tribune*, March 19, 1874, 8).

Nor did Chicago workers accept the law of supply and demand uncritically. Against theories of formal political economy, workingmen often counterposed the authority they amassed with real-life experience. In a letter to the editor of the *Tribune*, Gilbert Gurney, a workingman, wrote, "If we cannot all spell, we can all think. Men do not think in words. If we do not all shrivel up and volatize when the 'laws of supply and demand' are shaken at us, it is because we have eyes and ears, and see, and hear, and often feel. We know that theory is one thing and practice another,—sometimes having a resemblance, and sometimes not. We know that men's ideas of education are rapidly changing; and we begin to think that an adept at carpentering is as much a scholar as an adept in Latin or political economy" (*Chicago Tribune*, January 11, 1874, 6). That workers were skeptical of free market liberalism was not lost on the political establishment. The *Tribune* understood very well that Chicago's workers had rejected free contract and political economy outright, observing, "They are not, for the most part, political economists, and have little respect for the doctrines of Smith, Ricardo, Malthus, or Mill when in conflict with their own. Those of these who [have] any understanding of economic principles, like Karl Marx, the head of the International, do not accept our political economy any more than a Mohammedan accepts Christianity, if, indeed, as much" (December 25, 1873, 4).

Much more to workers' liking than free market liberalism was the antebellum critique of wage dependency as slavery, a fact that provides still further evidence that workers viewed the political establishment's liberal turn as a betrayal of the promise of the war. In a meeting where it was universally agreed that workingmen "had been a ball in the hands of politicians long enough," Mr. Watson of the Chicago Workingmen's Union said, "That they lived in an age of freedom was true, but there were forms of slavery worse than that from which the black men had been released. There were thousands of white slaves, who spent their whole lives putting money in the pockets of a few, and were worse off in old age than in youth." Watson then revealed even more of his antebellum prejudices, qualifying his remarks by insisting that he "loved Republicanism, not because it was the best, but because it was one step further on the ladder of progress . . . The object of the International was . . . to bridge that chasm by making every man his own master" (*Chicago Tribune*, March 18, 1872, 6). Watson thus characterizes international socialism as the next step after republicanism. For him, the two ideologies bled seamlessly into one another. Indeed, the "General Laws" of the "Social, Political, Workingmen's Association," Chicago's chapter of the International, could plausibly be read as either an old Wentworth editorial or a Marxist tract: "The economic submission of the laboring man to the rules of the grabber of working-materials—which are the fountains of life, constitutes the ground-work of slavery in all its varied forms . . . social privation, spiritual starvation, and political dependence" (*Chicago Tribune*, December 25, 1873, 1). Note, too, that as with the antebellum critique of dependency, the postbellum recuperation of the same was freighted with a racialized conception of civic standing. Now that the war had emancipated black slaves, there remained, Mr. Watson says, the task of undoing another form of subordination supposedly more horrific than bonded servitude, for it unnaturally enslaved white men. If the antebellum critique was driven by a notion of white male entitlement to land, then its postbellum counterpart married entitlement to a narrative of victimization, in which white male workers were inexplicably "passed over" while blacks received all the attention.

As the previous example suggests, Chicago workers viewed the emerging class conflict as the logical sequel to the Civil War. At a meeting several days into the 1867 eight-hour strike, for example, Eduard Schlaeger, the anti-slavery activist and socialist, proclaimed that the workers "had settled the black labor question, and now . . . would settle the white labor question." He went on to say, "The course of the *Times* and the *Tribune* showed them that they had nothing to hope from the old parties. They would both join when capital is endangered. Both were catspaws of the same power—capital" (*Chicago Times*, May 10, 1867, 5). To Taffy Taylor, a former rank-and-file Democrat and a striker at the Illinois Central Railroad, it seemed that "demagogues . . . liked to see them quarreling about this or that political party. He had himself been once a democrat, but he was nothing now but a workingman—one of the party of blistered hands . . . Capital gave them the challenge as the south did at Fort Sumter, and they had taken it up. Capital considered them as slaves" (*Chicago Times*, May 12, 1867, 4). Workers' disaffection from the major parties can be seen in the themes of betrayal, war, and racialized class (as opposed to northern sectional) identity. Whereas the Democrats were once the champions of the producer and Republicans the champions of free labor, now Mr. Schlaeger, formerly a Republican himself, called the parties "catspaws" to capital. The phrase, "one of the party of blistered hands," is telling in a similar way. Mr. Taylor has come to understand himself as a worker by being whipsawed by party demagogues, who liked to see him and his fellow workingmen "quarrelling." Finally, both speakers viewed the conflict between labor and capital as the natural successor to the Civil War. For Schlaeger, it was a matter of freeing white labor, now that black labor was free, and for Taylor, "the south . . . at Fort Sumter" was equivalent to "capital," which "considered them as slaves" and now "gave them" a new "challenge" to take up. Importantly, Eduard Schlaeger echoes Mr. Watson's sentiments above in that he frames the impending class struggle in both racial and class terms, as returning to the unfinished task of the "white labor question."

Their disaffection from the major parties, however, did not stop Chicago workers from turning to parties as an organizational solution to their problems. This underlines the importance of parties for shaping workers' politics in this period. That is, their alienation from the political establishment informed their identification as a class, and the organizational form they chose to pursue their ideological agenda, at least initially, was a party. A railroad striker named W.W. Boyle presaged just such an organization, when he declared, "Democrats were 'rottening out,' and republicans would soon 'rotten out.' Then the great laboring man's party would bury both of them and rise sublimely into power" (*Chicago Times*, May 11, 1867, 5). When upwards of 7,000 workingmen gathered at Vorwaert's Turner Hall to discuss solutions to mass unemployment in the city, a sometime Republican and now spokesperson for the Chicago International during the 1873 depression, was greeted with cheers when he declared that "the two political parties were dead, and the time had come for the workingmen to organize a party of their own and redress their injuries at the ballot-box" (*Chicago*

Tribune, December 22, 1873). By 1877, the workingmen had passed resolutions against the two-party system and called for the organization of a party for "working people." One such resolution read, "Resolved, That we, the working people of the City of Chicago and State of Illinois, do hereby repudiate the Republican and Democratic parties" (*Chicago Tribune,* August 24, 1877). These passages highlight once again the mounting hostility of Chicago workers to mainstream political discourse. Indeed, they go so far as to pronounce the parties "dead" and "rottening out." Relatedly, their disarticulation from the major parties appears to have been an important step in the process by which Chicago workers came to identify and organize as a class. Boyle viewed the process of rottening out as a necessary precondition for "the great laboring man's party" to emerge and bury its predecessors. Likewise, in 1873 the death of "the two political parties" was said to pave the way "for the workingmen to organize a party of their own." Lastly, the resolutions of 1877 suggest that workers found their voice as "working people" by coming together to "repudiate the Republican and Democratic parties."

It should come as no surprise, then, that the Chicago anarchists who were implicated in the Haymarket Affair would have echoed the immediate postbellum critique of the major political parties, on the one hand, yet moved beyond it to explicitly advocate for a new civil war, on the other. Albert Parsons, the future Haymarket martyr and editor of the Chicago anarchist organ, *The Alarm,* wrote, "The workers can therefore expect no help from any capitalistic party in their struggle against the existing system. They must achieve their liberation by their own efforts" (*The Alarm,* October 4, 1884). Similarly, in an editorial on the imminent presidential elections of 1884, Parsons held, "The real campaign begins where the political ends . . . One week more and the political phase gives way to the economic, where the daily wants of the working class incessantly clamor for relief" (*The Alarm,* November 1, 1884). In both these passages, Parsons signals the persistent disaffection of the Chicago labor movement with the major political parties. Moreover, as in the years immediately after the war, party politics continued to inform the movement's identification as a class. Thus, in the first passage, Parsons sets the "capitalistic party" against the workers, who "must achieve liberation by their own efforts," and in the second passage he distinguishes the "political phase" from the "economic" where the real campaign of labor begins.

But whereas the earlier Chicago labor movement worked toward organizing a workingman's party and engaged only in crowd action violence, the Chicago anarchists called programmatically for outright revolution. Comparing the revolutionary and civil wars with the impending war against capital, Parsons reasoned that because "two of the systems of slavery have been attacked by bloody war," "bloodshed" would be "necessary" "for the third" (*The Alarm,* December 6, 1884). The problem Parsons identified was the same as the problem posed by previous working class leaders in Chicago, namely, mounting economic dependency, but the solution had changed. Thus, Parsons noted, "Twenty years ago in the United States every poor man could choose between employing himself and seeking someone to employ him. Today not half of the poor men have got this power." He added that in response to "this terrible fact . . . the laborer must rise and crush it with his heel or he will soon be helpless. Votes and arguments are as nothing in the hands of the poor. Force and force only is his defense" (*The Alarm*, January 12, 1885).

Conclusion

We return now and for the last time to the implications of the above narrative. As I have indicated repeatedly, these hinge on the concept of political articulation, the process by which parties naturalize social divisions such as race and class and press the resulting coalitions into the service of reorganizing society.

The implications of this chapter for the literature on electoral politics are somewhat enigmatic. On the one hand, the political crisis over slavery and its aftermath confirm that parties have considerably more autonomy in generating social change than the dominant voter-centered scholarship would have us believe. For the latter, it is the cleavage groups on the ground that exert upward pressure on parties to represent them, yet as we have continually seen, parties have the capacity to define group identities and in so doing mobilize the mass electorate in pursuit of transformative social agendas. On the other hand, as the implosion of the Democratic Party in the 1850s suggests, electoral politics is not just about the successful articulation of social cleavages or the attainment of hegemony, the mass consent to rule. Hegemony by definition is impermanent and must therefore be constantly cultivated. When a party fails to do the work of articulation, the once taken-for-granted identities and understandings of "how things are and ought to be" fall apart. That process began in wartime and culminated during Reconstruction and the Gilded Age: the party system entered another moment of crisis—this time over the labor question—as workers of all ethnic backgrounds became unmoored from the mainstream party system. The behavior of parties in crises such as these further undermines the widely held notion that parties are passive. When sectors of the electorate reject partisan appeals, political elites do not necessarily pander to renegade constituents: because of the mechanism of party government, politicians, once elected, wield formal state power and may therefore authorize the use of force.

Like the literature on electoral politics, the scholarship on democratic transitions and expansions has generally viewed social groups, in particular social classes, as the prime movers of democratic change. By contrast, I have tried to demonstrate that in mid-nineteenth-century Chicago, parties were the decisive actors. The political crisis over slavery resulted from the factionalization of the Democratic Party and the articulation of a northern sectional coalition via free labor ideology, first by the Free Soilers and eventually by the Republican Party. The confluence of these primarily partisan dynamics worked to undermine the ability of entrenched political elites to deflect attention away from slavery. The ensuing dissolution of the mainstream party system and the emergence of antagonistic sectional parties was a vital precondition for what Charles and Mary Beard and later Barrington Moore referred to as the Second American Revolution. This is not to say that Moore was wrong to argue that the U.S. Civil War was a fundamentally bourgeois revolution, for the war certainly strengthened the hand of capital more than it did labor's both economically and politically. But for Moore, this was the work of the bourgeoisie as a class, not a class as articulated and mobilized by a relatively autonomous political party. Nor is another canonical work on democratization, Dietrich Rueschemeyer and John and Evelyne Stephens' *Capitalist Development and Democracy* (1992), necessarily wrong in its objection to Moore that the working class is a more consistent champion of democratic reform than the bourgeoisie. If this chapter on the right to work and antilabor violence does anything, it certainly affirms the Rueschemeyer thesis. Nevertheless, the chapter also reveals more complex dynamics with respect to the role of workers in democratic change that are as yet understudied. These include the ideological incorporation of workers by prodemocracy forces, and the bait-and-switch that may occur after a revolution when the gains promised to workers (e.g., cheap or free land) disappear with the war. In other words, workers are broadly involved in the achievement of democratic reform as Rueschemeyer et al suggest, but in the political crisis over American slavery they were mobilized as part of the Republican Party's free labor coalition. Further, Chicago workers only pressed for the expansion of their collective rights—that is, as a class unto themselves—once they broke loose from the major parties.

As I stated in chapter 1, scholars of working-class formation are divided into two broad camps: objectivists who argue that workers are always and already a class by virtue of their structural subordination in the capitalist system, and subjectivists who argue that workers must first identify as a class in the course of disputes with their employers before one can say that a class as such has formed. This book demonstrates support for both camps. Among the various cogs in the incipient free labor system, workers were structurally at the greatest disadvantage in mid-nineteenth-century Chicago and felt the brunt of depressed wages and unemployment during the downturns of 1837, 1857, and the postbellum period, especially the depression of 1873–1874. Moreover, workers established their own relatively autonomous organizations and trade assemblies, typically as a result of their lived experience on the job and on strike. This happened in every decade studied here. But class formation, as I have argued, also results from workers' interaction with political parties. It was the latter's perceived betrayal that at last enabled Chicago workers to arrive at their class identity and to justify various forms of antisystemic mobilization, including union organizing, strikes, third-party formation, and revolutionary activity. In other words, while not denying that workers are structurally disadvantaged or autonomously organized, I have argued that parties, too, may shape workers' identity. Indeed, the full arc of the narrative suggests that parties were decisive not only in articulating Chicago workers first as members of an aggrieved class of producers and then as northern free labor, but also in squandering the political allegiance of Chicago workers, thereby leaving room for socialists and others to articulate them as a class.

These claims about working-class formation come with two caveats. The first has to do with the ways in which class identity was ineluctably articulated with racial identity throughout this period in popular conceptions of civic standing. In previous chapters, for instance, we saw that workers viewed their standing as citizens in terms of their entitlement to land, without which they felt they would be forced into permanent industrial servitude akin (in their mind) to black bondage. In this chapter, we witnessed how even the most progressive revolutionaries framed the postbellum struggle for collective bargaining rights (i.e., to organize, strike, set hours) as a "white labor question," as if the emancipation of the hireling was unfairly forestalled to achieve the emancipation of the slave. In each case, white workers' class identity was formed in relation to the civic standing of African Americans.

Second, this periodization of working-class formation speaks back to the literature on American exceptionalism, which addresses the perennial question of why there is no socialism in the United States. It is the debate between Kim Voss and her critics that most concerns us here. To repeat, Voss (1993) famously argued that the Knights of Labor carried the seeds of a homegrown American radicalism that married republicanism with socialism, but that the Haymarket Affair of 1886–1887 and the antilabor violence it engendered forced the labor movement into a conservative crouch. In contrast to the Voss thesis, Daniel Ernst and Richard Schneirov suggest that the 1880s comprised the last gasp of an unforgiving regime of labor relations, after which a more just regime emerged. Voss's critics detect in the class accommodations of the turn of the twentieth century the origins of pluralist democracy, with its growing acceptance of the collective rights of labor. Like Ernst and Schneirov, I am somewhat critical of Voss in the limited sense that workers were undoubtedly able to force a more progressive synthesis of liberal democracy in later periods. The role of the American Federation of Labor in pressing for a pluralist conception of collective bargaining rights as documented by Ernst and the labor-capital détente orchestrated by the first Harrison administration in Chicago as documented by Schneirov are just two examples. The New Deal era is an even more illustrious case in point. On the other hand, I want to insist that the immediate postbellum order was not a one-off instance of sustained antilabor repression—impressive, but by the dawn of the twentieth century, over. What, I would ask, are we to make of antilabor violence after Carter Harrison was inaugurated mayor of Chicago in 1879 or the persistent justification of such violence as the protection of the right to work? How can we make sense of the persecution of countless workers and organizers throughout the early twentieth century, during and after the process in which the pluralist conception of labor rights set in? Finally, what can we say about the decades-long attack on the U.S. labor movement since the 1980s or about the structure of contemporary antilabor discourse, which echoes so eerily that of postbellum political elites? Are all of these mere coincidences or outliers in relation to the overarching pattern of prolabor pluralism? A more satisfactory approach is a dialectical one, in which American workers have had, and must therefore always be prepared, to defend their hard-won collective rights in the face of successive forms of individualistic liberalism, which achieved its modern expression in the postbellum concepts of free contract, corporate personhood, and right to work. In the epilogue, we fastforward to the present day to examine the struggle between individualistic and collective conceptions of worker rights, with special attention to the attack on collective bargaining in the American rustbelt and the racialization of the so-called middle class.

NEOLIBERALISM IN THE RUSTBELT

An important rationale for this book has been to reframe the nineteenth-century rise of antilabor democracy in Chicago and elsewhere as the ancestor of contemporary capitalism, which is often called "neoliberalism." Neoliberalism is the doctrine that a free market, unfettered by state regulation and unions, is the best mechanism for ensuring widespread economic prosperity. On that account, workers should be "free" to negotiate one-on-one with potential employers over the terms of their employment without the nuisance of unions and minimum wage laws, for example, which artificially inflate the cost of labor beyond what employers are willing to pay.

In this epilogue I address the question, "What can the origins of right to work teach us about the condition of American workers and the U.S. labor movement under neoliberalism?" To do this, I examine the present-day relationship between political parties and workers with respect to three controversies: the advent of right to work legislation in Michigan and Indiana; the passage of draconian public sector collective bargaining laws in Wisconsin and Ohio; and the racial logic undergirding these and other instances of neoliberal labor relations. Before I turn to the contemporary scene, however, I briefly preempt some concerns that my academic colleagues might have. Those who are not interested in the theoretical whys and wherefores can skip these remarks and move directly to the right to work section.

The premise for ending with an epilogue on the contemporary Rustbelt (i.e., the postindustrial midwestern United States) is a dialectical approach to labor politics over time, in which individualistic conceptions of worker rights have continually run up against collective conceptions. Such an approach is by no means a monocultural thesis akin to Louis Hartz's (1955) conception of the "liberal tradition," in which an unforgiving individualistic liberalism—because of the founding moment of the Civil War—dominates political culture from that point forward to the exclusion of all other political alternatives. A dialectic by definition is an ongoing struggle or tension between at least two broad social forces.

But neither is the dialectic between two competing monocultures: liberalism versus pluralism or socialism. They might roughly be referred to heuristically as individualistic and collectivistic interpretations of worker rights, but their forms are ever changing and contested internally within each camp. One need look no further than the internecine conflict between liberals, socialists, and communists in the American labor movement for evidence of the often heterogeneous tendencies that subscribe generally to the group or collective rights of labor. Likewise, the politics of libertarians, Tea Party conservatives, and the U.S. Chamber of Commerce are not always or even typically aligned on the meaning of individualism. And it is simply not the case that elites uniformly support individualistic interpretations of worker rights, whereas workers invariably support collectivist alternatives. There are, and have been, many prolabor elite reformers and reactionary workers.

Lastly, I am not quietly smuggling in a philosophy of history ascribed to Karl Marx called dialectical materialism. Though the overall approach is anchored in the ideas of a Marxist social theorist, Antonio Gramsci, my neo-Gramscianism is, as Stuart Hall (1983) once called his own, a "Marxism without guarantees." Some might still subscribe to the notion that the onward march of capitalism and the mounting deprivation of the working class will culminate in a final violent confrontation between the bourgeoisie and proletariat, but I most certainly do not. As I hope I have made clear by now, economic change is important to the degree that it tends to boost the heterogeneity of the political terrain, but economic change in and of itself has no inherent political meaning. The international crisis of capitalism known in the United States as the Great Depression, for example, gave rise to mass unemployment the likes of which the world had not yet known, but it was exploited (successfully, I might add) by parties as far apart as Democrats, Nazis, and Communists.

So what then do I mean? Two things really. First, any given moment in which collectivist interpretations of worker rights prevail is the result itself of a dialectic between organized sociopolitical forces. To use the previous example of Jentz and Schneirov's account of late nineteenth-century Chicago, I would argue that the Harrison administration represents the détente between workers who had for a time repudiated the major parties in favor of more radical organizations, on the one hand, and the political establishment—with its supporters among Chicago's middle class and incipient bourgeois elite—on the other. Similarly, Ernst's account of the rise of pluralism in the early twentieth century was, in my view, the result of four overlapping struggles: one between liberal and pluralist jurists; another between employer-proprietors and modern corporations; a third between capital and organized labor; and still another between the largely dominant Republican Party and the Democrats, who, seeking to disrupt GOP hegemony, looked to steal labor's support.

Second, the ascendancy of either collectivism or individualism is impermanent, because each entails the struggle for political hegemony, which is always subject to challenge. Thus, the Harrison administration was very quickly beset by the Haymarket Affair as the Chicago elite withdrew its support from the Democratic Party and the city's working class revolted against antilabor legislation and violence. Likewise, Ernst's pluralist moment was followed by a massive red scare that set in when the organized Left mobilized against the Wilson administration for reneging on its promise to keep the United States out of World War I.

In sum, a dialectical approach presupposes that a moment of ascendancy, whether individualistic or collectivistic, is 1) an artifact of previous struggles and 2) an impermanent state of affairs. This means that the present struggle between competing visions of worker rights cannot help but carry residues of struggles past, and that the present neoliberal incarnation of antilabor democracy is not the end of history.

The Right to Work in Indiana and Michigan

Recall that the right to work was a corollary of the postbellum doctrine of free contract. Workers could assemble and associate as unions and other organizations, but they could not prevent a coworker from exchanging his labor for wages under any condition. In this, Indiana's 2012 right to work law is postbellum boilerplate language. Section 8 of the act states that "A person may not require an individual to (1) become or remain a member of a labor organization; (2) pay dues . . . or (3) pay . . . a charity or third party . . . as a condition of employment or continuation of employment." In other words, the requirement to pay dues or fees cannot lawfully prevent the individual wage bargain. Section 9 voids any contract or agreement between the union and employer that violates Section 8, and Sections 10 through 12 then outline the repercussions "If an individual suffers an injury" as a result of a violation (General Assembly of the State of Indiana 2012, 3–4).

It would be a mistake to see this exclusively as a legal matter, for like Illinois's labor conspiracy laws of 1863 and 1887, Indiana's right to work law is a statute, authored by party politicians in the state house. Its passage was due in large part to the balance of political power in state government. The Republican Party held the governor's mansion, a 60-40 majority in the House, and a 37-13 majority in the Senate. Not a single Democrat voted in favor of the measure. On January 22, 2012, it passed the Senate by a vote of 28 to 22, with 9 of the 37 Republicans joining all 13 Democrats to oppose it (Sikich and Schneider 2012). Though Democrats attempted to stall the measure by depriving the House of a quorum, that body passed the bill on January 25 by a vote of 54-44 (Associated Press 2012). Moreover, Democrats viewed the law as a thinly veiled attempt on the part of Republicans to defund and disempower the base of their party. For example, Representative Ed DeLaney, an Indianapolis Democrat, said, "This is a transparent device to undercut the funding of the Democratic Party, OK? . . . If they want to eliminate us, why don't they just say it? Why are we pussy-footing around?" (Schneider 2011). The Indiana right to work law is also a partisan matter, because each party used the controversy as a strategy of mass mobilization: whereas Republicans argued that right to work legislation would bring jobs to the state in a moment of economic crisis, the Democrats held that the measure would lower wages and further shrink the already declining number of good-paying middle-class jobs.

It is this modern-day rhetorical battle that is perhaps most reminiscent of the postbellum period. Republican officials insisted that the right to work did not prevent workers from unionizing, yet they denied that anyone could make a worker financially support the union that was legally bound to negotiate on their behalf, thus institutionalizing the classic power imbalance of older labor conspiracy laws. Often supporters of the law invoked the nineteenth-century themes of tyranny, compulsion, and force to characterize dues collection. Thus, Republican governor Mitch Daniels said that "The vital right to organize is totally unaffected," but called opponents of the law, "advocates of compulsory dues." Similarly, Republican senator Luke Kenley specified, "Most of [the Republicans] see this as an individual right situation, as opposed to a labor issue" (Schneider 2011). The private sector weighed in on the Republican side. In a letter to the editor of the *Indianapolis Star*, CEO of Koch Enterprises, Robert L. Koch, wrote, "A right-to-work law simply protects employees from being forced to join or pay labor union dues and fees to get or keep a job. It doesn't end labor unions or collective bargaining at all. It protects the freedom of a worker to choose whether to support a labor union." Koch added that supporters of the law were simply "opposed to giving powers of compulsion to politically powerful labor union bosses" (Koch 2011).

Echoing the postbellum critique of the right to work as the right to starve or work forever for a pittance, prolabor Indianans dubbed the law "the right to work for less money." They also often invoked the notion of collective rights, especially of unions and workers as a whole. A prominent picket sign at protest rallies read, "Stop the War on Workers" (Schneider and Sikich 2012a). Union officials said that "the legislation is intended to weaken them. Unions must represent all workers in a bargaining unit, even nonmembers, so . . . the law would encourage workers not to join when they can get the benefits for free." They added that this would affect all workers negatively: "Weakened unions . . . would result in lower-paying jobs, higher unemployment and unsafe workplaces. Nonunion jobs also could become lower-paid positions . . . as companies no longer would have to compete with union wages and benefits" (Schneider and Sikich 2012b). Finally, if nineteenth-century Chicago workers organized to make and keep a life of economic independence attainable, then Indiana workers repeated a theme that might be called its modern-day equivalent: that collective bargaining was and remained their ticket to the middle class. At a statehouse rally on March 10, 2011, for instance, Paul Rausch, a steel worker, said, "Everything that I have I owe to that middle class wage." Indeed, speaker after speaker at the rally said their piece in front of a banner that read, "Hoosiers standing up for the middle class." Democrats on hand repeated the theme. Representative Bill Crawford of Indianapolis said, "we're standing for families, we're standing for the middle class" (wthr.com 2011).

The physical manifestation of worker opposition to the right to work law was also evocative of the past, as throughout 2011 and early 2012 Indiana workers protested in their thousands. For example, state police estimated that over 8,000 protestors attended the aforementioned rally; Nancy Guyott of the Indiana AFL-CIO called it "Day 18 in the largest sustained protest in Indiana's history." A local NBC affiliate at the time reported that unions had been "inside the Statehouse every day for weeks," and that was almost a year before the passage of the bill the following winter (wthr.com 2011).

In the end, the Republican Party passed the measure over the objections of Democrats, workers, and their unions. The outcome was not especially surprising given Republican control of all branches of government. The electoral might of organized labor had also diminished significantly in recent years: whereas 21 percent of all private sector workers were union members in 1989, in 2012 only 10.9 percent were (Schneider ad Sikich 2012b). Accordingly, Governor Mitch Daniels signed the bill into law on February 1, 2012, making Indiana the twenty-third right to work state in the nation and the first in a decade to pass such a law, following Oklahoma, which did so in 2001 (Davey 2012). As of this writing, the labor movement had successfully challenged the law on the basis that it demands "particular services" (i.e., union representation) "without just compensation" (*Sweeney, et al v. Zoeller, et al*). Republican attorney general Greg Zoeller filed an appeal with the Indiana Supreme Court on December 13, 2013 (Berggoetz 2013).

The Michigan right to work law is nearly identical to Indiana's. Section 14, Subsection 1, of the law prevents interference with the individual wage bargain: "An individual shall not be required as a condition of obtaining or continuing employment to do any of the following: (a) Refrain or resign membership in . . . a labor organization. (b) Become or remain a member of a labor organization. (c) Pay any dues . . . to a labor organization. (d) Pay any charitable organization or third party." Subsection 2 makes any contract or agreement that violates Subsection 1 "unlawful and unenforceable." Subsections 3 through 6 then outline the various penalties for violating Subsection 1, including a civil fine of not more than $500 and other liabilities such as legal fees and damages. Subsection 7 appropriates $1 million for implementation, enforcement, and education (Legislative Council, State of Michigan 2014).

Once again, the right to work law was as much a partisan affair as it was a legal one. A statute like Illinois's nineteenth-century conspiracy laws, the bill was authored and sponsored by party politicians and reflected Republican control of the executive and legislative branches of state government. In one day of a lame-duck legislative session, December 11, 2012, the bill passed the Senate by a vote of 58-52, the House by a vote of 58-51, and was then signed into law by Republican governor Rick Snyder, making Michigan the twenty-fourth right to work state in America. No Democrat voted in favor, while a total of six Republicans broke ranks to oppose the measure (Daum 2012).

As in Indiana and the historical case of Chicago, political actors used individualistic and collectivistic interpretations of worker rights to mobilize the mass electorate. Republicans and their allies in the private sector and conservative think tanks advanced a familiar individualistic view and insinuated that unions were tyrannical organizations with unchecked influence in the halls of power. "This is about being pro-workers, giving workers the choice," said Governor Snyder. Similarly, Charlie Owens, state director of the National Federation of Independent Business, predicted that Michiganders would remember "the historic vote that lawmakers made today establishing a worker's freedom to choose whether or not they want to belong to a labor union." And Paul Fisher, senior fellow of the conservative Heartland Institute, contrasted the new right to work Michigan with the one it supplanted by saying, "Michigan is poised to open up its labor market and to discover the dynamics of a free market which has been suppressed for far too long by the political class in concert with union leaders. Monopoly power created by union shops where workers must pay union dues or lose their jobs has caused long-term injury to industry in Michigan, resulting in high unemployment and a growing underclass leading to social deterioration" (*Lansing State Journal* 2012).

In contrast to these claims, Michigan Democrats framed the right to work law as an attack on a collective, most notably, the middle class. Thus, Democratic senate leader Gretchen Whitmer of East Lansing warned, "Passing these bills is an act of war on Michigan's middle class, and I hope the Governor and the Republican legislators are ready for the fight that is about to ensue." Minority Floor Leader Tupac A. Hunter of Detroit called the House and Senate bills "the latest in Governor Snyder and the Republican Majority's efforts to undermine the earning power of Michigan's middle class." Likewise, Rebekah Warren, state senator from Ann Arbor said, "Over the course of just a few days, we have witnessed yet another devastating attack on the middle class without any committee debate or public discussion" (*Lansing State Journal* 2012).

Workers and their unions also offered a collective or group centered view of worker rights. Recalling labor's nineteenth-century sardonic spin on the right to work, Katie Oppenheim, a nurse who works at the University of Michigan Health System, quipped, "The only right to work I or other nurses will have is right to work with no security, no rights" (Deruiter 2012). Richard Cummings, the president of the St. Clair County AFL-CIO wrote a letter to the editor of the *Lansing State Journal*, calling the legislation "the right to work for less" and "a sham to destroy workers' rights to a decent wage, dignity on the job and good health and safety standards and a voice in the workplace" (Cummings 2012). In addition, Michigan workers sounded the familiar refrain of unions as workers' best, and now disappearing, path to the middle class. For example, Blain Tarrant of Bath, Michigan, who attended a rally in Lansing with fellow members of Plumbers and Pipefitters Local 333, handwrote a slogan on the back of his jacket that read, "With a stroke of their pens, the politicians murdered Michigan's middle class" (Ahern and Lavey 2012).

Workers backed up their words with mass protests. In addition to the successive rallies held in Lansing in the weeks preceding, the rally on December 11, 2012—the day of the vote—was enormous and one of the largest in the history of the state capital. Officials estimated that about 5,000 union members marched from the Lansing Center that morning and joined another 5,000 protestors at the state house. Steve Benkovsky, executive director of the Capitol Committee, which oversees Capitol operations, later revised those numbers upward to 12,500. Most protestors reportedly came from a coalition of some thirty-three different unions, with additional supporters coming from Ohio, Indiana, Iowa, and as far as Maryland (Ahern and Lavey 2012; Ahern et al 2012; Daum 2012; Misjak 2012).

The workers were met with state violence and the threat thereof. Police used chemical agents twice to disperse protestors. State troopers dressed in riot gear, at times lined up four deep and reinforced by officers on horseback, drove workers back from the Capitol steps and other entrances. Three people were arrested when they refused to step away from the Romney state office building. Henry Bonga, a crane operator, and his wife reported that the police pepper sprayed them in the early afternoon as they and other protestors stood near the front door of the Romney building. Mr. Bonga said that the spray stung his eyes and continued to burn a half hour later, adding, "I'm sad because the state police are treating us like we're the enemy" (Ahern et al 2012).

As of this writing, the legal fight continues, primarily over whether or not state employees are covered under the law. In a 2-1 decision, a Michigan Court of Appeals ruled on August 15, 2013 that state employees were in fact covered. State employees appealed the ruling, and in January 2014, the Michigan Supreme Court agreed to hear the case (Egan and Davis 2014).

Public Sector Collective Bargaining in Wisconsin and Ohio

In this section, we explore a distinct set of cases, Wisconsin and Ohio, in which the terms of postbellum antilabor democracy were applied to public sector employees. We begin with the case of Wisconsin, in which the Republican Party under the leadership of Governor Scott Walker pushed through legislative limits on public sector collective bargaining. The 2011 Wisconsin law, Act 10, known infamously as the "budget repair bill," is more draconian than those of either Indiana or Michigan. Like its sister statutes, it is a right to work law. Section 219. 111.70 (2) acknowledges "the right of self-organization, and the right to form, join, or assist labor organizations," but the employee also "has the right to refrain from paying dues while remaining a member of a collective bargaining unit." Once again, neither union membership nor payment of dues can prevent the employer-employee relationship from being consummated. However, the Wisconsin law goes much further. Section 227. 111.70 (3g) prohibits public sector employers from deducting dues from the paychecks of employees, thus further crippling the ability of workers' organizations to stay alive. It then ties up the remaining resources of unions by making the latter prove, year-after-year, that the workers really want union representation. Section 242. 111.70 (4) (d) 3. b. states that a commission will conduct annual elections to recertify all unions. Beyond having to win a certification election every year, Section 320. 111.92 (3) (b) requires that unions must also bargain a new contract every year; existing contracts cannot be extended. If, in this process, workers are able to negotiate wages that are higher than a state sanctioned cap, Section 327. 118.245 requires that the increase be approved by a statewide referendum before it can be allowed to take effect. Finally, and most famously, the Wisconsin budget repair bill restricts collective bargaining to wages, thus stripping public sector workers of the right to bargain over hours, benefits, and working conditions. In effect, the law permits employers to unilaterally impose hardship on working people, for example, by cutting or increasing workers' hours, changing or eliminating health and retirement benefits, and disregarding worker safety. This feature of the law is enacted through a series of deletions enumerating the collective bargaining rights of discrete groups of workers. Thus, Section 95 46.2895 (8) (a) 1 is marked up (including strikethroughs of the original text) as follows: long-term care workers "whose wages, ~~hours and conditions of employment~~ were established in a collective bargaining agreement" must "abide by the terms of the collective bargaining agreement concerning the individual's wages ~~and, if applicable, vacation allowance, sick leave accumulation, sick leave bank, holiday allowance, funeral leave allowance, personal day allowance, or paid time off allowance~~" (State of Wisconsin 2011).

As with the contemporary cases of Michigan and Indiana and the historical case of Illinois, this piece of antilabor legislation was not exclusively or even primarily a legal matter, restricted to the rarified sphere of jurisprudence. As we have seen, such laws end up in the courts, but the courts review laws initially enacted and made possible in the arena of partisan struggle. Thus, the law might never have passed had it not been for the fact that Wisconsin Republicans controlled both the executive and legislative branches. Accordingly, the law carried in party-line votes. In the State Senate, the law passed by a vote of 18 to 1, with no Democrats present and one Republican dissenting. Senate Democrats had fled the state on February 17 to deny the Republicans the quorum necessary to decide matters of fiscal policy, but in a surprise parliamentary maneuver, the GOP skirted the quorum requirement by stripping the budget repair bill of fiscal items and passing both the limits on collective bargaining and the increases in employee contributions to health and retirement benefits (Spicuzza and Barbour 2011). The bill then cleared the State Assembly by a vote of 53-42. All Democrats voted against the bill, with four Republicans breaking ranks to join them (Davidoff and Czubkowski 2011). Governor Walker signed the bill into law on March 11, 2011 (Barbour and Spicuzza 2011; Spicuzza 2011).

Predictably, there was a stark divide in the nature of partisan discourse. In Wisconsin, the rhetoric of workers' individual rights was less in evidence, but the familiar rhetorical trope of tyrannical labor organizations was pervasive. Eliding their own collaboration with corporate groups like the Koch brothers, Republicans frequently accused Democrats of "taking orders from national labor leaders" (Spicuzza 2011). Their dependency on organized labor, Republicans often added, led to mass suffering. For example, Senate Majority Leader Scott Fitzgerald said, "There are still real people suffering in this economy, even though the labor unions' bullhorn has drowned them out in the past few weeks" (Barbour and Spicuzza 2011).

Against the theme of imperious unions, workers and their allies offered a collectivist alternative that emphasized group categories such as "working families" and attacked Republican Party backers as an elite minority. As ever, protesting workers viewed unions as their last remaining ticket to a modest middle class existence. Thus, in the aftermath of the GOP's Senate maneuver, president of the Wisconsin State AFL-CIO Phil Neuenfeldt said, "Senate Republicans have exercised the nuclear option to ram through their bill attacking Wisconsin's working families in the dark of night," adding, "Tonight's events have demonstrated they will do or say anything to pass their extreme agenda that attacks Wisconsin's working families" (Cullen et al. 2011). Similarly, Colleen Leinberger, a county employee, said she "grew up in a middle-class family of six" and "describes herself as a 'hardworking person' that has paid into the system through taxes." Governor Scott Walker, she said, wants to take "our money away and give it to the millionaires . . . We are going 50 years backwards . . . Now they can come in here and take everything away" (Davidoff and Czubkowski 2011). Likewise, Tod Pulvermacher of Spring Green traveled seven hours by tractor to the post-bill-signing rally in Madison to say that the bill was "anti-middle-class worker." He said that he hopes "we can change what was rammed down Wisconsin's collective throat" (Cullen and Simms 2011).

Mass resistance to the law was bigger in Wisconsin than elsewhere in the Rustbelt. For example, when Senate Republicans moved quickly to pass the stripped down budget repair bill, an estimated 7,000 workers rushed to occupy the state house on extremely short notice (Cullen et al 2011). On Saturday, March, 12, 2011, the day after Mr. Walker signed the bill into law, some 85,000 to 100,000 people converged on Madison from across the state (Cullen and Simms 2011).

Relative to Michigan, Wisconsin workers witnessed less state violence, yet there were documented incidents, especially at critical moments in the legislative process. In the hour leading up to final passage, police forcibly removed dozens of protesters from entrances and locked down the building reportedly due to safety concerns. Police effectively cleared the way for the bill to be debated and passed (Barbour and Spicuzza 2011). More in evidence than cases of actual violence were metaphors of violence applied to the democratic process. Democratic state senator Bob Jauch, for example, called his colleagues' parliamentary maneuver "legislative thuggery" and "a coup" (*Cap Times* 2011; Spicuzza and Barbour 2011). Madison Democrat Mark Pocan said that the process made him feel as if he lived in a "third world junta" (*Cap Times* 2011).

In the end, however, the Republicans and public employers prevailed. After successfully acquiring enough signatures to force a recall election of Scott Walker, Democrats and unions went down to defeat as Walker carried 53 percent of the vote to his challenger's 46 percent (Davey and Zeleny 2012). Although there was a short-lived Democratic majority in the State Senate, the November 2012 elections saw the GOP take back all branches of government, in part because that party had gerrymandered district lines to their electoral advantage in the previous session (Marley 2012). The labor movement's legal challenge to the law sparked a brief glimmer of hope. A Dane County judge struck the law down on September 14, 2012 on the grounds that it violated workers' rights to free speech and association (Treleven 2012), but on July 31, 2014, the Wisconsin Supreme Court upheld Act 10 in a 5-2 ruling (Treleven 2014; Wisconsin Gazette 2014).

We end this section with Ohio, the outlier of our four Rustbelt cases. It was there, in the Buckeye State, that the labor movement turned back the mounting challenge to workers' collective rights. Ohio's law, known by its legislative name, "Senate Bill 5" or just "SB5," was tougher than Wisconsin's budget repair bill. The two laws were similar in the sense that they contained right to work provisions, prohibited automatic payroll dues and fees deduction, and limited collective bargaining to wages. But Ohio's law included police and firefighters, whereas the budget repair bill exempted those groups. This meant that limiting collective bargaining to wages barred first responders from negotiating for safety equipment like bulletproof vests and fire-suppression technology. Another major difference was that school boards and legislative bodies like city councils could impose a contract on workers if bargaining or mediation failed. Specifically, in the event of an impasse, a neutral fact-finder would be invited to present recommendations, but if the report was rejected, then the employer could accept either its own last best offer or that of the union. In addition, the law banned all strikes, eliminated binding arbitration, prohibited union members from talking to elected officials during negotiations, removed all step increases (in favor of merit-based raises), eliminated sick days, and required public sector workers to pay at least 15 percent of their health insurance costs (Greenhouse 2011; Siegel 2011a, 2011b; Vardon and Siegel 2011).

Again, Ohio's law could hardly be called a judicial matter—like the other Rustbelt cases, SB5 was a signature Republican priority in a rare moment when the GOP controlled the executive and legislative branches of state government. Accordingly, the law passed due to the balance of partisan power. The Ohio Senate approved the bill on March 2, 2011 by a vote of 17-16, with all 10 Democrats and

6 Republicans voting in opposition. On Wednesday, March 30, 2011, the House passed SB5 by a largely party-line vote of 53-44. Governor John Kasich signed the bill into law the very next day. Perhaps rightly, Dale Butland, a Columbus Democratic consultant, said of SB5, "This is about one political party attempting to defund the opposition and destroy its electoral competitiveness . . . This is not about money for local governments or anybody else. It's a baldfaced power play" (Siegel 2011a, 2011b; Vardon and Siegel 2011).

But the political terrain in Ohio, like the law itself, was distinct from the fore-going cases. In contrast to Indiana, Michigan, and Wisconsin, Ohio's law barely cleared the upper house due to a large defection from the GOP caucus. Indeed, Senate President Tom Niehaus had to replace two Republicans (Bill Seitz of Cincinnati and Scott Oelslager of Canton, who were no votes) on two committees just so that the measure could reach the floor. Asked why he opposed the bill, Seitz, referring to the fact-finding process, asked why a legislative body would ever pick the union's offer over its own, calling it a "heads I win, tails you lose solution." Even a yes vote, Republican Karen Gilmor of Tiffin, complained that new members had not had a chance to discuss the bill. Republican senator Jim Hughes of Columbus voted against his party because of the inclusion of police, firefighters, and teachers (Siegel 2011a).

In typical fashion, supporters of SB5 combined an individualistic rhetoric with the insinuation that unions tyrannized taxpayers and workers. With respect to the right to work provision, Republicans held that "workers should not have to pay if they do not want to be in a union" (Siegel 2011b). Individualism was also redolent in Governor Kasich's insistence that union members should pay what a non-union worker pays for health insurance in the open market. "When Ohioans find out that your average private worker pays 23 percent of their health-care costs," he said, "and your average city worker pays 9 percent, that's not about enemy. That's about balance." Continuing to riff on the theme of balance, Kasich then attacked "union bosses" for their unchecked power over workers and tax-payers. In an email to potential donors, for example, the governor wrote, "There is a reason that the union bosses opposed these changes; because it strips power from the union leaders and returns it to the taxpayers and workers" (Vardon and Siegel 2011).

Against the themes of individualism and union tyranny, Democrats, workers, and their unions offered an alternative discourse centered on the middle class and workers. Democrats repeatedly dubbed SB5 "an attack on the middle class" and "middle-class families" that would "drive down middle-class wages." Workers struck a similar note. Public employee Mahalia Woods said she became a correction officer "to make a career, care for her kids and develop a good life." She added, "Senate Bill 5 would dry these opportunities up . . . Senate Bill 5 makes me feel like I did something wrong by becoming a public employee. Now we are being blamed for a budget gone bad" (Siegel 2011a, 2011c). It is perhaps no coincidence that the group that later organized to repeal SB5 chose a collectivist name and slogan: "We are Ohio" (Vardon and Siegel 2011).

In contrast to the other Rustbelt cases, workers demonstrated their resistance to the bill not so much in advance of the law's passage, but in a formidable ballot measure campaign, calling on the mass electorate to overturn the law. We are Ohio collected 915,000 signatures to put "Issue 2" on the statewide ballot, where a yes vote indicated support for the law, and a no vote indicated opposition. On Tuesday, November 8, 2011, Issue 2 failed by an impressive margin of 61 to 39 percent (Siegel and Vardon 2011).

Racial Contradiction and Organizational Isolation, Old and New

Free contract and right to work are not the only similarities between our time and postbellum Chicago. The first similarity is the importance of white privilege. In the antebellum context, the latter manifested itself in the feeling of entitlement to land and a life of self-sufficiency. Its contemporary incarnation, white entitlement to a middle-class lifestyle of property ownership and a high wage, emerged with the racial politics of the New Deal. A second and related continuity between the nineteenth century and the present day is the organizational isolation of labor (which helped to preserve white entitlements) from movements pressing for the civil rights of racial and ethnic minorities. Both of these continuities were anchored in the articulatory projects of political parties.

The Democratic Party had originally conceived many of its New Deal initiatives, including the collective bargaining rights now under attack, as a political strategy to construct and cultivate the support of a white suburban middle class constituency, while courting the black vote (then a decisive but unaffiliated bloc in northern swing states) with largely symbolic, rather than structurally redistributive, gestures. Thus, the Roosevelt administration officially forbade racial discrimination but turned a blind eye to racial loopholes in the implementation of the New Deal. For example, the National Labor Relations Act formalized the right to collective bargaining but exempted employers from having to recognize unions in the domestic and agricultural sectors, into which workers of color were segregated. This all but ensured that the good middle-class jobs that American workers are now losing were and are predominantly the jobs of white Americans. Similar loopholes secured white privileges in other New Deal programs, including the Federal Housing Administration, the GI Bill, the Social Security Act, Aid to Families with Dependent Children, the Agricultural Adjustment Act, and the National Industrial Recovery Act (de Leon 2011, 88; Frymer 1999, 94; Lipsitz 1998, 5; MacLean 2006, 15–16).

Though people of color technically have legal access to these programs now, the welfare state is dramatically diminished overall, and to the degree that it persists, its programs primarily serve the white middle class. According to the Congressional Budget Office, the poorest one-fifth of American households consumed 54 percent of social benefits in 1979; today they consume only 36 percent, while the lion's share goes toward "maintaining the middle class from childhood through retirement." Meanwhile, social welfare for the poorest citizens, among whom people of color are disproportionately represented, has largely been dismantled. After welfare reform became law under the Clinton administration, the amount of cash payment to welfare recipients decreased dramatically from $20.4 billion in 1996 to $9.6 billion in 2011 (Appelbaum and Gebeloff 2012; Congressional Budget Office 2011; Luhby 2012).

Moreover, working-age adults of color continue to suffer more job and asset insecurity than their white counterparts, and young adults and youth in this demographic experience more limited access to education and training for the putative jobs of the twenty-first century. In November 2008, when President Barack Obama was elected, the black unemployment rate was more than twice as high as the white rate. With respect to assets, the median wealth of white households was twenty times that of black households and eighteen times that of Latino households. Further, the Great Recession hit homeowners of color harder than it did white homeowners: inflation-adjusted median wealth among whites fell 16 percent, compared to a decline of 53 percent among Latinos and 66 percent among blacks. In terms of education, Orfield (2009) writes that 28.4 percent of white adults reported graduating from college in 2006, whereas only 18.5 percent of blacks and 12.4 percent of Latinos did. Approximately 40 percent of black and Latino K-12 students in the 2006–2007 academic year attended intensely segregated public schools where 90 to 100 percent of students were nonwhite, up from less than one-third in 1988 (Kochhar et al 2011, 1; Orfield 2009, 5–6, 13).

President Obama did not prove to be much help in these trying times. His political strategy has been to rearticulate the Democrats' New Deal coalition by foregrounding the concerns of the white suburban middle class, while doing just enough to keep people of color in his coalition. At a 2008 campaign stop in Indiana, for instance, Mr. Obama compared his own plans to end the Great Recession to President Eisenhower's embrace of New Deal deficit spending programs: "Now, back in the 1950's, Americans were put to work building the Interstate Highway system and that helped expand the middle class in this country. We need to show the same kind of leadership today" (Obama 2008a). Later, in a speech in nearby St. Louis titled, "An Agenda for Middle Class Success," he alluded to his future legislative agenda in this way: "we sent my grandfather's generation to college on the GI Bill, which helped create the largest middle-class in history. And that's what this country will do again when I am President of the United States" (Obama 2008b). In these speeches, Mr. Obama paints himself as the product and embodiment of the New Deal. In doing so, he elides the racial contradictions of postwar liberalism by framing the New Deal era as a golden age of American prosperity without any mention of Jim Crow segregation or the secondary status of black voters in the historical and contemporary Democratic coalition (de Leon 2011, 91).

Internal tensions within the 2008 Obama campaign confirm that the organization was doing what so many Democratic campaigns, including Bill Clinton's, had done before it; namely, court white voters while giving sufficient lip service to guarantee the black vote. The *New York Times* reported that Mr. Obama walked a "rhetorical tightrope—reassuring whites without seeming to abandon blacks." Senior aide David Axelrod confided that there was "a certain physics" to winning votes across racial lines, while another aide said, "there was certainly the feeling among some of the black staff that some of the white staff did not care about winning black votes." Cornel West recounted his early criticism of Mr. Obama and the campaign's subsequent attempt to reach out to him. Dr. West said, "He's got large numbers of white brothers and sisters who have fears and anxieties. He's got to speak [to] them in such a way that he holds us at arm's length; enough to say he loves us, but not too close to scare them away." He recalled that Mr. Obama expressed the fear that "he'd be pegged as a candidate who caters only to the needs of black folks" (de Leon 2011, 94; Thompson 2008).

If Latinos are not careful, they will join African Americans as another "captured constituency" within the Democratic Party, unwanted or unhoped for by the opposition and largely ignored by their own party (Frymer 1999). Already there are signs that this process is under way. Despite handing a majority of their ballots to Mr. Obama in 2008 and 2012, Latinos as of this writing have still not received their signature demand of immigration reform in year six of the Obama presidency. This is to say nothing of the fact that even with the president's Deferred Action for Childhood Arrivals program, which temporarily stops the deportation of qualified youth, Mr. Obama has deported undocumented immigrants at a faster rate than any other president in American history, including the much reviled George W. Bush (Lopez and Gonzalez-Barrera 2013).

Twentieth-century organized labor, which primarily represented white workers, followed a path parallel to, if more privileged than, that of African Americans. Until the New Deal, the Democratic Party had not been the natural home of the U.S. labor movement. Samuel Gompers, the longtime leader of the AFL, supported the Democrats only for pragmatic reasons, following the AFL's "voluntarist" policy of rewarding friends and punishing enemies, irrespective of party. Other prominent labor leaders, including John L. Lewis, head of the United Mine Workers, were diehard Republicans. Still others threw their support behind third-party alternatives like Minnesota's Farmer-Labor Party, which had, by the time of the Great Depression, elected several of its candidates to state and federal office. But the Democrats then did two things of great consequence to the future development of the labor movement. First, progressives in the party narrowly defeated the conservative Democratic appeal to make the 1932 presidential election against Herbert Hoover about prohibition. This cleared the way for Franklin Roosevelt and others to focus the polity on the Depression, class inequality, and the "forgotten man." Once in office, the Democrats passed labor-friendly legislation (e.g., the National Industrial Recovery Act and later the National Labor Relations or Wagner Act) and appointed labor leaders to prominent advisory posts. This had the effect of simultaneously incorporating labor into the party while also creating dissension within the labor movement. The internecine conflict over organizing turf (prompted by the labor board's power to define appropriate bargaining units) among other issues drained resources away from third party organizing, making the Democrats the only game in town (Eidlin 2014).

Though union members became middle-class property owners under the New Deal, many of them were conservative on racial issues and hawkish toward the Soviet Union during the Cold War (Fraser and Gerstle 1989). Accordingly, when progressive Democrats began pressing for school and residential desegregation and came out against the war in Vietnam, union members became available for recruitment by the Republican Party. Once in power, Republicans preserved some of the entitlements of the white middle class even as they dismantled the latter's unions. Instead of pushing back, the Democratic Party towed the neoliberal line, appointing free marketeers to high office, negotiating free trade agreements to the disadvantage of unionized manufacturing workers, and permitting welfare "reform" to unravel the social safety net. This public embrace of free market principles is made politically possible by the fact that organized labor, like communities of color, is a captured constituency within the Democratic Party, whose high-level operatives know very well that labor has had nowhere else to go since the 1930s (de Leon 2011; de Leon et al. 2009; Frymer 1999).

Once again, the Obama administration is no exception. The president never once traveled to the front lines of labor's crisis in the Rustbelt, preferring to send the occasional message via proxy. For example, when the Republicans passed the Michigan right to work law, Democratic state senator Glenn Anderson said, "Make no mistake about it, as President Obama said yesterday, passage of this legislation is about politics, not economics" (*Lansing State Journal* 2012). The true test of President Obama's resolve was his failure to deliver on the promise to pass the Employee Free Choice Act, which would have allowed workers to unionize after signing up a majority of the workplace as members, instead of going through a long and arduous election campaign, during which employers typically intimidate workers into voting against unionization.

Beyond generating racial contradictions and captured constituencies, the relationship between American workers and the party system has institutionalized still another problem akin to the challenges of the nineteenth century—the organizational isolation of the labor movement from communities of color, despite the latter's disproportionate representation among the lower strata of American society. Paul Frymer has referred to this situation as "a bifurcated system of power that assigned race and class problems to different spheres of government" (2008, 2–3). In the late nineteenth century, civil and labor rights were similarly construed as mutually exclusive issues. This was due in no small part to the social distance between African-American and affluent white abolitionists, on the one hand, and white working class trade unionists and radicals, on the other (Montgomery 1967; Stanley 1998). But it was also due to the way in which trade unionists conceptualized the labor question as the natural successor to the slavery question. Recall that during the war Andrew Cameron, the English-language editor of the *Workingman's Advocate*, differentiated between the slavery question, which was the responsibility of "Our brave soldiers in the field," and the labor question, which was fundamentally "a white man's question" (*Workingman's Advocate*, September 17, 1864). After the war, Cameron's German-language coeditor, Eduard Schlaeger, echoed this distinction at a rally for the eight-hour day, saying that workers "had settled the black labor question, and now . . . would settle the white labor question" (*Chicago Times*, May 10, 1867, 5). Note that though the struggle for racial equality remained far from over, organized labor viewed the civil rights agenda as passed or passing in a way very much reminiscent of contemporary postracial rhetoric about the civil rights movement.

Today, as in the nineteenth and twentieth centuries, social movements for labor, civil, and immigrant rights, are not mutually reinforcing, allied constituencies exerting combined upward pressure on the political establishment to rethink these struggles as linked. In this context, the Democrats do not stop at ignoring captured constituencies: they play one against the other. For example, the AFL-CIO recently negotiated a deal with the U.S. Chamber of Commerce on the U.S. Senate's immigration reform bill that would limit the number of immigrants who could work legally in the United States. Instead of taking a more inclusive stance by, for instance, demanding that all new immigrants become union members or at least have the right to unionize regardless of legal status, organized labor was maneuvered by the party system into accepting the logic of nativism, which turns on the unsubstantiated claim that immigrants take jobs away from "Americans" (Bennett 2013).

A new period of labor ascendancy can only be realized by rebuilding the movement in a way that at last overcomes the organizational isolation and racial contradictions that have been cultivated by the party system since the nineteenth century. This is not to discount political articulation, but on the contrary to counsel mindfulness of the awesome capacity of parties to shape workers' identity as they struggle for power. In this, Chicago's General Trades Assembly may have been onto something in 1864, when its members pursued a course of political independence from the two-party system. The attitude of the movement I envision lies somewhere between two competing sentiments from the leaders of that assembly, one from George K. Hazlitt, assembly president and once ardent Democrat, and the other from sometime Republican Eduard Schlaeger. Hazlitt said, "The workingmen of this city could not be dictated to by any man or men on the face of the earth, and could not be used by any party." To this, Schlaeger added, "the old political parties . . . must be made to obey the sovereign will of the people" (*Chicago Tribune*, August 21, 1864).

Notes

CHAPTER 1

1. This argument is typical of more sophisticated studies of American exceptionalism, which offer a historically sensitive explanation for why there is no socialism in the United States. Voss (1993), for example, argues that prior to the Haymarket Affair of 1886, which led to the violent suppression of the nineteenth-century U.S. labor movement, the Knights of Labor advanced a recognizable American variant of socialism. That claim has been called into question, especially by scholars of Chicago labor history, who argue that American workers were able to force a more progressive synthesis of liberal democracy by the end of the nineteenth century. See, for example, Jentz and Schneirov (2012) and Schneirov (1998).

2. In *Fear Itself* (2013), Katznelson traces the ethnoracial contradictions limiting American progressivism not to nineteenth-century ethnic machines as he did in *City Trenches*, but to the New Deal Democrats' Faustian bargain with the racist southerners in their party. In exchange for Congressional support for the New Deal, he argues, progressives promised to leave Jim Crow segregation unperturbed, thus curtailing the transformative impact of the welfare state (Katznelson 2013, 9, 15-18). As I note in the epilogue, I agree that the New Deal was shot through with racial contradictions, but I do not think they comprise "the origins of our time." Rather, the New Deal was a key episode in the ongoing struggle over the legitimacy of collective rights, going back to liberalism's initial ascendancy after the Civil War.

3. In this, Moore's notion that Midwesterners exchanged their political support for cheap land simply will not do, for Democrats had long made the same promise.

4. There are also good books on the effects of democratization in the contemporary Middle East, though there the debate is on whether participation in the democratic process moderates or further radicalizes Islamist parties (e.g., Schwedler 2006; Tezcur 2010).

CHAPTER 2

1. This is not to say that Jacksonian workers' organizations were uniformly Democratic. They were largely Democratic when they chose to endorse either party at all, but many of them retained an affinity for the Whigs. Some workingmen's organizations were swayed by the Whig notion that it was the divisive Democratic partisanship typified by the Bank veto, and not the Bank itself, which caused the protracted economic downturn of 1837. In the 1834 New York mayoral contest, "clerks, cartmen, sailors, printers, carpenters and blacksmiths" passed resolutions in favor of the Whig candidate, Gulian C. Verplanck, denouncing the Democratic Party for causing the "contraction of commerce, and consequent unemployment and dislocation of the currency" (Hugins 1960, 29–31). It should be noted here that Hugins has been criticized by Wilentz (1984) for claiming, very much like the Commons school of labor historiography, that the New York labor movement was motivated principally by economic concerns or "practical trade unionism" instead of status concerns anchored in republican political thought.

2. Note that in the context of New York State, which is Huston's case study, farmers had strong relationships with both liberal Whigs and Democrats (1998, 35).

CHAPTER 3

1. See also John Wentworth's speech, "Free Tea, Free Coffee, Free Harbors, and Free Territory: Remarks of Mr. John Wentworth, of Illinois, delivered in the House of Representatives, February 2, 1847." John Wentworth Papers, 1836–1888, Chicago History Museum, Chicago.

2. My quotations from the *Gem of the Prairie* come from the Arthur C. Cole papers in the Illinois History and Lincoln Collections at the University of Illinois, Urbana-Champaign.

3. Levine (1983, 178) argues that the slavery question was not a detour from, but an expression of, persistent international democratic sentiment among the German community. I am more ambivalent. To Levine's point, the issue of slavery extension did bind to 48er ideology as an enzyme does to a substrate, but the issue itself remained fallow until political parties cultivated it as a matter of contention. Consequently, instead of organizing job actions, or perhaps in addition to doing so, German workers spent their time organizing petition drives and traveling to conventions against slavery extension.

4. For a fuller discussion of the relationship between nativism and Republicanism, including its origins in the struggle between the GOP and the Know Nothing or American Party, see Gienapp (1987).

5. The reality was less straightforward. Small to middling farmers tended to vote for the Democrats in the South, whereas southern planters tended to vote for the Whigs (Wilentz 2005).

CHAPTER 4

1. Mr. Lincoln scolded the delegation and ordered them to return to Chicago and meet the quota, which they did.

2. Cameron himself was a Democrat, though other high-ranking Assembly officials like Hazlitt, were Republicans.

CHAPTER 5

1. As Victoria Hattam rightly points out prosecution of labor via the common law doctrine of conspiracy continued through the 1880s (1992, 47–48).

2. Daniel Ernst's account of the rise of corporate liberalism in the progressive era also acknowledges the role of party politics in forging legal tendencies. The eventual recognition of labor's group rights, Ernst argues, can be traced to "the revolt of insurgent Republicans, the election of a Democratic majority and a disciplined 'labor bloc' in the House of Representatives, and Woodrow Wilson's election in 1912," which, together, put labor conspiracy advocates "on the defensive," leading to "the passage in 1913 of a rider [on that year's Congressional appropriations bill] that denied the Department of Justice funds to prosecute organized labor" as a trust (1995, 8).

3. By 1880 the LaSalle Black Law had supposedly become a dead letter, yet organized labor never succeeded in repealing the law despite repeated attempts. Moreover, it bears mention that the law was used again in the twentieth century to prosecute workers (Beckner 1929, 10).

4. The Merritt Conspiracy Law was repealed in 1891, largely as a result of the lobbying efforts of the Illinois State Federation of Labor (Beckner 1929, 15–16). This victory was the first of several signaling the acceptance of a collective interpretation of worker rights.

5. For book-length historiographical accounts of the Haymarket Affair, see David (1936), Avrich (1984), and Green (2006). For shorter and more critical accounts of Haymarket, see Hirsch (1990, 73–80) and Schneirov (1998, 183–210). Kim Voss (1993) argues that Haymarket was the decisive moment at which the U.S. labor movement was transformed from a revolutionary to a reformist force.

6. I use the numbers for Cook County here to maintain continuity with the 1850 Census, which did not collect these statistics for Chicago. The figures cited here nevertheless reflect the growth of Chicago almost exclusively. Chicago accounted for 98.1 percent of the county's total product (U.S. Census Office 1883b, 960, 1047).

7. The figures for weekly board are actually for nearby Rock Island; the Census took sample rates from four regions in Illinois, with Rock Island representing the northernmost portion of the state. It is likely that weekly board was more expensive in Chicago; these are therefore fairly conservative estimates.

References

SPECIAL COLLECTIONS

The Alarm, Joseph A. Labadie Collection, University of Michigan
Gem of the Prairie, Arthur C. Cole Papers, Illinois History and Lincoln Collections
    University of Illinois, Urbana-Champaign
Robert W. Johannsen Papers, Illinois History and Lincoln Collections, University of
    Illinois, Urbana-Champaign
John Wentworth Papers, 1836–1888, Chicago History Museum

SECONDARY AND ANNOTATED PRIMARY SOURCES

Abramson, Paul R., John H. Aldrich, and David W. Rohde. 2010. *Continuity and
    Change in the 2008 Elections*. Washington, DC: Congressional Quarterly Press.
Ahern, Louise Knott, and Kathleen Lavey. 2012. "Capitol Draws Vast, Diverse Crowd to
    Protest." *Lansing State Journal*, December 11. Accessed February 21, 2014. http://
    pqasb.pqarchiver.com/lansingstatejournal/doc/1237139894.htm. . .tartpage
    =&desc=Capitol+draws+vast%2C+diverse+crowd+to+protest&pf=1.
Ahern, Louise Knott, Lindsay VanHulle, Kathleen Lavey, Laura Misjak, and Scott
    Davis. 2012. "3 Arrested as Police, Protesters Clash." *Lansing State Journal*,
    December 12. Accessed February 21, 2014. http://pqasb.pqarchiver.com/
    lansingstatejournal/doc/1237139291.html. . .ion=&startpage=&desc=3+
    arrested+as+police%2C+protesters+clash&pf=1.
Allen, Theodore W. 1994. *The Invention of the White Race*. New York: Verso.
Aminzade, Ronald. 1981. *Class, Politics, and Early Industrial Capitalism: a Study of
    Mid-Nineteenth-Century Toulouse, France*. Albany: State University of New York Press.
——. 1993. *Ballots and Barricades: Class Formation and Republican Politics in France,
    1830–1871*. Princeton: Princeton University Press.
Anderson, Perry. 1980. *Arguments within English Marxism*. London: Verso.
Andreas, Alfred T. 1886. *History of Chicago*. Chicago: A.T. Andreas.
Appelbaum, Binyamin, and Robert Gebeloff. 2012. "Even Critics of Safety Net Increas-
    ingly Depend on It." *New York Times*, February 11, p. A1. Accessed October
    23, 2012 http://www.nytimes.com/2012/02/12/us/even-critics-of-safety-
    net-increasingly-depend-on-it.html?_r=3&pagewanted=1&.
Ashworth, John. 1983. *"Agrarians" & "Aristocrats": Party Political Ideology in the United
    States, 1837–1846*. London, UK: Royal Historical Society; Atlantic Highlands,
    NJ: Humanities Press.
Associated Press. 2012. "Right-to-Work Measure Clears Indiana House." *USA Today*,
    January 25. Accessed February 19, 2014. http://usatoday30.usatoday.com/news/
    nation/story/2012-01-25/indiana-right-to-work-vote/52792100/1.
Banning, Lance. *The Jeffersonian Persuasion: Evolution of a Party Ideology*. Ithaca:
    Cornell University Press.
Barbour, Clay, and Mary Spicuzza. 2011. "Gov. Walker Signs Budget Bill Limiting Bargaining
    Rights, Rescinds Layoff Notices." *Wisconsin State Journal*, March 11. Accessed Febru-
    ary 26, 2014. http://host.madison.com/wsj/news/local/govt-and-politics/gov-walker-
    s. . .ts-rescinds-layoff/article_cef20214-4bff-11e0-b67d-001cc4c03286.html.

Beck, Paul Allen. 1974. "A Socialization Theory of Partisan Realignment." In *The Politics of Future Citizens: New Dimensions in the Political Socialization of Children*, edited by Richard G. Niemi and Associates, 199–219. San Francisco: Jossey-Bass.

Beckner, Earl R. 1929. *A History of Labor Legislation in Illinois*. Chicago: University of Chicago Press.

Bennett, Brian. 2013. "Business, Labor Leaders Reach Compromise on Immigration Reform." *Los Angeles Times*, February 21. Accessed March 3, 2014. http://articles.latimes.com/print/2013/feb/21/news/la-pn-business-labor-immigration-reform-20130221.

Benson, Lee. 1961. *The Concept of Jacksonian Democracy: New York as a Test Case*. Princeton: Princeton University Press.

Berelson, Bernard, Paul F. Lazarsfeld, and William McPhee. 1954. *Voting: A Study of Opinion Formation in a Presidential Campaign*. Chicago: University of Chicago Press.

Berggoetz, Barb. 2013. "Attorney General Takes Right-to-Work Law Appeal to Indiana Supreme Court." *Indianapolis Star*, December 18. Accessed February 17, 2014. http://www.indystar.com/story/news/politics/2013/12/18/attorney-general-takes-right-to-work-law-appeal-to-indiana-supreme-court/4116427/.

Bergquist, James M. 1971. "People and Politics in Transition: The Illinois Germans, 1850–1860. In *Ethnic Voters and the Election of Lincoln*, edited by Frederick C. Luebke, 196–226. Lincoln: University of Nebraska Press.

Black, Duncan. [1958] 1963. *The Theory of Committees and Elections*. Cambridge: Cambridge University Press.

Blau, Joseph L. 1954. *Social Theories of Jacksonian Democracy: Representative Writings of the Period, 1825–1850*. New York: The Liberal Arts Press.

Bonilla-Silva, Eduardo. 2003. *Racism without Racists: Color-Blind Racism and the Persistence of Racial Inequality in the United States*. Lanham, MD: Rowman and Littlefield.

Bourdieu, Pierre. 1989. "Social Space and Symbolic Power." *Sociological Theory* 7 (1): 14–25.

Boydston, Jeanne. 1991. *Home and Work: Housework, Wages, and the Ideology of Labor in the Early Republic*. New York: Oxford University Press.

Brady, David W. 1988. *Critical Elections and Congressional Policy Making*. Stanford: Stanford University Press.

Brodkin, Karen. 1998. *How Jews Became White Folks and What That Says about Race in America*. New Brunswick, NJ: Rutgers University Press.

Bronstein, Jamie L. 1999. *Land Reform and Working-Class Experience in Britain and the United States, 1800–1862*. Stanford: Stanford University Press.

Burawoy, Michael. 1989. "Marxism without Micro-Foundations." *Socialist Review* 89 (2): 53–86.

Burnham, Walter Dean. 1970. *Critical Elections and the Mainsprings of American Politics*. New York: Norton.

Campbell, Angus, Philip E. Converse, Warren E. Miller, and Donald E. Stokes. 1960. *The American Voter*. New York and London: John Wiley & Sons.

Campbell, Angus, Gerald Gurin, and Warren E. Miller. 1954. *The Voter Decides*. Evanston, IL and White Plains, NY: Row, Peterson.

Cap Times. 2011. "SHAME! SHAME! SHAME!" March 10. Accessed February 26, 2014. http://host.madison.com/ct/news/opinion/editorial/shame-shame-shame/article_10a66c10-a189-5b78-b8a6-3284c140ba32.html.

Carmines, Edward G., and James A. Stimson. 1989. *Issue Evolution: Race and the Transformation of American Politics*. Princeton: Princeton University Press.

Chen, Anthony S. 2009. *The Fifth Freedom: Jobs, Politics, and Civil Rights in the United States, 1941–1972*. Princeton: Princeton University Press.

Citron, Abraham F. 1969. *"The Rightness of Whiteness": The World of the White Child in a Segregated Society*. Detroit: Michigan-Ohio Educational Laboratory.

Cohen, Lizabeth. 2003. *A Consumers' Republic: The Politics of Mass Consumption in Postwar America*. New York: Knopf.

Congressional Budget Office. 2011. "Trends in the Distribution of Household Income between 1979 and 2007." Accessed October 23, 2012. http://www.cbo.gov/publication/42729.

Converse, Philip E. 1964. "The Nature of Belief Systems in Mass Publics." In *Ideology and Discontent*, edited by David E. Apter, 206–261. Glencoe, IL: Free Press.

———. 1966. "The Concept of a Normal Vote." In *Elections and the Political Order*, edited by Angus Campbell, Philip E. Converse, Warren E. Miller, and Donald A. Stokes, 9–39. New York: Wiley.

Cronon, William. 1991. *Nature's Metropolis: Chicago and the Great West*. New York: Norton.

Cullen, Sandy, and Patricia Simms. 2011. "Collective Bargaining Bill Signing Brings Largest Rally Yet to Capitol." *Wisconsin State Journal*, March 13. Accessed February 26, 2014. http://host.madison.com/wsj/news/local/govt-and-politics/collective-b. . .ally-yet-to-capitol/article_9f189108-4cbc-11e0-b9b8-001cc4c002e0.html.

Cullen, Sandy, Steven Verburg, Ron Seely, Dan Simmons, Devin Rose, Patricia Simms, and Dee J. Hall. 2011. "Thousands Storm Capitol as GOP Takes Action." *Wisconsin State Journal*, March 10. Accessed February 26, 2014. http://host.madison.com/wsj/news/local/govt-and-politics/thousands-. . .-gop-takes-action/article_260247e0-4ac4-11e0-bfa9-001cc4c03286.html.

Cummings, Richard. 2012. "Unions Protect Our Standard of Living." *Lansing State Journal*, December 11, p. A.9. Accessed February 21, 2014. http://pqasb.pqarchiver.com/lansingstatejournal/doc/1240385472.html. . .dition=&startpage=&desc=Unions+protect+our+standard+of+living&pf=1.

Dahrendorf, Ralf. 1959. *Class and Class Conflict in Industrial Society*. Stanford: Stanford University Press.

Daum, Kristen M. 2012. "Michigan's Labor Legacy Takes a Hit: Right to Work Signed into Law." *Lansing State Journal*, December 12. Accessed February 21, 2014. http://pqasb.pqarchiver.com/lansingstatejournal/doc/1237139886.htm. . .7s+labor+legacy+takes+a+hit%3A+Right+to+work+signed+into+law&pf=1.

Davey, Monica. 2012. "Indiana Governor Signs a Law Creating a 'Right to Work' State." *New York Times*, February 1, p. A12. Accessed Feb. 19, 2014. http://www.nytimes.com/2012/02/02/us/indiana-becomes-right-to-work-state.html.

Davey, Monica, and Jeff Zeleny. 2012. "Walker Survives Wisconsin Recall Vote." *New York Times*, June 5, 2012. Accessed February 26, 2014. http://www.nytimes.com/2012/06/06/us/politics/walker-survives-wisconsin-recall-effort.html?_r=0&pagewanted=print.

David, Henry. 1936. *The History of the Haymarket Affair: A Study in the American Social-Revolutionary and Labor Movements*. New York: Farrar & Rinehart.

Davidoff, Judith, and Kristin Czubkowski. 2011. "Tears and Resolve after Capitol Vote." *Cap Times*, March 11, 2011. Accessed February 26, 2014. http://host.madison.com/ct/news/local/govt-and-politics/tears-and-res. . .after-capitol-vote/article_2fa000f8-4b7d-11e0-ae3c-001cc4c03286.html.

de Leon, Cedric. 2008. "'No Bourgeois Mass Party, No Democracy': The Missing Link in Barrington Moore's American Civil War." *Political Power and Social Theory* 19: 39–82.

——. 2010. "Vicarious Revolutionaries: Martial Discourse and the Origins of Mass Party Competition in the United States, 1789–1848." *Studies in American Political Development* 24: 121–141.

——. 2011. "The More Things Change: A Gramscian Geneology of Barack Obama's 'Post-Racial' Politics." *Political Power and Social Theory* 22: 75–104.

——. 2014. *Party and Society: Reconstructing a Sociology of Democratic Party Politics.* Cambridge, UK: Polity.

de Leon, Cedric, Manali Desai, and Cihan Tuğal. 2009. "Political Articulation: Parties and the Constitution of Cleavages in the U.S., India, and Turkey." *Sociological Theory* 27: 193–219.

Deruiter, Greg. 2012. "Michigan Nurses Rally against Right to Work" *Lansing State Journal*, December 10. Accessed February 21, 2014. http://pqasb.pqarchiver. com/lansingstatejournal/doc/1237096805.html. . .=&startpage=&desc= Michigan+nurses+rally+against+right+to+work&pf=1.

Dorris, J.T. 1919. "Hon. Thomas E. Merritt." *Journal of the Illinois State Historical Society* 11 (4): 631–635.

Douglas, Stephen A. [1853] 1961. "To J.H. Crane, D.M. Johnson, and L.J. Eastin, Washington, December 17, 1853." In *The Letters of Stephen A. Douglas*, edited by Robert W. Johannsen, 268–271. Urbana: University of Illinois Press.

——. [1857a] 1961. "To John A. McClernand." In *The Letters of Stephen A. Douglas*, edited by Robert W. Johannsen, 403. Urbana: University of Illinois Press.

——. [1857b] 1961. "To Charles H. Lanphier and George Walker." In *The Letters of Stephen A. Douglas*, edited by Robert W. Johannsen, 405. Urbana: University of Illinois Press.

Downs, Anthony. 1957. *An Economic Theory of Democracy.* New York: Harper & Row.

DuBois, W.E.B. [1935] 1998. *Black Reconstruction in America, 1860–1880.* New York: Free Press.

Egan, Paul, and Scott Davis. 2014. "Michigan Supreme Court Takes Right-to-Work, State Employee Pension Cases." *Detroit Free Press*, January 30. Accessed February 21, 2014. http://www.freep.com/article/20140130/NEWS06/301300078/ Michigan-Supreme-Court-takes-right-to-work-case.

Eidlin, Barry. 2014. "Why Is There No Labor Party in the United States? Political Articulation and the Canadian Comparison, 1932–1948." Unpublished manuscript.

Einhorn, Robin L. 1991. *Property Rules: Political Economy in Chicago, 1833–1872.* Chicago: University of Chicago Press.

Enelow, James M., and Melvin J. Hinich. 1984. *The Spatial Theory of Voting: An Introduction.* Cambridge: Cambridge University Press.

Ernst, Daniel R. 1995. *Lawyers against Labor: From Individual Rights to Corporate Liberalism.* Urbana and Chicago: University of Illinois Press.

Eyal, Yonatan. 2007. *The Young America Movement and the Transformation of the Democratic Party, 1828–1861.* New York: Cambridge University Press.

Fehrenbacher, Don E. 1957. *Chicago Giant: a Biography of "Long John" Wentworth.* Madison, WI: American History Research Center.

Feller, Daniel. 2001. "A Brother in Arms: Benjamin Tappan and the Antislavery Democracy." *Journal of American History* 88: 48–74.

Fiorina, Morris P. 1981. *Retrospective Voting in American National Elections.* New Haven: Yale University Press.

Foner, Eric. 1970. *Free Soil, Free Labor, Free Men: The Ideology of the Republican Party before the Civil War.* New York: Oxford University Press.

——. 1988. *Reconstruction, 1863–1877.* New York: Harper & Row.

Foner, Philip S. 1977. *The Great Labor Uprising of 1877.* New York: Monad Press.

Ford, Lacy K, Jr. 1988. *Origins of Southern Radicalism: The Southern Carolina Upcountry, 1800–1860*. New York: Oxford University Press.

Formisano, Ronald. 1971. *Birth of Mass Political Parties in Michigan, 1827–1861*. Princeton: Princeton University Press.

Fraser, Nancy, and Linda Gordon. 1994. "A Genealogy of Dependency: Tracing a Keyword of the U.S. Welfare State." *Signs* 19 (2): 33–58.

Fraser, Steve, and Gary Gerstle, eds. 1989. *The Rise and Fall of the New Deal Order, 1930–1980*. Princeton: Princeton University Press.

Frymer, Paul. 1999. *Uneasy Alliances: Race and Party Competition in America*. Princeton: Princeton University Press.

———. 2008. *Black and Blue: African-Americans, the Labor Movement, and the Decline of the Democratic Party*. Princeton: Princeton University Press.

General Assembly of the State of Indiana. House Enrolled Act No. 1001. 117th General Assembly, Second Regular Session, 2012. Accessed February 1, 2014. http://www.nrtw.org/files/nrtw/Indiana_Right_to_Work_Law.pdf.

Gerteis, Joseph. 2007. *Class and the Color Line: Interracial Class Coalition in the Knights of Labor and the Populist Movement*. Durham: Duke University Press.

Gienapp, William E. 1987. *The Origins of the Republican Party, 1852–1856*. Oxford and New York: Oxford University Press.

Glickstein, Jonathan A. 2002. *American Exceptionalism, American Anxiety: Wages, Competition, and Degraded Labor in the Antebellum United States*. Charlottesville: University of Virginia Press.

Gramsci, Antonio. 1971. *Selections from the Prison Notebooks*. Edited and translated by Quintin Hoare and Geoffrey Nowell Smith. New York: International Publishers.

Green, James. 2006. *Death in the Haymarket: A Story of Chicago, the First Labor Movement and the Bombing That Divided Gilded Age America*. New York: Anchor Books.

Greenhouse, Steven. 2011. "Ohio's Anti-Union Law Is Tougher Than Wisconsin's." *New York Times*, March 31. Accessed March 9, 2014. http://www.nytimes.com/2011/04/01/us/01ohio.html?_r=0&pagewanted=print.

Guarneri, Carl J. 1991. *The Utopian Alternative: Fourierism in Nineteenth Century America*. Ithaca: Cornell University Press.

Hacker, J. David. 2011. "A Census-Based Count of the Civil War Dead." *Civil War History* 57 (4): 307–348.

Hall, Stuart. 1983. "The Problem of Ideology: Marxism without Guarantees." In *Marx: A Hundred Years On*, edited by Betty Matthews, 56–85. London: Lawrence & Wishart.

Hansen, Stephen L. 1980. *The Making of the Third Party System: Voters and Parties in Illinois, 1850 to 1876*. Ann Arbor: Research Press.

Hartz, Louis. 1955. *The Liberal Tradition in America: an Interpretation of American Political Thought since the Revolution*. New York: Harcourt.

Hattam, Victoria C. 1992 "Courts and the Question of Class: Judicial Regulation of Labor under the Common Law Doctrine of Criminal Conspiracy." In *Labor Law in America: Historical and Critical Essays*, edited by Christopher L. Tomlins and Andrew J. King, 44–70. Baltimore: Johns Hopkins University Press.

———. 1993. *Labor Visions and State Power: The Origins of Business Unionism in the United States*. Princeton: Princeton University Press.

Heller, Patrick. 1999. *The Labor of Development: Workers and the Transformation of Capitalism in Kerala, India*. Ithaca: Cornell University Press.

Hiers, Wesley. 2013. "Party Matters: Racial Closure in the Nineteenth-Century United States." *Social Science History* 37 (2): 255–308.

Hirsch, Arnold R. 1983. *Making the Second Ghetto: Race and Housing in Chicago, 1940–1960.* Cambridge: Cambridge University Press.

Hirsch, Eric L. 1990. *Urban Revolt: Ethnic Politics in the Nineteenth-Century Chicago Labor Movement.* Berkeley: University of California Press.

Holt, Michael F. 1999. *The Rise and Fall of the American Whig Party: Jacksonian Politics and the Onset of the Civil War.* Oxford and New York: Oxford University Press.

Hotelling, Harold. 1929. "Stability in Competition." *Economic Journal* 39: 41–57.

Howe, Daniel Walker. 1979. *The Political Culture of the American Whigs.* Chicago: University of Chicago Press.

——. 2007. *What God Hath Wrought: The Transformation of America, 1815–1848.* New York: Oxford University Press.

Hugins, Walter. 1960. *Jacksonian Democracy and the Working Class: A Study of the New York Workingmen's Movement, 1828–1837.* Stanford: Stanford University Press.

Huston, James L. 1987. *The Panic of 1857 and the Coming of the Civil War.* Baton Rouge: Louisiana State University Press.

Huston, Reeve. 1998. "Land and Freedom: The New York Anti-Rent Wars and the Construction of Free Labor in the Antebellum North." In *Labor Histories: Class, Politics, and the Working Class Experience,* edited by Eric Arnesen, Julie Greene, and Bruce Laurie, 19–44. Urbana: University of Illinois Press.

Ignatiev, Noel. 1995. *How the Irish Became White.* London: Routledge.

Jackson, Kenneth T. 1985. *Crabgrass Frontier: The Suburbanization of the United States.* New York: Oxford University Press.

Jentz, John B. 1991. "Class and Politics in an Emerging Industrial City: Chicago in the 1860s and 1870s." *Journal of Urban History* 17: 227–263.

Jentz, John B., and Richard Schneirov. 2012. *Chicago in the Age of Capital: Class, Politics, and Democracy during the Civil War and Reconstruction.* Urbana: University of Illinois Press.

Johannsen, Robert W. [1973] 1997. *Stephen A. Douglas.* Urbana: University of Illinois Press.

Katznelson, Ira. 1981. *City Trenches: Urban Politics and the Patterning of Class in the United States.* New York: Pantheon.

——. 2005. *When Affirmative Action Was White: An Untold History of Racial Inequality in Twentieth-Century America.* New York: Norton.

——. 2013. *Fear Itself: The New Deal and the Origins of Our Time.* New York: Liveright.

Katznelson, Ira, and Aristide Zolberg. 1986. *Working-Class Formation.* Princeton: Princeton University Press.

Key, Francis Scott. 1814. "The Star Spangled Banner (The Defense of Fort McHenry)." Norman: University of Oklahoma College of Law, Historical Documents. Accessed February 5, 2003. http://www.law.ou.edu/hist/ssb.html.

Key, V.O., Jr. 1955. "A Theory of Critical Elections." *Journal of Politics* 17: 3–18.

——. 1959. "Secular Realignment and the Party System." *Journal of Politics* 21: 198–210.

——. 1966. *The Responsible Electorate: Rationality in Presidential Voting, 1936–1960.* Cambridge: Belknap Press of Harvard University Press.

Key, V.O., Jr., and Frank Munger. 1959. "Social Determinism and Electoral Decision: the Case of Indiana." In *American Voting Behavior,* edited by Eugene Burdick and Arthur J. Brodbeck, 281–299. New York: Free Press.

Kimeldorf, Howard. 1988. *Reds or Rackets? The Making of Radical and Conservative Unions on the Waterfront.* Berkeley and Los Angeles: University of California Press.

Kinder, Donald R., and D. Roderick Kiewiet. 1981. "Sociotropic Politics: The American Case." *British Journal of Political Science* 11 (2): 129–161.

Kiper, Richard L. 1999. *Major General John Alexander McClernand: Politician in Uniform*. Kent, OH: Kent State University Press.

Klinghard, Daniel. 2010. *The Nationalization of American Political Parties, 1880–1896*. New York: Cambridge University Press.

Knoke, David. 1976. *Change and Continuity in American Politics: The Social Bases of Political Parties*. Baltimore and London: Johns Hopkins University Press.

Koch, Robert L., II. 2011. "Right-to-Work Law Is Right for Indiana." *Indianapolis Star*, December 20, p. A.15. Accessed February 17, 2014. http://pqasb.pqarchiver.com/indystar/doc/912281479. html?FMT=FT&FM...tion=&startpage=&desc=Right-to-work+law+is+right+for+Indiana&pf=1.

Kochhar, Rakesh, Richard Fry, and Paul Taylor. 2011. "Twenty-to-One: Wealth Gaps Rise to Record Highs between Whites, Blacks and Hispanics." Washington, DC: Pew Research Center. Accessed March 3, 2014. http://www.pewsocialtrends.org/files/2011/07/SDT-Wealth-Report_7-26-11_FINAL.pdf.

Lambert, Josiah Bartlett. 2005. *"If the Workers Took a Notion": The Right to Strike and American Political Development*. Ithaca: Cornell University Press.

Lansing State Journal. 2012. "Reactions to Passage of Right-to-Work Legislation." December 12. Accessed February 21, 2014. http://pqasb.pqarchiver.com/lansingstatejournal/doc/1237144306.html...rtpage=&desc=Reactions+to+passage+of+right-to-work+legislation&pf=1.

Lassiter, Matthew D. 2006. *The Silent Majority: Suburban Politics in the Sunbelt South*. Princeton: Princeton University Press.

Laurie, Bruce. 1989. *Artisans into Workers: Labor in Nineteenth-Century America*. New York: Hill and Wang.

Lause, Mark A. 2005. *Young America: Land, Labor, and the Republican Community*. Urbana and Chicago: University of Illinois Press.

Lazarsfeld, Paul F., Bernard Berelson, and Hazel Gaudet. [1944] 1948. *The People's Choice: How the Voter Makes Up His Mind in a Presidential Campaign*. 2nd ed. New York: Columbia University Press.

Legerbott, Stanley. 1961. "The Pattern of Employment since 1800." In *American Economic History*, edited by Seymour E. Harris, 281–310. New York: McGraw-Hill.

Legislative Council, State of Michigan. 2014. Employment Relations Commission (Excerpt). Act 176 of 1938—Am. 2012, Act 348, Eff. March 28, 2013. Accessed March 7, 2014. https://www.legislature.mi.gov/(S(dq2l0pn1ghngtg55uskd5pic))/documents/mcl/pdf/mcl-423-14.pdf.

Leonard, Gerald Flood. 2002. *The Invention of Party Politics: Federalism, Popular Sovereignty, and Constitutional Development in Jacksonian Illinois*. Chapel Hill: University of North Carolina Press.

Levine, Bruce. 1983. "Free Soil, Free Labor, and *Freimaenner*: German Chicago in the Civil War Era." In *German Workers in Industrial Chicago, 1850–1910: A Comparative Perspective*, edited by Hartmut Keil and John Jentz, 163–182. DeKalb: Northern Illinois University Press.

———. 1992. *The Spirit of 1848: German Immigrants, Labor Conflict, and the Coming of the Civil War*. Urbana and Chicago: University of Illinois Press.

Lipset, Seymour Martin, and Stein Rokkan. 1967. *Party Systems and Voter Alignments: Cross-National Perspectives*. New York: Free Press.

Lipsitz, George. 1998. *The Possessive Investment in Whiteness: How White People Profit from Identity Politics*. Philadelphia: Temple University Press.

Lopez, Mark Hugo, and Ana Gonzalez-Barrera. 2013. "High Rate of Deportations Continue under Obama despite Latino Disapproval." Pew Research Center, Washington, DC. Accessed March 3, 2014. http://www.pewresearch. org/fact-tank/2013/09/19/high-rate-of-deportations-continue-under-obama-despite-latino-disapproval/.

Luhby, Tami. 2012. "Welfare Spending Cut in Half since Reform." CNNMoney, August 9. Accessed October 23, 2012. http://money.cnn.com/2012/08/09/news/ economy/welfare-reform/index.htm.

MacLean, Nancy. 2006. *Freedom Is Not Enough: The Opening of the American Workplace*. New York: Russell Sage Foundation and Harvard University Press.

Mann, Michael. 1973. *Consciousness and Action in the Western Working Class*. London: Macmillan.

——. 2012. *The Sources of Social Power, Volume 3: Global Empires and Revolution, 1890–1945*. New York: Cambridge University Press.

Manza, Jeff, and Clem Brooks. 1999. *Social Cleavages and Political Change: Voter Alignments and U.S. Party Coalitions*. Oxford and New York: Oxford University Press.

Margo, Robert A. 2000. *Wages and Labor Markets in the United States, 1820–1860*. Chicago and London: University of Chicago Press.

Marley, Patrick. 2012. "GOP Retakes State Senate and Full Control of State Government." *Milwaukee Journal Sentinel*, November 7, 2012. Accessed February 26, 2014. http://www.jsonline.com/news/statepolitics/gop-retakes-state-senate-and-full-control-of-state-government-cf7dluk-177591051.html.

Marx, Karl, and Friedrich Engels. [1848] 1998. *The Communist Manifesto: A Modern Edition*. London and New York: Verso.

McCoy, Drew. 1980. *The Elusive Republic: Political Economy in Jeffersonian America*. New York: Norton.

Merrill, Samuel, and Bernard Grofman. 1999. *A Unified Theory of Voting: Directional and Proximity Spatial Models*. Cambridge: Cambridge University Press.

Merry, Robert W. 2009. *A Country of Vast Designs: James K. Polk, the Mexican War, and the Conquest of the American Continent*. New York: Simon & Schuster.

Meyers, Marvin. 1957. *The Jacksonian Persuasion: Politics and Belief*. Stanford: Stanford University Press.

Miller, Warren E., and J. Merrill Shanks. 1996. *The New American Voter*. Cambridge and London: Harvard University Press.

Mills, Charles W. [2002] 2004. "Racial Exploitation and the Wages of Whiteness." In *The Changing Terrain of Race and Ethnicity*, edited by Maria Krysan and Amanda E. Lewis, 235–262. New York: Russell Sage Foundation.

Misjak, Laura. 2012. "Right-to-Work Protesters March toward Capitol." *Lansing State Journal*, December 11. Accessed February 21, 2014. http://pqasb.pqarchiver. com/lansingstatejournal/doc/1237139263.html. . .startpage=&desc=Right-to-work+protesters+march+toward+Capitol&pf=1.

Montgomery, David. 1967. *Beyond Equality: Labor and the Radical Republicans, 1862–1872*. New York: Knopf.

Moore, Barrington. 1966. *Social Origins of Dictatorship and Democracy: Lord and Peasant in the Making of the Modern World*. Boston: Beacon Press.

Morrison, Michael A. 1997. *Slavery and the American West: the Eclipse of Manifest Destiny and the Coming of the Civil War*. Chapel Hill: University of North Carolina Press.

Mudge, Stephanie L., and Anthony S. Chen. 2014. "Political Parties in the Sociological Imagination: Past, Present, and Future Directions." *Annual Review of Sociology* 40 (forthcoming).

Neem, Johann N. 2008. *Creating a Nation of Joiners: Democracy and Civil Society in Early National Massachusetts*. Cambridge and London: Harvard University Press.

Nelson, Scott Reynolds, and Carol Sheriff. 2008. *A People at War: Civilians and Soldiers in America's Civil War, 1854–1877*. New York and Oxford: Oxford University Press.

Nichols, Roy Franklin. 1948. *The Disruption of American Democracy*. New York: Macmillan.

Nie, Norman H., Sidney Verba, and John R. Petrocik. [1976] 1979. *The Changing American Voter*. Cambridge and London: Harvard University Press.

Obama, Barack. 2008a. "Remarks of Senator Barack Obama: Reclaiming the American Dream" (January 29). El Dorado, Kansas. Accessed January 28, 2011. http://www.barackobama.com/speeches/.

———. 2008b. "Remarks of Senator Barack Obama: 'A More Perfect Union'" (March 18). Philadelphia. Accessed January 28, 2011. http://www.barackobama.com/speeches/.

O'Donnell, Guillermo, and Philippe C. Schmitter. 1986. *Transitions from Authoritarian Rule: Tentative Conclusions about Uncertain Democracies*. Baltimore: Johns Hopkins University Press.

Officer, Lawrence H. 2009. *Two Centuries of Compensation for U.S. Production Workers in Manufacturing*. New York: Palgrave Macmillan.

Oliver, Melvin L., and Thomas M. Shapiro. 1995. *Black Wealth/White Wealth: A New Perspective on Racial Inequality*. New York: Routledge.

Orfield, Gary. 2009. *Reviving the Goal of an Integrated Society: A 21st Century Challenge*. Los Angeles: Civil Rights Project/Proyecto Derechos Civiles at UCLA.

Paige, Jeffrey M. 1997. *Coffee and Power: Revolution and the Rise of Democracy in Central America*. Cambridge: Harvard University Press.

Parkin, Frank. 1979. *Marxism and Class Theory: a Bourgeois Critique*. New York: Columbia University Press.

Pessen, Edward. 1967. *Most Uncommon Jacksonians: The Radical Leaders of the Early Labor Movement*. Albany: State University of New York Press.

Pierce, Bessie Louise. 1937. *A History of Chicago*, Volume I. Chicago: University of Chicago Press.

———. 1940. *A History of Chicago*, Volume II. Chicago: University of Chicago Press.

Pierson, Paul. 2004. *Politics in Time: History, Institutions, and Social Analysis*. Princeton: Princeton University Press.

Pocock, J.G.A. 1975. *The Machiavellian Moment: Florentine Political Thought and the Atlantic Republican Tradition*. Princeton: Princeton University Press.

Pomper, Gerald M. 1972. "From Confusion to Clarity: Issues and American Voters, 1956–1968." *American Political Science Review* 66: 415–428.

Przeworski, Adam. 1977. "Proletariat into a Class: The Process of Class Formation from Karl Kautsky's *The Class Struggle* to Recent Controversies." *Politics and Society* 7: 343–401.

Przeworski, Adam, and John Sprague. 1986. *Paper Stones: A History of Electoral Socialism*. Chicago: University of Chicago Press.

Quist, John W. 1998. *Restless Visionaries: The Social Roots of Antebellum Reform in Alabama and Michigan*. Baton Rouge: Louisiana State University Press.

Redding, Kent. 2003. *Making Race, Making Power: North Carolina's Road to Disfranchisement*. Urbana: University of Illinois Press.

Riley, Dylan. 2010. *The Civic Foundations of Fascism in Europe: Italy, Spain, and Romania, 1870–1945*. Baltimore: Johns Hopkins University Press.

———. 2011. "Hegemony and Democracy in Gramsci's Prison Notebooks." *California Italian Studies* 2 (2). Accessed September 1, 2014. http://escholarship.org/uc/item/5x48f0mz.

Riley, Dylan, and Manali Desai. 2007. "The Passive Revolutionary Route to the Modern World: Italy and India in Comparative Perspective." *Comparative Studies in Society and History* 49 (4): 815–847.

Roediger, David R. 1991. *The Wages of Whiteness: Race and the Making of the American Working Class.* New York: Verso.

Rueschemeyer, Dietrich. 2003. "Can One or a Few Cases Yield Theoretical Gains?" In *Comparative Historical Analysis in the Social Sciences,* edited by James Mahoney and Dietrich Rueschemeyer, 305–336. Cambridge and New York: Cambridge University Press.

Rueschemeyer, Dietrich, Evelyn Huber Stephens, and John D. Stephens. 1992. *Capitalist Development and Democracy.* Cambridge, UK: Polity.

Schneider, Mary Beth. 2011. "Daniels Back 'Right to Work." *Indianapolis Star,* December 16, p. B.1. Accessed February 17, 2014. http://pqasb.pqarchiver.com/indystar/doc/911174844.html?FMT=FT&F. . .&edition=&startpage=&desc=Daniels+backs+%27right+to+work%27&pf=1.

Schneider, Mary Beth, and Chris Sikich. 2012a. "Right-to-Work Protestors Boo Ind. Governor's Address." *USA Today,* January 11. Accessed March 6, 2014. http://usatoday30.usatoday.com/news/nation/story/2012-01-11/indiana-right-work/52495786/1.

———. 2012b. "'RIGHT TO WORK': The Battle." *Indianapolis Star,* January 8, p. B.1. Accessed February 17, 2014. http://pqasb.pqarchiver.com/indystar/doc/916155101.html?FMT=FT&. . .edition=&startpage=&desc=%27RIGHT+TO+WORK%27%3A+The+Battle&pf=1.

Schneirov, Richard. 1991. "Political Cultures and the Role of the State in Labor's Republic." *Labor History* 32: 376–400.

———. 1998. *Labor and Urban Politics: Class Conflict and the Origins of Modern Liberalism in Chicago, 1864–1897.* Urbana and Chicago: University of Illinois Press.

———. 2008. "Chicago's Great Upheaval of 1877: Class Polarization and Democratic Politics." In *The Great Strike of 1877,* edited by David O. Stowell, 76–104. Urbana and Chicago: University of Illinois Press.

Schneirov, Richard, and Thomas J. Suhrbur. 1988. *Union Brotherhood, Union Town: The History of the Carpenters' Union of Chicago, 1863–1987.* Carbondale and Edwardsville: Southern Illinois University Press.

Schwedler, Jillian. 2006. *Faith in Moderation: Islamist Parties in Jordan and Yemen.* Cambridge: Cambridge University Press.

Schwenk, Nikolaus. [1856] 1988. Letter to Christian Schwenk dated at Chicago, November 15, 1856. In *German Workers in Chicago: A Documentary History of Working-Class Culture from 1850 to World War I,* edited by Hartmut Keil and John B. Jentz, 26–27. Urbana and Chicago: University of Illinois Press.

———. [1857] 1988. Letter to Christian Schwenk dated at Chicago, November 17, 1857. In *German Workers in Chicago: A Documentary History of Working-Class Culture from 1850 to World War I,* edited by Hartmut Keil and John B. Jentz, 28–33. Urbana and Chicago: University of Illinois Press.

Seigenthaler, John. 2004. *James K. Polk.* New York: Times Books.

Sellers, Charles. 1991. *The Market Revolution: Jacksonian America, 1815–1846.* New York: Oxford University Press.

Siegel, Jim, and Joe Vardon. 2011. "Unions Get Revenge." *Columbia Dispatch,* November 9, p. 1A. Accessed February 28, 2014. http://nl.newsbank.com/nl-search/we/

Archives?p_action=doc&p_docid. . .f353ff38f384a&s_accountid=AC011402281
4171222505&s_upgradeable=no.

Siegel, Jim. 2011a. "Senate Bill 5 / Fight over Collective Bargaining Bill Heads
to House after Heated Debate." *Columbia Dispatch*, March 3, 2011, p. 1A.
Accessed February 28, 2014. http://nl.newsbank.com/nl-search/we/Archives?p_
action=doc&p_docid. . .f353ff38f384a&s_accountid=AC011402281417122250
5&s_upgradeable=no.

———. 2011b. "Assembly Sends SB5 to Kasich." *Columbia Dispatch*, March 31, p. 1A.
Accessed February 28, 2014. http://nl.newsbank.com/nl-search/we/Archives?p_
action=doc&p_docid. . .f353ff38f384a&s_accountid=AC011402281417122250
5&s_upgradeable=no.

———. 2011c. "Ohio House Passes Senate Bill 5; Collective-Bargaining Bill Sent Back
to Senate." *Columbia Dispatch*, March 30. Accessed February 28, 2014. http://
www.dispatch.com/content/stories/local/2011/03/30/ohio-house-expected-to-
approve-sb5-this-afternoon.html.

Sikich, Chris, and Mary Beth Schneider. 2012. "Senate Oks 'Right to Work'; Dems
Stall Final House Vote." *Indianapolis Star*, January 24, p. B.1. Accessed February 17, 2014. http://pqasb.pqarchiver.com/indystar/doc/917322635.
html?FMT=FT&F. . .ate+OKs+%27right+to+work%27%3B+Dems+stall+final
+House+vote&pf=1.

Skogan, Wesley G. 1984. *Time Series Data for Chicago, 1840–1973*. Ann Arbor, MI:
Inter-university Consortium for Political and Social Research.

Skowronek, Stephen. 1982. *Building a New American State: The Expansion of
National Administrative Capacities, 1877–1920*. New York: Cambridge
University Press.

Skubick, Tim. 2012. "GOP to Introduce Right-to-Work Bills with Snyder's Support."
CBS Local News, December 6. Accessed June 6, 2013. http://detroit.cbslocal.
com/2012/12/06/gop-expected-to-introduce-right-to-work-bills-with-snyders-
support/.

Slez, Adam, and John Levi Martin. 2007. "Political Action and Party Formation in the
United States Constitutional Convention." *American Sociological Review* 72 (1):
42–67.

Smith, Eric R.A.N. 1989. *The Unchanging American Voter*. Berkeley: University of California Press.

Smithies, Arthur. 1941. "Optimum Location in Spatial Competition." *Journal of Political Economy* 49: 423–439.

Sombart, Werner. [1906] 1976. *Why Is There No Socialism in the United States?* White
Plains, NY: International Arts and Sciences Press.

Somers, Margaret R. 1997. "Deconstructing and Reconstructing Class Formation
Theory: Narrativity, Relational Analysis and Social Theory." In *Reworking Class*,
edited by John R. Hall, 73–105. Ithaca: Cornell University Press.

Spicuzza, Mary. 2011. "GOP Senators Vote to Start Imposing Fines on 14 Missing
Democrats." *Wisconsin State Journal*, March 10. Accessed February 26, 2014.
http://host.madison.com/wsj/news/local/govt-and-politics/
gop-senato. . .issing-democrats/article_a7027bea-4aa0-11e0-8e6d-
001cc4c03286.html.

Spicuzza, Mary, and Clay Barbour. 2011. "Budget Repair Bill Passes Senate, Thursday Vote Set in Assembly." *Wisconsin State Journal*, March 10. Accessed
February 26, 2014. http://host.madison.com/wsj/news/local/govt-and-
politics/budget-rep. . .e-set-in-assembly/article_8747fa04-4a74-11e0-8e6b-
001cc4c03286.html.

Stanley, Amy Dru. 1998. *From Bondage to Contract: Wage Labor, Marriage, and the Market in the Age of Slave Emancipation.* Cambridge: Cambridge University Press.

State of Wisconsin, 2011. Conference Substitute Amendment 1, To Assembly 11. State of Wisconsin 2011–2012 Legislature, January 2011 Special Session. Accessed February 26, 2014. http://docs.legis.wisconsin.gov/2011/related/amendments/jr1_ab11/jr1_csa1_ab11.pdf.

Steinfeld, Robert J. 1991. *The Invention of Free Labor: The Employment Relation in English and American Law and Culture, 1350–1870.* Chapel Hill: University of North Carolina Press.

Steinmetz, George. 1992. "Reflections on the Role of Social Narratives in Working-Class Formation: Narrative Theory in the Social Sciences." *Social Science History* 16: 489–516.

Stokes, Donald E. 1963. "Spatial Models of Party Competition." *American Political Science Review* 57 (2): 368–377.

Sugrue, Thomas J. 1996. *The Origins of the Urban Crisis: Race and Inequality in Postwar Detroit.* Princeton: Princeton University Press.

———. 2008. *Sweet Land of Liberty: The Forgotten Struggle for Civil Rights in the North.* New York: Random House.

Sundquist, James L. 1983. *Dynamics of the Party System: Alignment and Realignment of Political Parties in the United States.* Washington, DC: Brookings Institution Press.

Sweeney, et al. v. Zoeller, et al. (Lake Superior Court [2013]). Accessed February 19, 2014. https://portal.iuoelocal150.org/Documents/2013-0905_order_judge_sedia%5B1%5D%5B1%5D.pdf.

Tezcür, Gunes Mürat. 2010. *Muslim Reformers in Iran and Turkey: The Paradox of Moderation.* Austin: University of Texas Press.

Thompson, E.P. 1963. *The Making of the English Working Class.* New York: Vintage Books.

Thompson, Ginger. 2008. "Seeking Unity, Obama Feels Pull of Racial Divide." *New York Times*, February 12, p. A1. Accessed March 10, 2014. http://www.nytimes.com/2008/02/12/us/politics/12obama.html?pagewanted=all&_r=0.

Thornton, J. Mills, III. 1978. *Politics and Power in a Slave Society: Alabama, 1800–1860.* Baton Rouge: Louisiana State University Press.

Tomlins, Christopher L. 1992. "Law and Power in the Employment Relationship." In *Labor Law in America: Historical and Critical Essays*, edited by Christopher L. Tomlins and Andrew J. King, 71–98. Baltimore and London: Johns Hopkins University Press.

Treleven, Ed. 2012. "Judge Strikes Down Walker's Collective Bargaining Law." *Wisconsin State Journal*, September 15, 2012. Accessed February 26, 2014. http://host.madison.com/news/local/govt-and-politics/judge-strikes-down-walkers-collective-bargaining-law/article_ded3b708-feb5-11e1-a29a-001a4bcf887a.html.

———. 2014. "In 5-2 ruling, Supreme Court issues final word on Act 10." *Wisconsin State Journal*, August 1, 2014. Accessed September 28, 2014. http://host.madison.com/news/local/govt-and-politics/in---ruling-supreme-court-issues-final-word-on/article_0d448a2d-dd28-5a57-abeb-f32e114d80c3.html.

Tuğal, Cihan. 2009. *Passive Revolution: Absorbing the Islamic Challenge to Capitalism.* Stanford: Stanford University Press.

Unger, Irwin. 1964. *The Greenback Era: A Social and Political History of American Finance, 1865–1879.* Princeton: Princeton University Press.

U.S. Bureau of the Census. 1961. *Historical Statistics of the United States, Colonial Times to 1957.* Washington, DC: U.S. Government Printing Office.

U.S. Census Office. 1840. *Sixth Census of the United States, 1840. Volume 3.* New York: N. Ross Pub.

———. 1850. *Seventh Census of the United States, 1850. Volume 4. Compendium.* New York: N. Ross Pub.

———. 1860. *Eighth Census of the United States, 1860. Volume 1. Population.* New York: N. Ross Pub.

———. 1860. *Eighth Census of the United States, 1860. Volume 3. Manufactures.* New York: N. Ross Pub.

———. 1883a. *Compendium of the Tenth Census (June 1, 1880), Part I.* Washington, DC: Government Printing Office.

———. 1883b. *Compendium of the Tenth Census (June 1, 1880), Part II.* Washington, DC: Government Printing Office.

———. 1883c. *Statistical Report of the Railroads in the United States.* Washington, DC: Government Printing Office.

———. 1886. *Report on the Statistics of Wages in Manufacturing Industries; With Supplementary Reports on the Average Retail Prices of Necessaries of Life, and on Trades Societies, and Strikes and Lockouts.* Washington, DC: Government Printing Office.

Vardon, Joe, and Jim Siegel. 2011. "Kasich Signs SB5, but Fight Isn't Over." *Columbia Dispatch*, April 1, p. 1A. Accessed February 28, 2014. http://nl.newsbank.com/nl-search/we/Archives?p_action=doc&p_docid. . .f353ff38f384a&s_accountid=AC0114022814171222505&s_upgradeable=no.

Voss, Kim. 1993. *The Making of American Exceptionalism: The Knights of Labor and Class Formation in the Nineteenth Century.* Ithaca: Cornell University Press.

Watson, Harry L. 1981. *Jacksonian Politics and Community Conflict: the Emergence of the Second American Party System in Cumberland County North Carolina.* Baton Rouge: Louisiana State University Press.

———. 1990. *Liberty and Power: The Politics of Jacksonian America.* New York: Hill and Wang.

Welter, Rush. 1975. *The Mind of America, 1820–1860.* New York: Columbia University Press.

Wilentz, Sean. 1984. *Chants Democratic: New York City and the Rise of the American Working Class, 1788–1850.* New York: Oxford University Press.

———. 2005. *The Rise of American Democracy: Jefferson to Lincoln.* New York: Norton.

Wilson, Major L. 1974. *Space, Time and Freedom: The Quest for Nationality and the Irrepressible Conflict, 1815–1861.* Westport, CT: Greenwood Press.

Wisconsin Gazette. 2014. "Wisconsin Supreme Court upholds anti-union law." *Wisconsin Gazette*, July 31, 2014. Accessed September 28, 2014. http://www.wisconsingazette.com/wisconsin-gaze/wisconsin-supreme-court-upholds-anti-union-law.html.

Wood, Gordon S. 1969. *The Creation of the American Republic, 1776–1787.* New York: Norton.

———. 1992. *The Radicalism of the American Revolution.* New York: Knopf.

Woodward, C. Vann. 1951. *Reunion and Reaction: The Compromise of 1977 and the End of Reconstruction.* New York: Oxford University Press.

Wright, Erik Olin. 1990. *The Debate on Classes.* London: Verso.

wthr.com. 2011. "Thousands Attend Union Rally at Indiana Statehouse." NBC Local News, March 10. Accessed March 6, 2014. http://www.wthr.com/story/14223321/largest-protest-expected-at-indiana-satatehouse-today.

Wu, Yiching. 2014. *The Cultural Revolution at the Margins: Chinese Socialism in Crisis.* Cambridge: Harvard University Press.

Index

Page numbers ending in *f* and *t* indicate figures and tables.